Under My Skin

◆

My Father, Frank Sinatra
The Man Behind the Mystique

Under My Skin

✦

My Father, Frank Sinatra
The Man Behind the Mystique

Julie Sinatra

iUniverse, Inc.
New York Lincoln Shanghai

BIO
Sinatra
Frank

Under My Skin
My Father, Frank Sinatra The Man Behind the Mystique

Copyright © 2003–2007 by Julie Sinatra

iUniverse books may be ordered through booksellers or by contacting:

iUniverse
2021 Pine Lake Road, Suite 100
Lincoln, NE 68512
www.iuniverse.com
1-800-Authors (1-800-288-4677)

ISBN: 978-0-595-43478-7 (pbk)
ISBN: 978-0-595-68589-9 (cloth)
ISBN: 978-0-595-87805-5 (ebk)

Printed in the United States of America

For my father, Francis, who gave me his song,

And, my mother, Dorothy, who delivered my ship,

And, for my son, Dan, who is my future.

We all start out with our full potential

It is 1996 and the press releases, softened by the family line,

begin to allude to his illness. It is a time when people dress up

to meet with friends around intimate tables in fashionable little

out of the way cocktail lounges somewhere in America

and across the world to spend an evening out

while talking about Sinatra.

The Voice comes back into the arenas

And the jubilance of the Rat Pack,

Now only an echo in Vegas, is transported on the words:

"I was there when Frank …"

Contents

PART I

ILLUMINATION

"TO SEE THE REAL WORLD YOU MUST

TURN YOURSELF UPSIDE DOWN." Old Native American Proverb

CHAPTER ONE

Twilight, June 9, 1996, Cave Creek, Arizona ...

*T*he sun had already slipped off the shoulders of the Seven Sister Mountains, a row of hills west of the small garage size adobe tackroom where I made my home, as I finished feeding my horses, Checkers and Missy Starr.

Walking back the short distance to the, "bunkhouse," as I preferred to call it, the string of Christmas bulbs I'd hung up for lighting at nights were visible through the barn size door I kept open onto an adjoining screened-in covered patio, to extend my living space. The tiny clear lights were shimmering against the interior mud colored walls. Across the room a second barn size door was ajar. The opening framed a deep lavender sky as a backwash for the stately Saguaros glowing in the surrounding landscape, outlined by the last brush stroke of sunset that had turned their needles pink.

It's too hot to cook, I said to my German Shepherd, Harley, who had momentarily left his puppy chow to greet me. I'll make some macaroni and cheese later, and I'll save you some. He was looking at me, smiling as much as a dog can smile. I wanted some coffee and put a cup of water to heat in the microwave, which sat on some adobe bricks I had drystacked for a make-shift kitchen counter top. I turned on the TV., which was tuned to CBS where I had watched the late news the night before.

I was about to turn the channel to PBS, when a mini-series on the life of Frank Sinatra came back from commercial. I had never really followed his career. My only impression of him, formed back in the fifties when I was a teenager and news coverage had shown him hitting some guy in a restaurant, was that he was a hot head. I distinctly remembered my mother sneering, "Way to go, Big Shot!" and mumbling something about the Mafia ... so I didn't think I wanted to watch the series. I still had my hand on the channel selector when I thought, "After all, he is a very successful music person, and I am a music person ... Maybe I'll learn something." And what I did learn would change my life forever ...

I came into the show when a very young and ambitious Frank Sinatra was agreeing to an all or nothing at all contract with Tommy Dorsey who then took him to California to record a solo for a movie being made by Paramount. They were ready to record the song on an empty soundstage when Frank said he needed an audience to sing to in order to perform the song.

A glamorous young starlet standing in the background was motioned to come and sit in a chair in front of the stage. She sat down and crossed her legs, and dipped her chin slightly as she looked up at him with a demure smile, which was, in addition to her physical appearance and the mannerisms she had just displayed, suddenly way too familiar to me. I was vaguely aware that I had just stood up from my chair.

Why does she look so much like me? No! Like my mother! A prominent photograph of my mother, taken before I was born when she worked as a hostess at the El Rancho, a fancy lounge in early Las Vegas, abruptly flashed through my mind. She was on a chair at the aisle end of a u-shaped booth table occupied with men dressed in business suits, in the same cross-legged pose, young and glamorous and dressed to the hilt with that same recognizable smile on her face the starlet had just displayed. "What in the hell is going on here?!" I protested out loud.

The scene in the movie abruptly changed to the two of them rolling around in a passionate exchange of kisses. A phone rang. Frank answered and learned he had just become the father of little Nancy. The somewhat now disheveled lady sat up on the bed next to him, with my mother's distinct pout on her face as she listened to his excitement, which excluded her.

"What about us?" she asked when he hung up the phone. He retorted in the negative, and her expression then changed to my mother's classic one she always uses for anticipated disappointments. Then the starlet got up, tossed a mink coat over her shoulder, and made her exit, walking quickly and decidedly away.

By this time I was drowning in missing puzzle pieces from my own life flooding into my mind ...

Tom Lyma, the man who was my mother's husband when I was born, the man who was supposed to have been my father, boasting to me during a visit with him as a child about being acquainted with Frank Sinatra. Lyma, a salesman whose company supplied food for the upscale resorts saying he knew the businessmen who backed Sinatra's early solo career because they were owners of the restaurants he serviced, and they had introduced him to the famous singer ...

Once while playing with my cousins at my Aunt Iva's house when I was 12 or 13 she had called me in from the backyard. I was bewildered as she sat me down and said, "I'm going to put on a record of Frank Sinatra. You should at least hear his music, Julie."

When I got back home I told my mother that Aunt Iva had played a Frank Sinatra record for me. "What did Iva say about Sinatra?" she asked in an unexpected demanding tone.

I told her Aunt Iva had said, "That's my Frankie!" My mother tossed her head back and huffed out "Her Frankie?!" The song that played in my memory of that day was "Witchcraft".

Then, almost like a slap, I saw the moment I first learned that I was an illegitimate child …

I was 17. Home in Long Beach, California, in 1960 for my Christmas break from San Jose State. My mother's third husband, Carroll Hunter gave me the shocking news.

"You're a pinko like your father," he said when I told him I wished I would have been old enough to vote for President Kennedy. "Tom Lyma never uttered a word of politics that I can remember," I said in rebuttal. Then Hunter said the thing no one else had ever said to me. "Lyma was never your father. Your father is that pinko saloon singer."

Saloon singer? I thought to myself. "My real father is someone who sings in a bar somewhere?"

Before I could phrase that to Hunter he spat out, "That's where your mother is now. I can't understand why she's still having an affair with him after all of these years!"

The next obvious question was on my lips when my mother suddenly appeared coming through the front door just a few feet from where Carroll and I were standing. I should have gotten to the bottom of it right then and there, but I didn't. I had witnessed several violent fights between this couple including an afternoon when I arrived home from high school earlier than usual and my mother, believing I was Hunter, opened the door and pointed a hand-gun at me. She quickly withdrew it saying, "Oh, I didn't know that was you, Julie, I thought it was Carroll" and walked away. You didn't cross this woman without paying a price. Knowing what my loaded question would likely blast off, I put it aside for a time when she couldn't connect Hunter to it.

My boyfriend when I was sixteen had given me a stuffed dog I had named Francis, after my boyfriend's middle name. My mother went berserk when I held it up in front of her, telling her what I named it.

"You named that animal Francis, just to mock me. Didn't you Julie?"

I feebly attempted to defend what made no sense for me to have to defend. "How can naming a stuffed dog Francis, mock you?!"

She walked away fuming, "I'm warning you, Julie!" I dismissed the incident as her craziness …

A recent visit with my son, Dan, whom I hadn't seen for four years. He was in his 30's and his physical appearance had changed from how I remembered him. He was a little portly and his hair had already receded from his forehead. As he came through my door I remembered thinking that he had reminded me of someone else who seemed familiar, but I couldn't think who. One of my songs I'd had Dan sing some time ago had gone over to an author who needed music for a book he hoped would become a movie and he phoned me excited about my son's singing voice. "He sounds a little like Elton John, but more so like someone much more famous than that, but I can't think of who it is." At that time I had mused over who could be more famous than Elton John ... now it hit me ... Frank Sinatra!

Finally, still standing and staring into the following scene of the movie, I remembered that in my 30s I had gone over to my mother's house. My half-sister, Lisa, whom I hadn't seen for a while, was there. "Julie," she said, looking at me intensely, "you look a whole lot like Nancy Sinatra." Mother was at the kitchen sink and quickly interjected: "No, Julie looks like Jane Fonda."

"My God!" I shouted into the walls of my bunkhouse. "I am f—-ing Frank Sinatra's daughter!" My legs suddenly felt like Jell-O and I sat back down.

I lit a cigarette and focused my attention on the mini-series as it was continuing. There was a scene that showed Frank Sinatra arguing with his agent and another man. They were confronting him about a baby girl who had been born in February, 1943. Sinatra insisted that the lady was married and that her husband was the father. One of the men said something about this being just like what happened in 1938, as Sinatra stalked out of the room. It must have been an earlier segment in the movie, so I didn't know what had happened in '38. I did know that I was born in February, 1943, and this assured me I hadn't just gone crazy arriving at this conclusion of my true paternity.

Harley looked up at me expectantly. I gave him a doggy biscuit, and made myself a peanut butter and jam sandwich, which I ate standing up. I felt excited and drained at the same time. I retrieved my coffee and sat down for my front row seat, to watch the life story of my father ... the man who had been hidden from me for 53 years ... the man who would turn me upside down.

CHAPTER TWO

Confirmation ...

F rom what you know so far you're probably expecting me to do something to let my father know I'm out here and, because my poverty is already obvious, jump at a chance to be bailed out of it. The truth is just having discovered that my whole life has been a lie is taking some getting used to, not to mention the shock from finding out I am the daughter of a world famous icon—and as far as the money is concerned—I'm assuming he must know about me and will remember me someday in his Will along with his other children. It's also true I had a lot of questions but Tom Lyma was dead, Hunter was long gone, and my mother, who had successfully crushed each approach I'd made over the years to learn who my real father was, would probably have a field day with me now. That left Frank Sinatra himself. He's not listed in a directory ... Did you ever have his home phone number?

The bunk-house had its usual glow from the morning sun coming through a sky-light on the roof that was softened by filtering through a large cotton painter's drop cloth tacked up across the width of the room to create a ceiling beneath the exposed rafters. The same humdrum of my swamp cooler could be heard combating the desert heat as early as 7 am. But as I got out of bed, the feeling of excitement still with me from my discovery a few days before signaled that nothing was the same. I looked up at myself in the bathroom mirror as I brushed my teeth, and a stranger looked back at me with a girlish shyness and twinkle in her blue eyes. I was seeing myself really for the first time. People have forever commented on my eyes, which I now identified as my father's—"Ole Blue Eyes"!

After watching his whole story it was clear to me that my father had put three hundred years of living into one lifetime. He was amazing, yet complicated. I saw how romantic and vulnerable he reportedly was involving his love for Ava Gardner. I also watched how cold he could be when he faced that his marriage to Mia Farrow was not going to work. The abruptness in which he had divorce papers delivered, slammed down in front of her, where she was on a movie set, without any warning was startling, until I recognized under different circumstances I had surprised my 4th husband under the same pragmatic. We apparently had in common that we both didn't believe in dragging something on when it was in fact over. The viewers of his movie had been invited to witness his brutal temper aroused at something phony—lashing out at an Italian slur. Because he drank—when he drank too much he could be cruel—yet I saw that he could also be a prince among men, generous and supportive. He expected respect and he insisted others be treated with like respect, regardless of nationality, race, or religious preference. He acted under his own code for this and he never missed a beat, as he unwittingly began to change America's behaviors still buried in Puritanism in the 40's and 50's. He changed the rules at hotels and casinos—and got his way—A Jewish band member checked into a restricted hotel—Sammy Davis Jr. gambled along side him in the casinos where Blacks weren't allowed. Had he known what he was seeding there would begin to change the world?

I traveled back in my mind to a theatre arts class I attended in college. I was assigned to do a scene about a grand French lady and her maid. A black girl in the class was paired with me. I still kick myself about letting her choose the role of maid for herself—I missed the opportunity to lift her away from her painful assumption. She should have played the grand lady—I should have been the maid. Like my father, I am color-blind and choose my friends based on the kind of person they are, never on regards to their skin or how they find their God. My ego had been in the possession of my youthful clumsiness that day when I took the bigger part and missed the larger role.

And his life, included in all its elements, as it did—US Presidents,—heads of state around the globe—Mafia bosses—Hollywood movie moguls—major music label record producers, and kinship with other famous celebrities—was immense.

Even if I could contact him, what would I say. I didn't know if he had simply turned away from me as a young man focused on his way up when I was born and his career began to skyrocket. Had he kept abreast of me via secret communications with my mother as I was growing up—did he ever want to know—or had my mother been the one to cut him out of the picture? And what if I somehow succeeded—would he see me as a phony wannabe? Or, if he knew who I was, would I be considered an intrusion and recipient of his notorious anger? At this point I was too fragile for any of that. I turned my attention instead to an event portrayed about him that I was able to correspond to my own life where, under similar circumstances, we had handled things in equal ways.

This one period especially in my father's life affected me deeply. It was a time when everything he had accomplished was shattering around him …

By the time I was three months old in 1943 Frank Sinatra was performing to screaming bobby-soxers all over the country. Before the year was over he had become a household name. But by 1952 his singing career was all but gone. The boyfriends and the young husbands of his worshipping fans had returned home from World War II and 'the boy next door' who crooned their longings and filled the gap for their missing loved ones was beginning to go out of style. By 1952 the blossoms of his singing and acting careers had fallen from the vine. Full of his young ambition my father had reached the top so quickly that he wasn't able to look back and see where he had just come from. Worse yet, he was breaking another old rule about success—the one that says you have to be able to do it again. The marriage to Ava Gardner took place the day after his divorce from his first wife and mother of Nancy Jr., Frank Jr. and Tina, in 1951. Before a year had fully passed, in 1952, the relationship that had always been too hot had become—Baby it's cold outside. The money was crumbling. He was still juggling with his obligations to continue to cover fully Nancy and the children's lifestyle in a large elegant home along with pay rolling his agents and the rest of the people who had been making Frank Sinatra possible on stage—and the venue was shrinking to occasional gigs in small clubs. It was heartbreaking to see him coming out of the exit door of a large auditorium where he had just performed for but a handful of people, entering the empty alleyway where so many times before security guards had to usher him to the safety of a waiting car through throngs of aggressive fans wanting to touch him—wanting a piece of his clothing to keep. Now, here he was walking alone.

It was painful watching his verbal attacks on Ava, fueled by the anger at himself for failing as 'the man'—punctuated by her meteoric rise in her acting career—She was paying the bills and resented having to prop up his emotions that were pulling her down. Clearly he was losing her and he had already lost everything else. As I had watched my father tumbling toward oblivion I was reminded of the nightmare I had just survived in my own life.

I looked around at my surroundings and realized even though I was living in a building meant to store saddles and bridles, it was a miracle I was here at all. I recently experienced a ten-month bout of homelessness in which I had somehow managed to keep my two beloved horses and dog together with me. For six years previous I had struggled and self-healed from what had been diagnosed as probable Multiple Sclerosis. This had been combined with a very bad marriage ending with my fourth divorce as I had "married the same man just with a different face," so a line in one of my songs goes—all alike on some level to the abusive relationship I had always had with my mother. The MS was finally the eminent culmination of having been someone lost to myself, and becoming homeless under those circumstances was inevitable. Old friends were mystified that I was actually stronger after coming through it all—to answer their queries, I would say simply,

"Necessity breeds capacity." But that isn't the whole of it. What I saw my father do next would show me something inside of myself that I had never really been able to identify ...

Warn down almost to his skeleton, Frank Sinatra insisted, persisted to producer Harry Cohn who saw him as washed up, a lost cause, that the role of underdog Maggio in the movie about to be made, "From Here To Eternity," had all but been written for him. He agonized for months, waiting for the liberating call that he knew had the potential to put his life back up on a new track carrying as well the chance to save his marriage with Ava, before he was granted the audition. I could feel the ice on the surrounding walls as he passed by the shaking heads making it obvious they believed he was just going to waste their time. The audition had been granted as a result of Eva begging Cohn's wife, and it was just an exercise. There hadn't been any intention of actually considering Sinatra for the part which he must have sensed when he saw the pair of dice, the stage prop he was supposed to pick up as part of his action, were not even there. But my father reached down inside of himself and ignited the spark that had been waiting for this moment when he would create the re-birth for his life. He picked up two olives from a bowl, shook them and blew on his hands and rolled them down the bar—the Oscar and the rest is history.

I had seen the film, "The Godfather," and I was aware of the innuendo. But I had just witnessed how my father had reached out and took action in the midst of personal despair, something I had also done as I had created each day's chance to bring my family of pets and myself to renewed normalcy. The necessity and the capacity were there, true, but he could have easily never recognized that 'spark' I knew I had also used to rekindle my own life. That he got the part as a gift from some don was crap.

I made a mental note to check out the video of "From Here To Eternity" and watch it. When it had come back around in the theatres in the late 50's I was a teenager. My mother had forbidden me to go and see it, telling me it had love scenes in it that were too mature for me. Now as I remember it, she had always managed to steer me way away from anything about Frank Sinatra. When his television show came up on our living room set, there was something else I had to do such as homework up in my room. I had been only somewhat aware that he had made movies in addition to being a famous singer. Sadly, I realized I had missed everything about my father.

Dad's audition photo for role of Maggio—note the spark of determination

November, 1996

Summer had gone to another side of the world, and the challenge of how to heat the bunkhouse was foremost in my mind, until the evening news on November 11, 1996, announced that Frank Sinatra had been admitted to a hospital in Los Angeles because of a, "pinched nerve." For the past five months the only way I expressed being his daughter was to get new strings on my guitar and go out and sing in public—but not under my true maiden name of Sinatra—I wasn't ready for that yet.

I realized I didn't know how old he actually was. In my memory of seeing his face he must have been close to 40. But, now I was in my fifties. He had to be nearly 80. Suddenly making contact with him became more important to me than anything else in the world. Why had I wasted all this time? Several times during these weeks I thought about phoning my mother and confronting her with my discovery—Maybe she had his phone number. But I never called her. The truth had come in like a thunderbolt, so it wasn't that I had doubts about it. I had doubts about her.

So I contacted the next person I could think of—a program director at CBS Television. I hadn't looked at the credits when the mini-series had aired. If I could find out who produced it, it might lead me to at least my father's office phone number. Oddly enough, the woman I was transferred to in New York had trouble locating the tape. "It's strange that it wasn't in the file where they're always kept, but I found it," she finally announced.

I dialed the number she gave me for the production office and got an answering machine that announced I had reached Tina Sinatra and Lisa Tan. At the beep I took a deep breath and said, "I am calling after having viewed the mini-series about Frank Sinatra last June here in the Phoenix area. My name when I was born on February 10, 1943, was Julie Ann Lyma. My mother was Dorothy Lyma, and her husband at the time I was born was Thomas Vincent Lyma. I have some questions about the mini-series. Please call me." Then I left my phone number.

Within an hour, an astonishing short period of time to get a call back from any Hollywood production office especially that of a Sinatra, Lisa Tan was politely asking what "they" could do for me.

"This is very personal, Lisa …" I began.

"Would you like to speak with Tina?" she offered.

I started to cry and was struggling not to let it be noticed on the other end of the line. "No, I think it would be better if I wrote her a letter," I managed. Lisa gave me the address and we hung up, after she instructed me to mark my envelope personal and confidential to Tina.

I couldn't believe how shook up I became. I couldn't bring myself to tell Tina over the phone that we were sisters. I wasn't sure if she already knew. After getting a call back so quickly from her office, I pondered whether or not it could be possible that I was the only member of the family who had not known all these years. My God, this is going to be the hardest thing I have ever tried to do in my life.

I wrote version after version until I finally realized that the letter I was trying to write to Tina Sinatra wouldn't come together for me because it was Frank Sinatra I needed to write to. I sat down that night and typed a letter to my father and a cover letter to Tina. I didn't announce who I was, somewhat because I believed he already knew. It wasn't my intention to upset him now over something that he did or did not do all those years ago—I just told him about my music and how important it was to me. I assumed he knew the rest. I mailed it on December 11 …

December 11, 1996

Ms. Tina Sinatra
Warner Bros. TV
4000 Warner Blvd.
Burbank, California 91522

Re: Personal and Confidential

Dear Ms. Sinatra:

I viewed the mini-series on Frank Sinatra you were Executive Producer for, last June 9th and
11th of 1996 on CBS. CBS in New York gave me the phone number for Warner Bros. in
Burbank, and I was connected to your production office. I spoke briefly with your assistant
and expressed my desire to write to you.

My Mother's husband at the time period of 1942-43 had personal and business relationships
with people that may have made it possible for Mr. Sinatra to have known my Mother for a
brief time when he first began his solo recording sessions. I was born, Julie Ann Marie Lyma,
February 10, 1943, in Sacramento, California. My Mother's husband's name was Thomas Lyma.
My Mother's name was Dorothy Bonucelli Lyma. The segment of the movie covering this time
period may have put little missing puzzle pieces together to fit into my life. My interest in writing
to you at this time is not to disturb whatever remains in the past. I do not wish to impose myself
in any way now in the present. In the off-chance there is any connection with Mr. Sinatra, I
would feel regret if the time should pass that allows me to say hello and convey that I have been
given all I needed to overcome any difficult passages in my life, all I needed to be able to enjoy
who I am today, at the age of 53.

You are welcome to read the enclosed letter to Frank Sinatra. I would appreciate very much
your passing it on to him.

Thank you for your time.

Julie Alex-Rider (Speelman)

Julie Alex - Rider
P.O. Box 4650   Cave Creek, AZ 85331   (602) 488-8032

SKYWATER

December 11, 1996

Dear Mr. Frank Sinatra,

I'm writing to say hello, and share with you a little about the role my music played in my being able to enjoy complete recovery from Multiple Sclerosis. When I was a small child living in the country north of Sacramento, California, I used to make up songs and sing them for my horses and pets. I loved to sing and perform, and the school choir teachers would choose me for the solo's. In college, I majored in Theatre Arts and did some singing there, and in the 60's I sang folk songs and played the guitar in Southern California. The music got buried somewhere in the years of bad marriages and other distractions. In 1986 I contacted MS and was forced to leave working and stay at home to do the necessary combat to win back my health. I turned to my piano and guitar and began writing and singing again. The more time I spent with my music, the less strong the symptoms of MS became. During those years, I read something about how music is healing for a neurological illness...apparently the brain likes to entrain most easily to rhythm. Just working the lyrics in my head must have helped, but singing did the most because of the breathing it requires. Breath is life, right? Today I'm well and there is no sign I ever had MS. I play out Friday and Saturday nights at the Carefree INN, in the neighboring village of Carefree, Arizona. I do all my own original material and play the guitar for accompaniment. I'm active in conservatio efforts in the area here, and have been invited to sing one of my songs at a concert the Conservation Land Trust is putting on with Michael Martin Murphy and the Phoenix Symphany Orchestra in May here in Cave Creek. I live just north of Phoenix in a beautifull part of the Sonoran Desert, and my surroundings and love of nature have their influence on the songs I write. A studio musician I was working with recently described my songs as, "folk-rock desert prairie music". Whatever it is, it gives me good energy and people seem to like the words. When I was young I was nick-named, "blue skies", for my eyes, and because my music acts like the rain that renews life, I call the collection of songs I've written, "Skywater".

I live in a small adobe rented bunk-house on a property that allows me to have my horses, Checkers and Missy Starr, and my German Shepherd, Harley, with me. The animals played a huge role in my recovery also, especially Checkers. He has outstayed three husbands, he's smarter, doesn't drink, and is better looking than they. He's been with me 22 of his 24 years, and I needed to become well and strong enough to keep him and the rest of us together. There was a cat, Alexander, now deceased who was a great pal also. When I realized I had truly come through the MS, I honored this bunch by re-naming myself, Julie Alex-Rider. I was born, Julie Ann Marie Lyma, on February 10, 1943, in Sacramento, California. My son, Dan, inherited my passion for music and sings great. He loves the mountains and just moved from the Chicago area to Durango, Colorado, where he is trying his hand in writing a science fiction novel. He drove across the country in a snow storm, following his heart and doing it, "his way". When you take a look at it, that philosophy can't hurt a thing.

Get yourself a horse and a dog, keep singing (breath).

Best wishes,

Julie Alex-Rider

Julie Alex - Rider
P.O. Box 4650   Cave Creek, AZ 85331   (602) 488-8032

Christmas Eve, 1996

The little adobe felt empty of the season's tidings. My son, Dan had sent me a candle that I kept lit Christmas Eve. I still didn't feel ready to share my news with him yet. I hadn't shared it with anyone. I was stepping on my lower lip by Christmas night when it was obvious that my phone was not going to ring. I wasn't going to hear somebody say to me from the other end of the line, "Hi Kid, It's your Dad."

I hadn't heard from anyone in the Sinatra family after sending my letters. I started to think I never would. My eyes traveled to the top of my piano, to the chewed corner of a coveted Navajo blanket draped over the top, to the door too warped to shut all the way. Sometimes even birds flew inside. Who would ever believe I was whom I was, living there like some nut dropout from the mainstream. The desert night was cold as I crawled into bed and pulled a heavy down cover over me loaned by a friend. I felt overwhelmed thinking about the buffer zones constructed around my father. "He's just too famous," I said softly to myself, as I watched the stars through the open door next to my bed dance in a little night wind, blurred by the tears I couldn't keep from coming, until I fell asleep.

On New Year's eve my phone rang around 8 pm, Arizona time.

"Julie, this is your mother. I'm calling you because I need help. I am short money I need and I want you to send me at least $50. That should do it." Her voice was a little hesitant and her speech reflected a froggy tone from her throat.

"Hi Mom," I answered flatly. I had not had any contact with her for over three years. In a quick instant in my mind, I realized that this was an opportunity to confront her about my true birth father.

"I can't send you any money right now, but I have a real estate escrow going on that will close in a week or so and I'll send something to you then. By the way, I was invited to write a letter to Tina Sinatra."

"Oh," mother said, her voice suddenly brightening up. "Frank will know me as Lyma. I was Dorothy Lyma at that time."

"Then it's true," I embarked. "Frank Sinatra is my true father and where I got my music ability."

"Yes," she answered in a very quiet voice.

I felt the word pass through my ears and enter my whole body. Yes. I knew it, but I had needed this confirmation more than I realized all these past months.

"Why wasn't I ever told?" I asked. "Was it to protect me or something?"

"That's right," she said with a darker voice that had changed to an unpleasant tone including a hint of sarcasm.

"Well your privacy is your own," I said, and my attempt to bring the conversation back up on a brighter note again worked.

"By the way," she used my previous expression as a retort. "We used to celebrate our birthdays together. Frank's is December 12, and mine is December 9, as you know. I am a year and three days older than he is."

Something rocked my ability to continue the conversation any longer with her. This was all about her and them. There wasn't the slightest consideration or sensitivity from her where my feelings were concerned.

"Mom, I have to go now." I said. "I'll send you the money when I can."

"Cancel this call," she said and we hung up.

I was aware of the misfit of her expression, but I didn't understand it at that time.

The phrase "Cancel this call" would haunt me in the near future.

I wrote what was said during our conversation on a piece of scrap paper that was handy next to the phone. I wanted to have it all down as a keepsake. I had included the reference to my music in my confrontation with her because of an odd event that had taken place with my mother within the first few days of that period when I had become homeless in 1992.

I had gone over to my mother's house to drop off the houseplants I could no longer keep with me and found her on the phone with my Aunt Elsa, her brother's wife. From what I could overhear it seemed Elsa, a German woman who cared strongly that things are always put right, was arguing my case. My mother kept insisting I didn't need anything and I overheard her say, "Julie doesn't need to know anything about that. She can still drive her car." I wanted to get on the phone with my Aunt, but mother waved me off and ended her conversation. I went outside and began unloading the plants onto the driveway. Mother walked out toward me with a strange expression on her face and stated simply, "Julie you don't get your music from anyone in the family." I had been conditioned by this time to her lifelong attempt to crush my desire to perform my songs. So when I should have asked, "Well, where did I get it then?" instead, I let it brush by me and what very probably had been an opportunity to have learned about my father during a time before he became ill, was lost.

But now I had a renewed feeling of celebration, and I didn't want to spoil it with what could have been. I stayed up to watch the ball descend in Time's Square in New York, counting the way to the first of my New Years and then slept like a baby. The next morning I woke up knowing the letter I needed to write:

Dear Tina Sinatra,

I knew in my heart when I wrote the letters I sent you dated December 11, 1996, that I was Frank Sinatra's daughter. Now I have just had the confirmation from my mother that that indeed is the truth. I am writing you now because I want to meet my father before it is too late ...

CHAPTER THREE

New world emerging …

*T*ina Sinatra's response arrived in my mail a few days later—a cannon's blast to issue the order to "cease and desist" any further contact with her. It came as a letter accompanied by the photos I'd included to show my likeness, penned by attorney Robert Finkelstein.

The message was easily translated: Cease to exist.

I phoned my son, Dan, sharing my discovery and my intention of meeting his famous grandfather. I wanted him to join me in going out there in person. One look at both of us would show the truth, but Dan was preoccupied with moving back to the Chicago area from Colorado and stated, "I'm a generation away from it. This is your thing, Mom."

Next I shot a letter off to Mr. Finkelstein putting him on notice that the clock was ticking while he was playing a game that could result in a father and daughter not having a chance to meet each other … It made me feel better anyway. I knew I needed some level headed advice because I also knew I wasn't going to jump in my "Z" and fly the mission to Burbank I would more than likely be forced to eject to avoid crashing at the gates of Warner Brother's TV.

Rod de Szendeffy had leased the space to me I had used shortly as my broker's office doing real estate. He was a realistic person and I hoped he knew me well enough that he would probably not think I was a nut when I phoned him and told him I needed some guidance about what I was facing.

"It's more than a coincidence that you thought of me to call about this Julie," Rod began. "What you could not have known is that I had tried for some years to meet my real father and he passed away about two months before I had been able to locate where he lived."

I was surprised at his story and also aware that these little synchronicities will pop up from somewhere, maybe the Divine, to help align matters and move things forward. Rod reminded me that his wife, Carol Lynne was an attorney and he said he would get back to me after talking with her. In the meantime I was in for another surprise.

It was late in the afternoon when a woman I had recently become acquainted with after showing her home in Carefree she had on the market phoned me. She had been widowed a handful of months earlier and in spite of her loss she was trying to move forward. She deserved some support and we started a friendship. She wanted me to see the acreage she planned to build a new house on and we located a boulder that had a petroglyph on it, left by the ancient native tribe who had lived there long before. The rock scraped picture was of a spiral representing a new world emerging—re-tokening 800 years later. I was gazing into an orange sunset when I decided to tell her about learning I was Frank Sinatra's daughter.

"You look just like your father!" Gayle exclaimed and it seemed with specific reference.

"Yes, I have discovered that," beseeching her next comment, and she continued.

"I know your father and his wife, Barbara. I know you could not have known that, Julie."

"What? How?"

"Well I'm not really a friend or anything, what I mean is, I met them and visited with them when I attended a special dinner with my late husband out at the Center for Abused Children that Barbara volunteers at. We were guests invited because my brother—in—law is a priest who knows Barbara's work there and he is also a very close personal confidant to her."

"This is amazing," I said, dizzily.

"Your father, Frank Sinatra, is a wonderful man, just a wonderful man," Gayle went on. "He has given a lot of money to help those children. He changed from the way he had been when his mother died in a plane accident some years ago. He went back to the Catholic Church—And, his singing was just wonderful! Did you ever see him in concert?"

I explained to her that I had been steered way away from anything about him by my mother as I grew up and knew very little about him and had never seen a concert in person. Her enthusiasm was apparent as she shared more.

"He was a great performer. He was wonderful with an audience, and the Rat Pack was very entertaining. People just loved him." Her repeating use of past tense caught my attention.

When I expressed my desire to meet my father and asked her whether or not her brother-in-law would consider speaking with Barbara on my behalf Gayle withdrew from her previous tone.

"Oh, I don't know. I just don't think there is anyway I could get involved in that. You're going to need a top attorney to help you with this, Julie. It's going to be very hard for you to accomplish meeting your father. I just don't know the

Sinatra's well enough to help you. I know they live in Beverly Hills, up on Foothills Road or something like that."

I wanted to interrupt to ask if she had my father's whole address. The dinner she attended must have been a fund-raiser and she probably got a thank you note—maybe even from my father or Barbara. Gayle allowed no opening for me to jump in ...

"They sold his house he loved so much out in the Palm Springs area last year. He is not just ill now, he is seriously ill. He had to be lifted by helicopter to then be flown out to Los Angeles when they left the house. They sometimes also live at their address in Malibu, on the beach there."

"How seriously ill?" I braved while still clinging to some optimism. I had caught a glimpse of this on the news one night. A musician who played in his orchestra was interviewed after visiting with Frank Sinatra at his home. The man shared that Frank was up and around but would probably not return to going out on the road with his music again.

"He has heart trouble, heart attacks. He is very ill and is being kept under wraps." Gayle continued.

When she finished talking I felt the dynamics of a pendulum swinging, saw the salt seeping down to the bottom section of the hourglass. My heart sank into the prayer—"Please don't let me be too late."

"I do have an attorney," I stated to her, addressing her earlier comment. "She is not a top LA lawyer, but is local here. Her husband knows me and I have credibility with them so I feel comfortable about being represented by her. He's acting as her paralegal and the first step is going to see my mother in Vista." Gayle wished me luck and I had no idea she was to play a large role in all of this in the near future.

When Rod phoned me a couple of days later I understood that attorneys want to communicate with attorneys and I signed the agreement for Carol Lynne to represent me with Rod as her paralegal. It was naïve I guess but I could not help asking why sisters couldn't communicate with sisters.

I had asked Tina for a quiet private avenue in which to meet my father, if he wanted it. She should have been able to see that the photographs of me as a child and recent ones as well revealed the likeness to Frank Sinatra. There had been a repeat airing I had watched back in June of the TV show Magnum P.I. in which he guest starred as a retired New York police detective tracking down the killer of his little granddaughter. In a close up of him holding a picture of the child I had been struck with the irony of his portrayal of grief over the loss of the little girl, as it was the first time for me to see him as an actor. But a feeling of excitement had also been sparked when I discovered the physical features we both had in common—Our blue eyes of course, but not just the color, also the shape, and our mouths were the same—the bone structure of our faces—we had the same skinny arms, and our hands looked almost identical including the shapes of our fingernails. So, I knew I looked like my father. Gayle had just recognized that and even months before when I had performed my music singing with my guitar, a young man in the audience had come up to me and asked if I had been famous back in the sixty's. "You look like someone famous," he stated when I had just smiled back.

The trip to California was at hand a week later when Rod phoned me.

"Hi Julie, this is Rod. I'll pick you up at 8 AM tomorrow morning. I'm bringing a tape recorder to get down everything your mother has to say while we're there. You will need the facts from her surrounding your birth to convince the family about who you are".

I was kicking myself for not pinning Gayle down to possibly get my father's home address. With second thoughts I realized after hearing how ill he was that a letter might not be presented to him directly. It would be better to have more facts about me to convince Barbara that I truly had a right to ask to meet her husband.

Rod seemed so confident about going over to my mother's, but I still had the physic bruises from those parting words she used after confirming Frank Sinatra was my father. I was still haunted by her phrase: "Cancel this call."

CHAPTER FOUR

Mid-February, 1997

I knew my mother would be at home because she always was. But I was nervous about what Rod and I would be walking into since I had not been able to reach her by phone before we flew over there. She often had her phone unplugged to keep my half-sister, Lisa who lived with her from making expensive long distance calls. Rod agreed to pull off the freeway in a little beach town after leaving the airport in San Diego before driving the rest of the 30 miles or so northeast to Vista. I needed a cup of coffee for fortitude before arriving at my mother's house, a place I had vowed for years I would never go to again. Coming down the off-ramp into Lacadia I could see the ocean in view a few blocks ahead. I sat outside of the café so I could hear the sound of the waves, their repeating rhythm helped me to center myself. Rod was anxious about the time and we left to continue on to our destination. It seemed like just a handful of minutes passed when he pulled in mother's driveway at her California bungalow style home located at the edge of a Barrio. Her garden as usual was bursting with flowers—red carnations, purple pin cushions and pink Mexican poppies arranged as if they were growing as wild flowers in a small field framed by colorful terracotta pots of geraniums and various succulents—all blooming because of the mild climate. She looked up with just the faintest look of surprise as Rod and I came through her door.

"Hello, Little Girl," she greeted, never having called me that before.

I introduced Rod to her as Lisa and her friend got up from the dining table where mother was sitting and announced they were on their way out somewhere. Rod explained why we had come and asked mother if she objected to his taping the conversation. Luring us into the tempest she agreed not to object and proceeded to disjoin my already fragile optimism by delivering a violent blow as she added, "but you should know that my daughter suffers from fantasies."

Resolute I would not be set adrift I quickly retorted, "Where do you get an idea like that? You have already confirmed that Frank Sinatra is my father."

"Don't you remember the phone call we had recently when you called me for money?"

"No, well, yes,—But we didn't discuss Frank Sinatra, Julie."

I pulled out the little scrap of paper I had written down that conversation on when it happened and read it to her.

"Yes," she said. "I remember the conversation but I never said Frank Sinatra was your father, though I may have said something about our sharing birthdays the same month."

"I can't believe you are lying about this, Mother, what is your reason for doing this?"

"We used to go to the Springs," she stated and trailed off, not elaborating. "You ruined my fun life when you were born," she shouted, then glaring at me, "After you were born I couldn't go around to the resorts anymore—they considered me for singing at one time because I was Italian. They thought all Italians could sing."

"I don't remember you ever singing," I said back set adrift by this time by my own emotions. Her face looked hurt and I felt sorry.

I got up from the dining table and went into the kitchen and poured myself a cup of coffee from her 1950's vintage coffee pot. Rod was listening to her as mother told him my cousin Pat had once told her that "Julie was around the bend," in reference to the explanation I had given about not having the money to travel to my aunt's funeral because of MS cutting off my income. I didn't feel like arguing and I hoped Rod would soon begin what we came for. In view was a scalloped edged mahogany table in the living room where a little ruby colored glass duck sat half buried by an ashtray's overflow of cigarette butts. I began looking for a dust cloth to clean it up with when my mind slipped back to a day when my step-daddy, Harry had visited my mother and I before they were married when I was four. The white Santa Barbara style house with a Spanish tiled roof and rose bushes lining it's front entry path on "T" Street in Sacramento washed over my eyes …

I was picking up one of the two little glass ducks that had fallen on the floor accidentally swiped off mother's table where I had been dusting—getting to be a "big girl." The table stood nearby a soft jade green stone fireplace that had a carved relief above the firebox. It was glowing from the late summer light coming through a large arched picture window draped on each side by wine colored velvet panels. One of the ducks had shattered upon hitting the tile that buffered any hot ashes from the hardwood floor. The other was in tact having fallen upon a mostly blue and rose colored Karestan carpet I used to enjoy laying on and staring up at the carved timber sized crossbeams that supported the high church like ceiling. I returned the safe little duck to the table, but mother had seen what happened and I was still upset when Harry arrived …

"Hocky!" I squealed, jumping off the last step of the stairs that led down from my bedroom. Bounding over to him where he was already seated in one of mother's chairs, I climbed up on his lap and hugged him, sighing my nickname for him again. "Hocky I want you to meet this little duck," I said as I climbed down and retrieved it from the table. "It's very sad because it's all by itself. I broke its friend. It was mother's favorite." I was becoming almost hysterical. "I was careless!" Harry looked sympathetic as my mother suddenly interrupted, upsetting me even more by lying to him.

"You broke two of the ducks, Julie. There used to be three of them." She turned to Harry and explained how it happened while I was dusting for her.

"No!" I screamed. "I didn't break the other one. A man did it! Accidents happen!"

Harry had intervened that day by suggesting we all go for a ride in his Nash to William Lands Park where we could see real ducks … I realized that since there had been no man present when the duck got broken in my mother's house, the incident must have triggered a previous memory of traumatic proportions where I had or I had been present when something had been broken somewhere else—somewhere my mother needed me not to remember.

I found something to clean up the ashtray with as mother turned her attention from Rod and called out to me.

"Julie, you've never dusted for me before."

"I was the one who did most of your dusting and vacuuming as I recall Mom." Then within full mutiny I added: "I see you still have this little glass duck."

"There used to be three of them," she retorted with a smirk.

"Three? I thought there were only two. I remember breaking one of them when I was very little."

"No—I need to correct you.," and she went on telling it her way still fifty plus years later. I was about to confront her with what man broke the other one and where did that happen when Rod interjected.

"The tape is running, Dorothy, and I have some questions to ask you. Is that okay?"

"Yes." She smiled up at him turning sideways and crossing her legs. She now had that same demure expression on her face I had recognized on the night of my discovery.

"Rod, you are looking at the same scene I saw portrayed in the Sinatra miniseries." He nodded.

"The night you confirmed he was my father was good for you too—to finally have let that out, Mother."

Her face changed to an expression that said "I'm in power here, Little Girl," as she attacked.

"It's not true. You had a nightmare about it." You already mailed the letter and I said, Oh we have a birthday together!," she spouted angrily. I wondered why she had used the word, "nightmare"?

I read the little scrap of paper out loud again.

"No. I haven't used the name Lyma for years." She stated in reference that Frank would know her as Lyma—that she had been Dorothy Lyma at that time.

"You confirmed that Frank Sinatra was my father and the world hasn't fallen apart, right?"

"The sun is still out." Rod interjected. I had almost forgotten he was there.

"I have a bad neck that's coming up a little bit," she complained, then, recovering herself added quickly, "I'm sorry, I just remember about his birthday. It's just that way." Then quietly chuckling, she said, "I'm sorry. I never met him."

Clearly she wanted to sink my ship, but I was not ready to go down with it.

"Why did I get a call back from Tina Sinatra and the invitation to write her the letter?"

"They called you?"

She actually seemed thrown off her course by what I had just said to her. "I didn't know they'd called you. Before you talked to me that had happened?"

Tina produced the movie I saw you being portrayed in as a starlet, mother."

"What name did they give the starlet?" She asked carefully.

"Just 'starlet," I answered and her face changed to one of relief.

Rod spoke up. "Dorothy, Julie got that call back within ..." I cut in. "Fifteen minutes or so after I left my message and the name, Lyma".

"The whole thing is foreign to me," mother chuckled.

"You can imagine how this must be for Julie." Rod added.

"It seems that along the way there have been some people involved who knew that Tom Lyma, in spite of the birth certificate, was not the true natural father of Julie," Rod directed to mother.

Mother chuckled and looked over at me. "When your son Dan had his first haircut he looked like Tom Lyma's son, Don."

"Dan looks like me, Mom, so he couldn't look like Don Lyma—a person I am not even related to." I stated firmly, hoping to shake her from her lying.

"Did you have a lot of contact with Tom Lyma after the divorce?" Rod asked me.

"No. I didn't even meet him until I was seven years old. Mother was married to Harry who owned a drugstore in Sacramento. Mr. Lyma or Tom as I was told to call him, got out of a car parked behind my mother's when we arrived. He walked over to me and bent down and kissed me on the lips saying he had waited a long time to meet me. I had been horrified by this."

"Years ago you talked about this, Julie, and I corrected you." Mother argued. You were two and we were already divorced when Mr. Lyma's girlfriend picked you up from our house on "T" Street where you stayed a few days with them once. Don't you remember that?"

No. Of course a two year old didn't remember.

"When you divorced did you stay in the "T" Street house?"

"Yes," mother answered Rod. "He had a house a few miles away from mine where he lived."

"There's been some discussion that has occurred concerning the possibility that Mr. Lyma had some knowledge or connection to the group that has been known as the Mafia."

"I don't think so." Mother grinned at Rod. "He was a little shot who wanted to be a big shot. He was my boss before I married him and he worked as a traveling salesman that sold Italian stuff to restaurants."

"Did you know him very long before you married him?" Rod asked.

"Yes two or three years. I guess my typing wasn't so good so I decided I'd better marry him." She said chuckling.

Rod shared with a chuckle back, and cleared his throat. "Do you think he ever had any doubt that he was Julie's father?"

"No. I never got that at all. He would boast of her that she had pretty eyes to people."

"Were Tom's eyes blue?"

"No. Brown." Realizing she had trapped herself, mother became agitated. "I don't really know what this is coming to. Why are we doing this?"

"We're here to find out," Rod began but mother cut him off.

"I don't think Frank Sinatra was ever known to be in Sacramento!" She shouted.

I got up from the dining table and walked to the back of the house. I was hoping I could locate those early photos of mother in her glamorous days to show Rod. The ones I remembered weren't in sight but one I had never seen before was sitting in a frame on her dresser. She had always been either a blonde or redhead. Her hair was cut short and in curls and she was a brunette. I took it back out and showed it to Rod. "Wasn't she beautiful?" I directed to him.

"She still is." Rod stated as mother smiled back without an explanation of the picture that had been hidden for years. Did it surface only now because the cat had been left out of the bag? A photograph she could look at every day now to remind her of that time with Frank Sinatra?

She was calm again and Rod was moving on so I decided to go outside. Maybe he would do better with her if I wasn't present. I could hear what was being said through the open screen door.

"Why do you remember sharing a birthday with Frank Sinatra?"

"I don't know. It has always stayed with me."

"Do you remember Tom Lyma's birthday?"

"I think it was January."

"Harry's?

"No." She wasn't sure about Carroll Hunter's either.

"Frank's is right next to me, on the 12 of December for him and the 9 for me."

She wasn't sure about mine also, only Frank Sinatra's.

Before I wandered a little out of earshot I heard her tell Rod that all her brothers and sisters had died—that she alone was the only one with any information about "that time," as she called it. I was sadly aware that I had not been informed of their passing on. She had taken over all the correspondence with them, saying years ago that it was easier for them to get the news from just one letter. So I hadn't stayed in direct contact with anyone on her side of the family. I realized that this had been a control tactic for the secret, lest it be leaked by a sympathetic relative. I smoked a cigarette out in the driveway and noticed that the plants I had left in her care when I became homeless had been allowed to die, while the rest of her garden flourished. I stepped back over to where I could overhear them talking. Rod was asking her if she had ever had an affair while she was married to Mr. Lyma. She admitted she had done so, but evaded stating the man's specific name. Rod chose wisely by continually asking her about "the man" as opposed to asking her about Frank Sinatra. She described "the man" as tall with broad shoulders and dark hair. She said his eyes might have been blue …

From Rod's taping:

There was a man in your life at the time of 1942 and 1943?

Uh-huh.

And that man's name you don't recall although you said it was English, a short name?

Yes. Short. George or maybe Frank.

And you had an affair with this man while you were married to Tom Lyma?

Yes.

Can you talk a bit more about this? Like, when you met him? Julie would have been conceived in May or June of '42, for instance?

I think I met him in the late 30's or 1940. I don't know now. I met him coming from a movie.

From the movies you said? Do you remember what you saw?

No. But it was black and white.

And you said you then saw him a couple of times a month, for a couple of years?

Something like that, yes.

Could that man have been Julie's father?

I never thought of it. It never entered my mind.

Was the timing such that it could have been?

I don't know, maybe.

Okay, was there anyone else during that period of time?

No. The last name was English, four or five letters. The first name might have been George or Frank, and there was a cousin involved.

What was the cousin's name?

I don't remember, but it was similar or the same. I don't know.

Whose cousin?

I don't remember.

Now Tom Lyma was involved in selling food to restaurants. Did he travel out of town?

Sometimes, Saturdays or Sundays. He said he needed a rest period from working hard.

Where was that?

Sacramento mostly, but throughout California and Nevada.

Did he go to Las Vegas and Los Angeles too?

Not often.

Do you remember when you married Mr. Lyma?

I don't know.

Do you know where you were married-what city that was in?

Carson, no. It was Tijuana, in Mexico.

Can you remember how many years difference it was after you divorced Tom and married Harry?

Maybe four years.

So you married Harry in 1947?

Yes, somewhere in there. Julie liked him.

He was the one who got her the horses?

Yes.

What did Tom Lyma think when you were pregnant with Julie?

He was proud.

When were you divorced from him?

I don't know, before Julie was two I think.

And the man you said you had the affair with around 1942—you said he had a black Buick in the 30's model?

Yes. Not too flashy. Not too plain.

Did you keep up with Frank Sinatra's career at that time?

Never. I didn't like him when he was singing. He was skinny. I liked Bing Crosby at that time. Sinatra looked better when he was older.

Did you see that man again when you were pregnant with Julie, or after she was born?

No. He moved away to somewhere in California. He didn't live in Sacramento.

When did he tell you he was moving to this new place?

I think I read it. I read it.

In a newspaper or magazine?

Uh-huh.

Is that when the relationship broke off between you?

No. It was before that I think.

When you told him you were pregnant with Julie?

No. I broke it off when I became pregnant. *I don't think he knew …*

She had nothing else to add and we left for the airport. Rod agreed that it was hard to understand her behavior in not wanting to clear the air and come forward to help me meet my father. He thought perhaps the "secret" had been her way of having control over her daughter's life. What ever her reason I felt betrayed once again by my own mother. My father could be dying and her stalling could keep me from ever being able to meet him. Staring out the plane's window, fighting back my tears, the only "fantasy" that came to my mind was a little girl from Kansas confronted by a wicked witch in the Wizard Of OZ. Each time "Cancel this call" ran through me I wanted to grab a pail of water and throw it on her.

Father and Daughter

Grandson, Daniel Hunter Brown

Grandfather, Francis Albert Sinatra

Dan and Frank 30's something…

CHAPTER FIVE

Back for the facts Jack ...

O h I know what you must be thinking—And you're right. It was dumb to go over there without first having prepared ourselves with even just a little knowledge about where Frank Sinatra was and who the people were that surrounded him during the period of 1942 through February of 1943—Especially when my mother was already known for her unpredictable behavior. As Rod put it, "She is a crafty alcoholic who succeeded in leading me astray several times." I was hoping that this hindsight would not act as a bridge to no where when I began reading Kitty Kelly's "His Way," The Unauthorized Biography of Frank Sinatra, after the trip. I was counting on how a person who lies always includes some truth—she would have left some clues.

"Hi Julie. This is Rod. I ordered a copy of the mini-series and it came in. I'll bring it over for you to look at again. Do you have a video machine?"

"Yes I do."

"Good. It might help if you viewed it again knowing what to look and listen for—in case you might have missed something that will be of help."

Kitty Kelly had made quite a point about the lawsuit my father lost after trying for two years to stop her book. She also eluded to the idea that the mini-series was made to combat what she would possibly be presenting about him. Frank Sinatra wanted to "tell his own story." So, when I viewed the video and saw that the scenes regarding my mother had been re-arranged to be shorter, omitting the part about the baby girl who was born, I realized why the gal in New York had found the taping of it pulled from the usual file. Apparently there had been more than one version and the wrong one had been shown. I had already passed the early '40's in Ms. Kelley's book. There was nothing about an illegitimate child being born Frank fathered. There was no accusation about this for the mini-series to combat as it did not even air the first time until 1992—a few years after Kelley's book came out—During the period I had been homeless and had no television. The segment about the divorce with Mia Farrow had been changed to portray something less harsh, maybe for the same pragmatic. But there was a starlet who caught my attention in Kitty Kelley's book, named Alora Gooding. Alora's timing in her affair with Frank Sinatra was reported as having begun in 1940, lasting a couple of years. This was a match for the dates my mother had given. There was more.

A picture of what must have taken place began to form as I read about "the man" with the "English sounding name," as mother had called him. He was George Evans, my father's early publicist who, besides deserving the credit for the strong promotion that spurned his career to stardom, also was the person who struggled to maintain the sellable image of Frank Sinatra as the boy next door. Evans, who was based out of New York, relied on Nick Servano to keep an eye on Frank's womanizing—an affair would have been trouble in the press—a pregnant starlet, a disaster.

Nick Servano was acting as my father's personal manager and valet. He was on hand, it was reported, when Frank Sinatra met with Alora Gooding upon his arrival with Tommy Dorsey's band in Hollywood, October, 1940. Frank and Alora moved into the Plaza Hotel and were living together. The Plaza was not far from the Palladium Theatre where the band was currently appearing for the theatre's grand opening, but they had come mainly to appear in the movie, Las Vegas Nights where my father sang the song, "I'll Never Smile Again" without credit. This must have been the movie my father and mother came out of when they met, mother had told Rod about. The mini-series placed them together back in June of 1940. Maybe the song had to be pre-recorded for the movie at that time to be ready to dub in for filming in the fall. According to Kelly, my half-sister, Nancy was born on June 8, 1940. The mini-series showed Frank and the starlet together when the call came about her being born in New Jersey where he had his home with his wife, Nancy Barbato Sinatra. It looked like my mother and father had met at least for the second time in October and that's when the affair took off.

According to Kitty Kelly, Nick Servano had visited Alora Gooding when she had left Hollywood to be treated for Tuberculosis—He said in Saracen, New York. Could Saracen have been misheard for Sacramento? Or was Servano deliberately misleading Kelly? My mother had directed her third husband, Carroll Hunter to a section of Sutter's Hospital in Sacramento once when the three of us were out for a Sunday drive, a popular recreational activity during the 50's when gasoline was cheap and the pace of living was slower. She had pointed out a building there and whispered that it was the TB Unit to him. She had never discussed having TB with me—something which took place in the period of her life she'd kept secret. My older cousin Bob had told me about how my mother was always watchful over my health when I was little. My mother told me that I had pneumonia when I was born at Sutter Hospital and was kept there for a couple of months. Was she pregnant with me when she had TB? No date was given regarding Alora's bout with TB in Ms. Kelly's book.

In May of 1941 Frank Sinatra was named as Top Band Vocalist by Billboard Magazine, surpassing, Bing Crosby. During this time my father was on the road with Dorsey and was back and forth between the East and West coasts. In January, 1942, he gave notice to the bandleader that he planned to leave and begin his solo career. This would account for my mother saying they saw each other only a couple of times a month during the affair she reported lasted two years with the man named, "George or Frank." In Kelly's passages, Nick Servano is blamed for aiding Frank's womanizing by Nancy Sr., who has found a photo of Alora Gooding in her husband's wallet when he was home. Nick was instantly fired and a cousin was now to be the personal valet. My father's full name I discovered only now by reading this book, was Francis Albert Sinatra. The cousin had the same name of Frank Sinatra and was usually called "Junior." So, I had found the mystery men. My merriment sobered as I realized this meant the family probably had a way to recognize who I was, and they chose not to. I had included an early photograph of my mother when I'd sent all the pictures out there with my letter to Tina.

Just before Tommy Dorsey let my father out of his contract. The arranger, Axel Stordahl, took him into a recording studio in Hollywood. Frank Sinatra sang three songs. My mother had the sheet music for two of them in our home— "Night And Day" and "The Lamplighter's Serenade." She never had any other song sheets—Was this when she had been considered for singing?—maybe, as a backup chorus singer or something? There were no Frank Sinatra records in our home, but my mother had several recordings by Lena Horne. She seemed to act as though she had known the beautiful singer personally, saying how she'd "liked" Lena Horne—I thought I also remembered that she had added, before trailing off—"because she was always nice to me."—when I played one of her records and commented that I liked her voice. Kitty Kelly, in her research for her book, had discovered Lena Horne among the artists that George Evans represented during that period. Nick Servano had told Kelly Frank had rehearsed madly for this recording session privately at the Plaza—maybe mother was still there sharing in his early excitement about going solo and left Hollywood before the actual recording of the record, possibly months later. In January, 1942 when the record was finished she would have been 8 months pregnant with me, and she had stated she had already broken off the affair. The record reportedly convinced my father and Axel Stordahl that a solo career for Sinatra was guaranteed to succeed.

A further segment in "His Way" got me off the hook for having "ruined" my mother's "fun life." I spotted a photograph of what I was 99.9999 percent sure was of her taken at a New Year's party held in Frank Sinatra's home in 1946 where he had moved his family, Nancy Sr. and Nancy Jr., and Franklin Wayne Emanual Sinatra who had been born in January, 1944. This was what mother must have been referring to when she told Rod she had read in a newspaper or magazine that the man she had the affair with had moved to a new home in California.

My mother's half face was shown in the photograph taken of an unnamed starlet according to Kitty Kelly's account who was sitting up on a stair, ironically, just above Ava Gardner. My mother's hair was very blonde and she was dressed in a gorgeous gown and looked as glamorous as any big star. I wasn't used to seeing her that way and the photo did throw me a bit.

The picture appeared in the book shortly following a passage where it had been reported to Kelly that a starlet had been seen to be wearing a diamond dinner ring by Nancy Sr., one she'd recently given to Frank to take somewhere to be cleaned. I believe that was the ring my mother had shown me when I was a teenager and we were living in Long Beach.

Arrow points to Julie's mom sitting behind Ava Gardner.

She had called me into her bedroom one afternoon and I followed her to her closet area where she had a chest of drawers. She opened the top drawer and took out a box of jewelry. She picked up the ring that I remember was oval in shape or perhaps diamond shaped, and handed it to me to see. I think I remembered it had a small group of larger diamonds with tiny ones surrounding it—but it wasn't round. She said it had been given to her by my, "father." Since she always referred to Tom Lyma as Tom to me because that is what I had always been told to call him—never "father," this had stood out as not fitting that norm. She included showing me a jade pennant on a gold chain and said it was also given to her from my "father." My mother never wore the ring or the jade necklace. They had been put away just like the fancy gowns and shoes that, as far as my memory went, had always hung in bags with sachets of moth balls in an out of the way closet. When I was little I would go and retrieve one—It was like playing dress up with glamorous ghosts from her unexplained past …

In the mini-series there was a scene like this that depicted Marilyn Maxwell, an actress Frank Sinatra allegedly had an affair with, as being caught wearing, not a ring, but a bracelet that once belonged to Nancy Sr. at the same party. Nancy Sr. became as any wife would, very upset and threw her out of her house … Marilyn Maxwell was a blonde too, but she was not the woman in the photograph. Maybe Nancy Sr. ushered two gals out of there that evening …

Less than a week had gone by since Rod and I returned from seeing my mother when my phone rang on March 2, 1997.

"Julie, this is Gayle. I've been thinking about this thing about you and your father, Frank Sinatra, and it interests me. I've changed my mind about becoming involved, that is if you still want me to be." She began saying this without so much as a hello, almost like someone on a mission.

"If you can be of any help at all I would appreciate it." I stated back wondering where this was going to lead—hoping it was sincere.

"What did your mother have to say when you went over there?"

"She spent most of the day attempting to put her cat back in the bag." She refused to give any clear facts surrounding the time of my birth that would help convince my father's family that I am for real."

"I can possibly help you where your credibility is concerned through my brother—in—law, but you can't ever let anyone know this—Okay?"

"I want this to remain quiet and private within the family. Can you arrange for a meeting for me with Barbara?"

"I don't know if that can happen. Your father had a serious heart attack back in January, and he is still very ill. Barbara probably would not meet with you any-time soon."

"I could just sit quietly with him ..." She cut me off.

"I don't know. Are you seeking anything material?"

The motive for her call had been suggested by the question and I told her that I was not and that I wanted to see my father while we were both alive. "What is the prognosis for his recovery?" I asked, barely getting a word in as she took back the control of our conversation.

"I'm not privy to that information. Did your mother give you any facts at all?"

"She made reference to his being my father in round about ways—Rod told me she had cemented my credibility even though that had not been her inten-tion."

"I see. I need to get off the phone." Gayle was finished with the interview and we hung up.

I felt insulted over the question about whether or not I was "seeking anything material." But we live in a culture where people think everything is about money—at least the ones do that have it. What kind of relationship could begin between my father and I, if we got the chance to have one, if he believed I was only interested in asking him for money? There was no way to hide the fact that my finances were lacking—I hoped Gayle had not shared how I was living. I never told her how precarious my situation actually was—and I didn't intend to. The fact is at this time it had just become worsened. My landlord who lived in

California had been renting a condo in town whenever he came to continue work on building the main house on the property. On March 1st he stopped by my little abode to give me two months notice for moving me out. He planned to live there himself. My rent was way below what it would cost to live in a regular home with horse facilities, and my earnings would not cover it. I was anxious from facing separation from my horses and I knew I had to solve this soon—but I was not going to do it by "seeking anything material" from my father.

I phoned Rod and shared my conversation with Gayle.

"It looks like a back avenue has opened for this," he said with some interest adding—"What did you tell her?"

"The truth."

Rod shared that his wife Carol Lynne still wanted to pursue this as my attorney and had written a letter to Robert Finkelstein stating her representation for my desire to meet my father. He assured me she had made it clear that I was not looking for any litigation. I needed an attorney to help me but I couldn't help worrying over how it would seem to my father's family. I decided to phone Tina's office again and tell her personally that my only motivation in coming forward at this time was because I wanted to meet my father. The call lasted only a few seconds as Lisa Tan upon hearing it was me on the other end of her line, quickly stated that their attorney had advised them not to speak with me, and abruptly hung up the phone.

On March 5th, I got another call from Gayle—very short.

"There's going to be something on television tonight at 6:30 on Channel 3 about your father. I know this because I've been watching TV all day when it was announced that Barbara would be on talking about her husband's heart attack."

Barbara Sinatra asked the fans to be, "patient." She explained he was recovering but it would be a couple of months before he would be his old self again. The segment was shot in their home but he did not appear even for a walkthrough in the background or a wave hello. Still this gave me hope that he would be all right again and maybe also it was Barbara's way of saying to me as well that if I could just be patient I would be able to meet with him. I crossed my fingers, and making my mother less of a liar, I fantasized about a walk on the beach in Malibu talking quietly with my father.

Further evidence of my mother's fun times in Hollywood surfaced when I watched the video of the movie, "Anchors Aweigh." Because it had been made in 1944 during the years I suspected my mother was still in Hollywood and I was beginning to act like a private eye searching the truth of my own life, a supportive friend rented it for me. I was on target and located her in the beginning part. The movie was first released by MGM in 1945 and my father starred in it along with Gene Kelly and Kathryn Grayson. My mother as an extra in her role was not credited, but she was playing a switchboard operator with her hands busily connecting the calls, including the one Gene and my father were making from the docks where they had just been given leave from their ship in the Navy. The two of them played sailors out on the town looking for gals. Kelly was the confident leader in this and Sinatra was his apprentice—still within that image of the naïve innocent lad.

Frank memorizing his lines at lunch break on the set of Anchors Aweigh *with screenwriter Isobel Lennart*

My mother had bright red hair for the part and a light blue suit on. Her back was turned from the camera but I spotted her right away—wouldn't you know your own mother even if she was turned away from you? This also fit with another of my missing puzzle pieces as I once got a job as a switchboard operator during the 60's after I was divorced from my son's father. Mother had joked with me saying she had also once had a job doing that—I knew she had never worked outside of our home as I grew up and had only worked once for a short time as a receptionist who greeted people when they came into the Rancho Los Alamitos hospital where Jerry Lewis used to visit and cheer up the crippled children. She did not operate a switchboard there. Her getting a job suddenly without ever having worked before always had seemed odd, as I knew from my own work history how many employers looked for an experienced person to hire ... George Evans, my father's publicist had also been the agent representing Dean Martin and Jerry Lewis ...

"Anchors Aweigh" was a big hit and did a lot for my father's acting career.

He was reportedly, good friends with Gene Kelly who taught him how to dance for the part that called for a lot of it. He also performed the beautiful song, "I Fall In Love Too Easily," among the few he sang in the movie.

So, my mother was there—was I around also?—or—did she leave me with a baby-sitter up in Sacramento? There were never any photos that I ever saw that showed where and how my mother and I had lived before we were in the "T" Street house in Sacramento. My own photographic history begins when I was four, in 1947.

Me—"T" Street House   Mom in 1947

I did recall a time when Harry was my stepfather and we lived in the country outside of Sacramento during the early 50's. Gene Kelly was scheduled to be coming to Carmichael to scout for a child talent for a part in a movie he was planning and my elementary school teacher phoned my mother about it. I was usually the one my teacher chose to sing the solo parts in the glee club and she must have believed I had talent. Mother pooh-poohed it over the phone and I overheard her and was upset about not getting to go to the audition. Gene Kelly could very possibly have recognized her and possibly me as well—that could have threatened her … But it was my mother who had enrolled me in tap dancing and ballet lessons when we still lived in the Sacramento house. Was she just finding somewhere to place my excessive energy—Or did she have plans at one time to return to Hollywood—and was grooming her child to become the next Shirley Temple? I was five or six when I tap-danced as one of the 'brooms' in a chorus line of children for a Halloween event at the Shriner's Auditorium in Sacramento—I looked the part as I was the very thin one amongst the others plumped by their baby fat—like Frank Sinatra stood out as so skinny as he danced in Anchors Aweigh—and for at least one time I was a hoofer just like my father.

So why didn't she ever go back to her fun glamorous life? When Kitty Kelly interviewed Nick Servano for her book he reportedly told her that Frank had wanted to divorce Nancy to marry Alora, but Evans and additionally, Frank's mother Dolly raised holy hell with him over it. My mother and father apparently had at one time a very real love relationship. What happened?

Rod had phoned my mother to talk with her about the information I had gathered. I hoped it would open her up. He reported back that she was someone he believed wanted to tell her story but was more locked up than before. He was not able to present anything I had found.

"Your mother once again spent the conversation trying to discredit you, Julie. Clearly she carries a deep resentment for you."

"She always has."

"I don't think she will ever come forward to help you meet your father."

The air was cold blowing through the tack room, accenting the chill I felt from his words. After we hung up I took my dog Harley for a walk to get out in the sunshine. I was trying to think back again wondering what it was that could be blocking her—and why still all these years later? What ever it was I knew I would have to try to bring it to the surface. My exile had gone on for too long separating me from the man I could feel the growing connection with to allow something from way back in the past to interfere now—My father and I deserved a healing together.

I remembered how I had been surprised at her words "Julie had a nightmare about it." during one of her denials that she had confirmed Frank Sinatra was my father. Was this said to preempt my bringing up another old memory she was ready to correct? There had been an incident that began around the time of my fourth birthday. It remained a mystery that had never been resolved each time I had brought it up to my mother. It had the makings of a bad dream for a child— It surely must have been a nightmare for her.

CHAPTER SIX

Wool jodhpurs that itch …

M y mother sometimes went out of town when I didn't go with her. I remember the heart-shaped cake with pink frosting my mother had baked a day early for my birthday, on February tenth. She was going on another one of her trips and the cake and I were going out to my grandmother's where I would be spending a whole week. I didn't mind because I liked visiting the ranch in Floren and being out in the country. I got to play on the old surreys that my Uncle Bobby kept stored in one of the barns, and I liked exploring down the steps of the musty wine cellar. I was even more excited about going this time because my cousin Patti was going to be there too and I would have someone to play with. I remembered how unprepared I was as a child for the ending this visit would have and the upsetting event that followed it in 1947 …

"Nina. Nina!" my grandmother shouted down to me from a second-story window as I ran for the back steps leading up to the kitchen. The Victorian farmhouse sat in the center of the ranch surrounded by acres of fields planted with grapevines that spread out under a sky uninterrupted only by the tall branches of the walnut tree in the yard. Patti ran out to meet me and within seconds we each had a wedge-shaped anise cookie bar that our grandmother had given us along with her usual warm smile.

My grandmother Julianna Maria Bonucelli was a soft spoken lady who came from Italy and didn't speak English but Patti and I both understood as she gestured she wanted us to help her cut the strips of ravioli dough she had rolled out in a flat sheet on a floured wooden table in the center of the kitchen. I remember everything smelled good there, from the cast iron stove where the tomato sauce was simmering mixed with the burning aroma of wood smoke—mixing with the fragrance of the fresh garden picked herbs and parsley she used to season the minced spinach and ground pork with that would become the filling inside the raviolis.

I never met my grandfather Bonucelli—As the story goes when it was told to me by my mother when I was much older—after the family had come to America from Canada and started the ranch for the purpose of raising grapes for the local wine makers in California—Grandfather made trips back to Tuscany, a northern region of Italy where they originally had vineyards. My grandmother had mostly raised their children on her own. On one of these occasions towards the beginning of World War II, he was in Florence when the Nazi officers took over the family villa there and he was killed. The oldest son who had not married stayed to work the ranch with my grandmother and had taken the role of patriarch of the family.

Uncle Bobby always wore the same cotton shirt beneath his jean overalls that bore out the faded blue color of his eyes against his red tanned face. He smelled of grass and fresh tilled dirt and diesel oil as he lifted me up to sit on the fanny-shaped iron tractor seat and scolded "Why you have to be first?" at my over active enthusiasm. Patti and I had gone out to tell him dinner was almost ready. He picked up Patti and carried her all the way back to the house. After dinner she got to be on his lap where he rocked in his chair by the wood stove while I waited for my turn that never came. My aunt took Patti home a day later and I had to sleep downstairs in a bedroom in the part of the house that was never used anymore instead of the warm room next to the kitchen where we both got to sleep before. It was dark there with the curtains always kept closed across the windows and there were pieces of furniture that stood in a living room with sheets over them. My grandmother tucked me in at nights so I felt better but I wanted my mother to come and take me home also.

I was down in the back yard on a wooden swing that Uncle Bobby had painted green when my mother finally arrived. She barely took notice of me as she went up the steps behind me. My grandmother came out to the back porch and they were both talking together when suddenly their voices were at a high pitch. It seemed my grandmother was bawling out my mother for something and my mother kept defending her side of their argument. This all went on in Italian so I couldn't understand but clearly my mother was in trouble with my grandmother. I had never witnessed anger coming from my gentle grandmother before.

On the way home I explored the rejection, I was too little to know the word for, I'd received from my Uncle Bobby with my mother.

"Uncle Bobby doesn't like me—he only likes Patti."

"Patti's father died and Uncle Bobby feels bad about it," mother offered.

"Do I have a father?"

This question went unanswered and she stated impatiently—"Uncle Bobby prefers Patti because she's quiet."

A short time after we had been home again my mother announced we were going someplace where I would not be able to use a bathroom. I had to have an enema that I remember I screamed through. It was a very cold day and I also had to wear my wool jodhpurs that itched to go on the bus over to a very large house that had a wall built around it. We stopped in front of some wide cement steps that led up to a long covered porch.

"Julie, do not follow me. Mother has business to do and I want you to wait for me down here." mother gave her firm order as she went up the steps where she disappeared behind a shiny dark wooden door. She seemed very upset about something and I knew I had better obey her. I was standing down in a courtyard next to a tree with bare branches and the wind was blowing but the voices of more than one man yelling at my mother were not dampened by it. I ran up the steps. "Don't hurt my mother!" I screamed. A man opened the door and leaned out waving me away. Through the opening I could see my mother standing up in front of a desk where a man in a suit was glaring at her. Two more men also in business suits were sitting on a sofa across the large room against the wall.

"What about Julie?" I heard my mother ask in an agitated tone, as the man at the doorway growled for me to go back down and wait for my mother. I don't think anyone else there had noticed me. I was scared and did as I was told as he stepped back inside and shut the door. I hadn't heard how her question about me might have been answered. Mother eventually came out and we went home. She was too upset to even talk to me.

From time to time I would bring this early childhood memory up to my mother. She always gave the same explanation—she had gone to see those men to discuss her divorce from Mr. Lyma—that they were business associates of his. But now I had the court records of their divorce at the suggestion from Rod to obtain them—It took place in August of 1944—three years earlier than this incident—a mysterious meeting that had all the earmarks of having been a Mafia summons. What, if anything, did Frank Sinatra have to do with it?—It was within that context that she said: "Julie had a nightmare about it."

There had been a passage in Kitty Kelly's "His Way," that discussed a trip Frank Sinatra made to Havana, Cuba in February of 1947. He had repeatedly under gone investigations by the FBI for having made the trip there allegedly to bring money to the mob boss, Lucky Luciano, who had been exiled from the United States. I saw nothing that alluded to a woman being involved in Havana—no Dorothy Lyma/Alora Gooding was mentioned. But the timing of my father's trip was the same as my mother's. This couldn't be just a coincidence.

The answer was blowing all around me. I didn't see it and I didn't know it then, but it was in my destiny to eventually learn what happened—and the information that would solve this mystery would be forth coming from a highly unexpected source to bring me out of the dark.

April 7, 1997—Cave Creek, Arizona

"I knew when I first met you that you reminded me of someone famous, now I know who!" "Okay Sparky, but I want to keep this a secret for now," I said to the musician who was rehearsing with me at the time Rod called with an update.

Sparky had overheard our conversation in which I learned that the attorney, Robert Finkelstein admitted to my attorney, Carol Lynn in a phone call she made to him after getting no response from her letter, not in fact to be the lawyer representing Frank Sinatra or the family. To my surprise and alarm Rod said that Carol Lynn had been told that Frank Sinatra did not have an attorney representing him at this time, and she was told by Finkelstein that Barbara Sinatra's attorney would be the person for contact. Carol Lynn was writing our next letter to an Arthur Crowley … We were going to have to start all over again to plead my desire to meet my father. Two months had been wasted with the clock running while Finkelstein had treated this as if it was a tossed out tin can that rolled onto his path, one he just kicked down the road.

Grinning wildly, squinting his eyes and pointing a finger at me, mimicking a photograph I had seen of my dad in this pose, Sparky produced his next pronouncement, shifting my attention.

"Julie, you don't just look like Frank. You look a lot like Nancy too!"

He followed this by explaining he had once seen her in person when our father had gifted her with a radio station ownership in Arizona some years back. She was there to promote the station in a live performance she gave of her hit song, "These Boots Are Made For Walking."

I tried to imagine what it was like to have your father give you a radio station, but I couldn't relate to it. Our lives were so far apart.

Sparky left soon afterwards and my thoughts focused on an assignment that Rod had given me over the phone. He wanted me to write down all of the missing puzzle pieces that had first come to my mind when I watched the Sinatra mini-series and anything else I could remember from my childhood and beyond that might help to illuminate, as he put it, "that this has been working behind the scenes" all of my life. This information was to be included in a future letter Carol Lynn was already preparing that say more than just her first one to Crowley that just introduced her as my representative to him. It was her hope, Rod's hope, and mine that Crowley would be someone who would be the type of person to want to get to the bottom of this. I had joined in with Rod's optimism but I couldn't help thinking that he might turn out to be just one more lawyer who had no qualms about delaying a daughter who desperately wanted to meet her father, a man reportedly too ill to even have his own attorney representing him.

I had enclosed a letter to my father that had been sent out to Robert Finkelstein by Carol Lynn, asking him to pass it along. In it I said we couldn't do anything about what had gone before, but I hoped maybe now we could share a hug … Clearly it was never forwarded to Frank Sinatra. But the past was involved as the old adage implies. It was where I still had to go to find the door to my future.

CHAPTER SEVEN

Summer of 1947, Sacramento, California ...

A few steps across a small porch at the back of our kitchen in the "T" Street house was another door leading to what was originally intended for a maid's quarters in use now as an attached rental apartment. Most of the time it was vacant as the tenants traveled a lot. I remember a day I knew they were home.

"Don't pester them Julie! They are resting!" My mother who had just come out onto the porch caught me knocking on the door. She was whispering loudly and reaching for me when suddenly a stretched out arm appeared from behind the door as it slowly opened. Moving towards me, the hand quickly retrieved a little red wooden apple from behind one of my ears as I squealed and bolted through the opening.

"It's okay Dorothy," the handsome Mr. Christian laughed and assured my mother, who relented. "She can help me practice my magic act," he concluded. Mrs. Christian had cookies and she smiled at my merriment over each wooden apple or shinny new penny that appeared and disappeared, seemingly, at his command ...

My mother had once shown me a post card from the Christians that had come all the way from London, England. They had become famous enough eventually to play before the Queen. Until that happened they had been on a circuit, one casino lounge at a time in mostly Nevada in the 40's. She said she knew them from the time they had played at the Riverside Inn—a mobby owned hotel and casino in Reno, Nevada. Now, still reading and discovering people and places in my father's life, I learned that the Riverside Inn was where Frank Sinatra had made his debut singing the first time at this type of venue, in 1951—at that low time when, as he put it himself, "These guys were the only ones who gave me any work." The Riverside Inn was also one of those Tom Lyma serviced through his food company—the place where my mother and Tom first met one another, as she had put it during Rod's taped interview, when he "needed to relax" ... The link between the three of them was apparent via the tenants in our house, who could have been sourced from anybody from the Sacramento area, but were not.

This made me wonder if it could have been through my mother, based in her old connections, that my father met the backers for his solo singing career.

When I wasn't visiting the Christians, I liked to go over to our nice neighbor lady's house across our driveway and play her piano. She had shown me how to press down on each key to play the melody along as I sang the words she taught me to "Bell Bottom Trousers, Coats of Navy Blue," a popular song during World War II. I did this at the top of my lungs until she couldn't take any more—she would politely suggest we go out to the orchard in her back yard and pick apricots to take home to my mother.

An audience was hard to come by when I was four and my mother's orange tabby cat became my captive one. I would often sing to him from songs that played on the old

Philco radio we had. Even though he was her cat, he liked to sleep at the end of my bed, and that is where he was when my mother, dressed in a blue floor length hostess gown came waltzing into my room. She had a stranger with her, a man who smiled at the doorway who was wearing glasses. She picked up Red and began to dance around holding him up as her partner. I was startled as she began to sing. Her voice was low and brash. I had never heard her sing before. I was struck by how beautiful she looked as her now red naturally curly hair that once had been blonde, bounced over her shoulders in sync with the lyric, "Come on Red can't you come out tonight, come out tonight, and dance by the silvery moon …" A short time later the nice man became her husband and I got to have a daddy and a last name. Our exodus from her previous glamorous era would now be complete before I was old enough to have memories of it that I could re-call. We would be safe and secure with the man who was a druggist at the pharmacy down the street, where she purchased the little red pills she took every day hence forward—the uppers to lift her each morning from too much Jack Daniels on the night before when she would drown out what was too painful to remember.

But I was something she could not erase and within a few months after her marriage to Harry, my mother's resentment for me escalated. I attached myself to him. He was my harbor from wave after wave of the anger she directed onto me. I didn't have to misbehave to bring it on. I realized now that I must have been like a red flag waving in front of her, especially irritating when I would sing or dance through the house. "Stop that Julie!," she would growl. "Be yourself." I didn't know what that meant as a child but now I see how I was threatening her—acting like the father …

In more than one biography the telling was the same, that Frank Sinatra began singing at a very early age. He was already an entertainer before he was ten when my Grandmother, Natalie Della Sinatra would lift her little son up onto the bar in her speak—easy called Marty O'Brien's in Hoboken, New Jersey. Little Frankie sang the songs popular during the roaring twenties and was tossed pennies from the patrons. Dolly as she was called, also sang, sometimes played a guitar, often danced on the tables. My behaviors as a child could not have been otherwise. This was in my blood.

Harry Misfeldt didn't take long to come up with a solution for the tension between my mother and me. On my fifth birthday in 1948, a pony was waiting in an orange rental horse-trailer outside our house. Within an hour I was up in the saddle for my first ride at my Grandmother's ranch in Floren. "Babe" knew only two gaits: standing still and a dead full out run. Harry and my mother spent the afternoon racing into the pasture to grab the reins under the bridle to bring the wild-eyed pony to a stop ... but I wasn't scared. I loved the wind blowing through my hair and the feeling of freedom it gave me to be astride the thundering movement. I was hooked.

A fun discovery about my real father for me was when I read about his having been on a horse too for his first time in 1948. Frank Sinatra made the movie, "The Kissing Bandit," for MGM that year opposite Kathryn Grayson. My father played a buffoon galloping to her side and falling backwards off his horse into her garden—his sincerity eventually won him the gal.

Later in the year of 1948, Frank Sinatra recorded "Nature Boy" and "Sunflower," two songs among those he performed when he was with Columbia Records ... I was about to become 'nature girl' where sunflowers grew wild and taller than the fences surrounding our pasture beside our new country home in Carmichael, a small town north of Sacramento my step-daddy moved us to in 1949. It would be here where the foothills dotted with strong old oaks rolled beneath the majestic Sierra Nevada mountains that I would form a code to live by, the one that taught me to get back up on the horse every time my life fell.

"Just look straight ahead between the horses ears and picture this dime on the ground here. Squeeze and release your knees a little bit and shift your weight forward and walk him to it and picture stopping right on this dime before you straighten up and say 'whoa' to him," Marshall, my new teacher was giving me more in his lesson than just how to walk and stop a horse.

"I can already ride at the trot. I don't want to just walk this horse." My know—it—all remark was ignored.

"Think with the horse to become one with him. That is how you will become a champion rider," he urged.

This special gift of learning to use telepathy with the horse from Marshall Macgee, as passed down from the old ways in his Native American Sioux heritage, did make me a blue ribbon winner in a short period of time, adding to it of course, my commitment to practice daily. The true reward was the bonding that resulted in my being able to connect this way. The mutual respect and friendship I was able to enjoy with my new horse, "Lil Abner," named after the comic strip character because of Harry's light hearted sense of humor, replaced the rejection I received from my mother. With 'Abner' I had unconditional love and through that I gained self-confidence. Harry, whom I now called "Daddy," was gone from our house for long hours during the week. He still worked at the Rex-al Pharmacy in Sacramento, commuting by car 23 miles each way, unheard of in those days. This left me at the mercy of my mother. My morning chores, cleaning the stall and feeding the horses, kept me mostly out of her view. I was bathed, changed into school clothes and on the bus before I hardly even saw her. But after school I would return and she was always ready for me with a biting sarcastic remark or gruffly delivered orders for cleaning my room or helping her with laundry where my little hand was the one dangerously near the old wringers squeezing out the rinse water from the clothes I later hung up to dry on a line in the back yard. Her eyes were always on me, seething with hatred. I was afraid of her.

My safe place was out on my horse, practicing for a show, or riding, escaping really, on the endless trails far from our house.

On weekends when we didn't get up at the break of dawn to load horses into a trailer and drive miles to a horse show somewhere, I would saddle up after chores in the morning and ride all day into the wilderness on narrow grassy paths along side the American River. In this refuge alone on my horse, I began a life-long connection to the beauty and the creatures of nature. Once while my horse was drinking from a small stream I was sitting on a log resting when a little red fox ran from the space under it between my feet. It stopped and turned to look at me for a second and I said hello before it disappeared into some briar. Sometimes an eagle or a hawk flew above me, it seemed, coming along with me on the ride. When I wasn't playing the harmonica I carried in my jean pocket, I would make up songs about my horses or sing one I learned from the radio by Gene Autry, "I've Got Spurs That Jingle Jangle Jingle." But I wasn't a cowgirl. I always chose to be the Indian when I played cowboys and Indians games with the boys and girls who lived nearby.

I liked to ride bare-back during these games, pretending I was an Indian princess, but I no longer felt the wind blowing through my long hair. My mother kept it cut no more than a few inches from my scalp and in a tight frizzy perm. The first one of many was the day before she took me to Daddy's drugstore to meet Tom Lyma and countless haircuts followed by this treatment happened each time I was about to visit him. I still remember how cold and hard the tiles on our sink counter felt under me as she would hold me down and snip at my hair under the running tap water, also always cold. She would scream into my face to hold still and keep my eyes shut when she applied the hair permanent solution which fumed

Thomas Vincent Lyma 1957

and stung. Her excuse was that I had to look "neat and groomed" both to go visiting and to look right under my cowboy hat in the horse shows. I had no way of knowing I was being disguised to match the frizzy hair on Tom Lyma's head—to look alike with a man who had never been my father-to hide the silky light brown hair with natural strawberry blonde highlights passed down to me by my Grandmother Dolly Sinatra as she also did for my half-sister, Nancy, which has a lot to do with why we resemble each other.

The visits with the Lymas usually lasted only a day or two a couple of times per year. I never felt natural around him, somehow I sensed as a child that something was not right. He would show me photographs of his son Don, who had been killed in the Korean War and I felt sympathy for his loss, but I never felt connected as a person should visiting and learning about 'family.' I remember my mother arguing once over the phone with Tom who was insisting that she not let Harry adopt me as his own child. I don't know what Harry knew about my true paternity, but he did not adopt me. Tom must have been convinced by the frizzy perms that I was his, at least for a time.

Sadly, in August of 1954, Harry Misfeldt passed away from a sudden heart attack. For years I carried the scar from my mother's words when I asked her at that time, why he died. She had told me it was because I wore him out with going to all the horse shows. This was said when we left my Aunt Iva's house where mother told me my daddy had passed away. Iva bawled me out because my crying was upsetting my mother.

Nancy

Julie

My grandparents: Dolly and Marty Sinatra, and Grandmother and Grandfather Bonucelli

I was in my forties when I finally let that blame go, as a result of finally being able to identify my mother's closet alcoholism and the vulnerability I experienced as a child of an alcoholic. Harry had been very overweight, over 300 lbs and his heart valve gave out before the invention that could have saved him became available. But he did save my life by providing and thus creating the circumstances wherein I would bond with nature to eventually connect with my spiritual path. He liked my spunk he called, 'moxie,' and he taught me to come out smiling no matter what happened. I had watched how he reached out to kids in trouble, finding a ranch for a teenage boy to live on as a hired hand. He had been arrested for a petty crime and needed to learn responsibility and work off his steam. Harry believed this was a better alternative than putting the boy away in a juvenile facility. Harry signed on as his guardian, and the boy didn't let him down. I still have a tooled leather belt that he made with my name stamped on the back—a gift to Harry's little girl as a thank you. I saw the photograph of the baseball team Harry Misfeldt sponsored for boys from impoverished neighborhoods in Sacramento. He often used his spontaneous sense of humor to diffuse my mother's dark moods. Harry had natural sunshine. He wasn't my father, but he was my 'daddy'. He was in my life for seven years. At the least, Harry was an angel.

Something happened that would begin the life long estrangement between my mother and me on a trip to Southern California for the last horse show I ever competed in, a few months after Harry's death. Al Root, the local country sheriff who had an equestrian drill team I was a rider in talked my mother into going to the California State Equestrian Convention being held that year in Santa Barbara. The previous year I had taken fourth place in the State finals on Lil Abner, a high accomplishment for us as the underdogs. I competed against children with wealthy fathers who spent at least a thousand dollars to buy them a show horse. Lil Abner was bought at an auction where Harry paid fifty dollars for him. Now my next step was to try for the trophy in the state competition—the Oscar for horse-shows.

I remember feeling something was more wrong than usual with my mother's mood when we arrived at the motel after stabling the horses at the fairgrounds. Usually my mother was smiling and charming everyone when we were at horse shows, but this time her vibes were very dark. I avoided even talking with her and went to bed on a sofa while she slept in the bedroom. The next morning she was looking for a pair of spurs in our luggage, extra ones she had planned to loan another rider in the drill team whose horse needed some prodding. She couldn't find them and was becoming more and more agitated. We were back over at the fairgrounds standing in the alley between the barns when she realized the spurs were not in with the horse equipment either. She began shouting at me that I had made her forget to bring them. In another second she was running toward me screaming, "Julie! You little bastard! This is all your fault! You should never have been born!" Her face was wild with fury and she knocked me down on the ground and started choking me with her hands. Just before I passed out I saw two or three of the adult men there running over to us. That night it was decided that all the kids sleep on their saddles with the saddle blankets as pillows in the barn in front of the horse stalls, for fun, instead of going back to the motel. Marshall Macgee had also taught me about clearing my mind and using full concentration on the horse, and this was what I used to at least temporarily put the horrible incident behind me as I competed later that same day with the drill team who did win the state championship.

Julie on Lil Abner Sacramento State Fair—note the frizzy perm.

The next day when my individual championship class in Western riding was coming up, something else took place where I had my first lesson about betrayal. The father of a little girl who was my equal competitor came up to me when I was warming up my horse. He had another man with him and he wanted to see what 'Abner' could do. At this urging to show my horse off I complied and moved him through running sliding stops and spins imitating the routine for the upcoming class. A few moments later when we entered the show ring, Lil Abner, loyal and earnest to please me, but too worked up, too 'high' from the performance he had just given, began to anticipate my signals before I gave them. We were doing each routine beautifully, but not according to the judge's directions and we were disqualified—a heart breaking disappointment because I was riding that day for my Daddy. The other little girl won and the man who had been with her father who wanted to see what my horse could achieve, was a person my mother had contacted—that man arrived at our house in Carmichael too early a few weeks later as Lil Abner, sold to him without any warning, was in a horse trailer already pulling out of our driveway as I got off the school bus, running blindly through rivers of tears, screaming his name.

After all these years I realized how Santa Barbara was just too close, too near where the echoes stirred in the ocean air and the sights and smells rose up from what might have been with an anguish calling out what should have been that was lost to a woman who was not able to see herself as responsible for what ever it was that had happened to her ... it was maybe less painful that in my mother's mind it all became my fault.

Carroll Hunter came out of no where, and was married to my mother, it seemed, within a handful of weeks after we got back from the Santa Barbara trip. They had decided to move us down to Southern California to Long Beach once the rest of the horses and our home in Carmichael had been sold. I was given another one of those ugly perms, roughly delivered by my mother who had received on short notice that Tom Lyma wanted to take me on a day trip to Lake Tahoe. The trip included a stop at the Cal-Neva Lodge where I believe I had the only encounter with my real father, Frank Sinatra.

Tom and his wife Marguerite went into the lounge where children could not go and I was left in the lobby, to wait, as he put it, for him to complete business he had there in regards to his food company. Tom took me over to stand where the borderline between California and Nevada crossed through the middle of the lobby. A second after he disappeared into the bar a man, a stranger in a dark blue business suit came out of a door at the far end of the lobby and seeing me there, walked over to me.

"Hello little girl. What are you doing there?" he asked me smiling as he leaned down to be closer to my size. I remember how blue his eyes were.

"I'm standing on the borderline. I have one foot in California and my other foot is in Nevada." I sparkled and pointed down to my feet. "See how the rugs change?"

"Yes I see that too. Where are your parents?," he asked looking concerned.

"My daddy just died and my mother is at home. I'm here with Tom and Marguerite Lyma. They're in the bar where I can't go." The man had straightened up and his face quickly changed at the moment I said the name, "Lyma." He looked upset and I felt confused.

"I have to go to work now," He said as he turned and walked away quickly.

A split second later Tom and Marguerite appeared from around a corner of the hall area that opened from the bar back onto the lobby area. Tom's face was very serious and Marguerite gave me a pained smile. When we pulled out of the parking lot and turned back towards King Beach, a community along the lake, I spotted a wishing well on the sidewalk outside a small café. We decided to eat there and I put a penny Tom gave me into the well and wished my Daddy would come back.

I have read that Frank Sinatra had a chalet at the Cal-Neva during that period of time. It seemed to me looking back at it now, that if he had known I was his little girl who was standing in the lobby that day, he would have taken the opportunity to find out more about me. There would have been perhaps cautiously veiled questions to learn my favorite thing about school. Maybe I would have had the chance to tell him I loved to sing and to ride my horse. There might have been a slip about my mother or something that would have revealed that he already knew who I was … There was nothing. I believe that nice stranger was my father and when I was 11 years old we were face to face with one another for those brief minutes that God must have wanted to have stay in my memory. There we were, our blue eyes looking into blue eyes, without having a clue about being father and daughter. Secrets are daggers but the what-ifs are killers.

A few days before Mr. Hunter moved us all down to Long Beach, my mother told me my aunts and uncles were coming over to say good by. She wanted me to sing a song for them. This was confusing for me because it wasn't the normal protocol for me regarding my adult relatives. It was the usual practice that I be seen but not heard and I was often told not to talk with my aunts and uncles and just play with my cousins. Mother gave that instruction every time we went to visit them. She said my use of big words as a child annoyed them. That had always been okay by me because they seemed to make too big a deal out of what I looked like when we would arrive, more fuss than they made about it with my cousins. I felt uncomfortably under glass.

I don't remember the song that was picked but I do recall standing in the doorway between our living room and dining area to perform it. They all just sat there at our dining table while I sang, staring at me like stones.

Our first day in Long Beach, I discovered that all my photos of Harry Misfeldt were missing. My mother said that Carroll threw them out and I was supposed to call him "Dad." The second day he came home drunk and announced as he passed by me in the living room that he would kill me if I ever got in his way. Great. I would spend the next five years walking on eggs and smiling through it to keep my scalp.

My mother seemed happier than I'd seen her in years. She had two more children by Hunter. I was already 14 when she had Lisa and two years later she had Eric. I cheered up at getting to be a big sister, but there were too many years between us to have a typical sibling relationship. I was more like an occasional babysitter. A year or so more into the marriage however, my mother found out that Hunter had another wife and a few more children, and they were living and had been living before my mother met him in Northern California, in Santa Ana, east of Long Beach. Hunter had used up mother's money from the sale of our place in Carmichael quickly by supporting two families and investing in an ownership of a gas station which failed. That diamond dinner ring she once had shown me that she never wore that I strongly suspect had once belonged to Nancy Barbato Sinatra, had mysteriously disappeared along with some other pieces of jewelry. But Hunter had another reason besides the little money mother had to hook up with her.

Carroll had been working for some years on a manuscript for a fictional novel about his experiences in World War II. He was able to get it in front of Stanley Kramer, I believe now because of my mother's connection with Frank Sinatra. This happened in 1957, the same year Stanley Kramer produced the movie, "The Pride and the Passion" for United Artists where my father starred along with Cary Grant and Sophia Loren. I remember how my mother began making snide remarks about Sophia Loren around the house, saying she couldn't see why anyone thought of that Sicilian actress as being beautiful. Once again I don't believe in coincidence.

The explosive household was unbearable for me. The city itself seemed gray and alien, full of noise and sprawling with ugly concrete. In the first year or so there I grieved for the life left behind me. I missed bright blue skies and the smells of sweet wild grasses growing in the fields and the cheerful orange poppies that sprang up in the spring. I escaped down to the beach a couple of blocks away from the house. Watching the coming and going of the ocean waves I would often slip back into a summer's day, and with the magic of a child's imagination, weave my horse through the sunrays streaming to the moss laced trees on a gentle sloping hill, pretending once more that I was an Indian princess riding in a glorious wilderness.

Change is a natural force, sometimes delayed, but never corralled for long. Soon boys and wearing lipstick and choosing my own clothes dictated my interests. Listening to the radio pop stations and playing '45's of the latest Paul Anka hits on my 'hi-fi' filled hours I spent in the sanctuary of my bedroom where I dreamed about how the current boy I had a crush on would think of me as "Venus" and ask me to the high school dance.

Another song of a different style was a favorite I used to sing along with when it came on the radio. It was, "One For My Baby and One More For The Road," sung by Frank Sinatra originally for the movie "Young At Heart," with Doris Day made in 1955. As a teenager I had been singing along with my father.

By age fifteen I still had the body of a twelve year old. I wasn't developing those curves the other girls in school already had. I blamed this as the reason I wasn't one of the really popular girls, but I did get attention from the boys because of my singing and went out on my share of dates too. The music teacher for the school glee club chose me to learn a song I could sing solo at each of the school assemblies and football rallies before the games. This became very irritating to my mother. I was rehearsing the song, "High Hopes" at home when it erupted.

"Julie, I'm going to call your teacher and forbid her from picking you for her solo singer anymore," she growled, confusing me with her sudden anger as she had seemed amused before when I was practicing the song made popular by Doris Day—Que Sera Sera.

"I plan to be a singer when I grow up," I argued back. It was futile. She delivered her orders that I would not be allowed to become a singer and that I was to sign up for typing in school and learn to become a secretary instead.

She didn't make that phone call but I began to hide the fact that I was still singing from her. Choosing "High Hopes" had been an act of 'getting in her way,' threatening the secret once more without my knowing it. Frank Sinatra was on the radio singing that same song at the same time I was. It was a hit from the movie "A Hole In The Head" he starred in that was released in November of 1958. He was definitely behind the scenes for that one, and additionally another incident that had taken place that past summer during what would be my last visit back with Tom Lyma.

My hair had actually gotten long enough to wear it in a pony tail. Upon my arrival at the Greyhound Bus Station in Sacramento Marguerite announced that my mother had phoned her and insisted that I be taken to have a hair cut styled into curls before seeing Tom, again, so I would "look neat and groomed in appearance." I resented watching my hair fall onto to floor in the beauty parlour, but I remained quiet and polite. During the visit, mostly spent with Marguerite who took me school clothes shopping, I objected to a dress she picked out for me. I flatly refused to agree to it. Tom was furious about my giving his wife a bad time and drove me out to see my Uncle Bobby at the ranch he still lived on in Floren.

"What's a matta with you? You are an ungrateful girl and I'm ashamed of you after all Tom has done for you!" Uncle Bobby's words stung with puzzling injustice.

"I can't wear that dress she picked out because it's wool and wool itches me." My protest was waved off and I was sent outside when my uncle told me he and Tom had things to talk about in private.

When I was called back in Tom said we were going to the bus station. He had my suitcase already packed and in his car that I hadn't known about. He walked me over to the bus to take me down to Long Beach and said: "I don't want to see you again. Go back to your mother."

I was blown away believing I had just lost my own father because I didn't like a dress. When I arrived home my mother quickly sat me down to write a letter to Tom. She insisted that I begin it with the words, "Dear Daddy" and apologize for my rudeness. His letter came back in a flash protesting why I had suddenly called him "Daddy" when I never had before. He expressed that he believed my mother had put me "up to it," and repeated that he did not wish to hear from me again. Now all these decades later I can guess what the private conversation between Tom Lyma and my Uncle Bobby must have addressed.

Tom passed away during the spring of 1959. Marguerite phoned the news to my mother and I went up to Sacramento to attend only the rosary my Aunt Irene would bring me to. The instructions included I was not to talk with any of Tom's relatives or attend the funeral. My aunt pointed out a young woman there saying she was Tom's daughter Joan and I should go and say hello to her ... she didn't say I should go over because the woman was my sister. When I passed by the open coffin I looked down at him, a man who was supposed to have been my father who, lying there, still seemed to be more like just a stranger to me.

In mid April, 1997, my phone rang in the bunk house. "Julie, it's Rod. A letter responding to Carol Lynne's has just come back from Arthur Crowley. It's disappointing, I'm sorry to have to say."

"Has Barbara refused to meet with us?"

"Worse than that." Rod went on to explain that Arthur Crowley stated that Frank and Barbara Sinatra had never heard of me and wished no further contact from me.

Julie with high school sweetheart
Bobby

Julie age 16 with King

I was devastated. I groaned something out over the phone to Rod who was picking up on how upset I'd become.

"How are you coming along with your list of experiences that tie you in with your father? Carol Lynn is now already composing her next letter to Crowley and wants to include them," Rod implored adding, "We have to keep putting this in front of them."

"What's the use if he refuses to see me?"

"I don't think that is coming from him," Rod encouraged. "I believe he is ill and is not being told about you. I think this is Barbara's wish not to acknowledge you. I followed Frank Sinatra's career for many years and he has been known for his love for his children. I don't think he knows you are his child. If he did he would never tolerate the poor conditions you are living in."

"I'm not planning on asking him for money, Rod."

"You wouldn't have to."

"I remembered something that happened at the Cal-Neva Lodge at Lake Tahoe. I believe my father and I did meet, or at least were face to face with each other." After I shared all the details with Rod I asked him if he thought I had been taken there so my father could see how I was doing after Harry died.

"With what you've just told me it sounds like Sinatra just stopped to say hello to a little girl. I think Lyma took you there because he was beginning to suspect you were not his … he wanted to see what kind of reaction Frank would have to you. If you want this chance to meet him now you can't give up. Your father never gave up."

Before we got off the phone Rod told me he had made a copy of the video taping from the concert I performed that I'd been rehearsing with Sparky and other musicians for. Carol Lynn was planning to include it as well with her next letter to Crowley, which went out on April 14 th. I woke up every day waiting for word to come that my father wanted to see me. On April 28th, Crowley wrote a letter back to Carol Lynn saying that my mother becoming upset because I named my stuffed animal "Francis," did not prove I was Sinatra's daughter. He ignored all the evidence we had sent out and chose to dismiss it by isolating one part of it. He stated that he had sent it all over to the "Sinatras," but I didn't buy that, not at all after the cheap shot he delivered, in fact I was so furious over his phoniness that his letter served as a strong catalyst to plummet me forward.

Sparky kept his promise during the concert I sent my father the video of, and didn't spill the beans about whom I found out I was, but I wondered myself why I was still keeping the secret. I had included a tribute song to my father, "It Was A Very Good Year," and changed a verse just for the performance to honor the Oscar he won for his role as Maggio in "From Here To Eternity" … hailing the underdog who never gave up. I sang under the name Julie Alex-Rider. Alex for a beloved cat and Rider to represent the horses and Harley, my dog named after the motorcycle … Did I need the secret because I still didn't know how to be Julie Sinatra?

The disappointment from Arthur Crowley's letter hurt my heart. I went outside to be with my horse Checkers—to be consoled as only he could do for me. His love didn't require that I prove who I was—I got my usual big camel-lipped kiss on my cheek and my hopes lifted a little higher. Maybe my father really didn't know about me as I had believed he must have. My mother, when Rod taped her, stated the man she had the affair with "never knew".

I thought about what Marshall Macgee had told me so many years ago about entering the arena and not looking at the competition, just keeping my mind on my own performance. The principle still applied. I was competing against people—my mother, the Sinatra family attorneys, my father's wife and his other children, all who wanted to defeat me, and a tougher one—time. But my real competitor was myself. This was no time to stay under camouflage—The fox was out on the fields, no longer hidden in the tangled briar.

Julie's mother Dorothy with Julie at Lake Tahoe

Julie at 19 married and pregnant
with Dan

PART II

TRANSFORMATION

"I have already agreed to be there and that is the same
as if I gave you my head and my heart" Western Apache

CHAPTER EIGHT

May, 1997

During those several months of homelessness, back in 1992, I began to rely on symbols and signs to help me determine what to do next or which way to go in order to have shelter and something to eat for myself and my animals. For an example, one night while living in a run down trailer some mice got in a broken window and jumped down to the end of my bed. I woke up screaming when I saw them and Harley ran over to the door and began insisting to go out. I opened it for him but he made it clear he wanted me outside with him. Within a few seconds later he looked up and stared into the night sky. A shooting star rushed overhead towards the east. I trusted that somewhere east of us was a better place where all of us could be together. It turned out to be that little adobe bunk—house with the horse facilities where we'd been secure for the past three years. But now we had less than a week left on the notice to vacate.

Once again I was grateful for the angels who look after me. A lot sold in time for me to have commission monies to move with from my real estate work. I picked up my check from the escrow agent Shawn, who was a business acquaintance who had attended my recent concert with his wife. He asked me about the Sinatra tribute song I had done. I told him I had just learned that past year that I was his daughter. He looked astonished for a moment and then he asked me if Frank knew?

Nothing affordable had turned up in the Cave Creek area. Two things were motivating me to look up in Northern Arizona for a place to live. The first was because seven bald eagles had appeared flying over the horse arena. They circled a few times and then flew directly north. To see that many of them together had been startling. This was outside of their normal behavior. The second reason had to do with a dream that came on the last night in California before the first morning of homelessness, on July 31st, 1992 …

I had asked before going to sleep, "Where is home?" a logical question to be on my mind given the circumstances I faced then. In a dream that came that night, I was doing some kind of ritual I later learned matched one the Apache girls would do to represent coming into womanhood. I was wearing a dress made of deer hide in my dream and motioned to lie down three separate times while an elderly woman, a different one each time, sprinkled corn pollen on me. When I stood up the last time I was suddenly in modern clothes and walked over to the back of a little house and stood on the patio there. A woman with distinctly Native American features including long black hair tied back behind her neck was sitting at a table with a red and white gingham cloth over it. I asked her, "Where is home?" She pointed out across a field and I could see a high cliff of red rock on a mountain sloping down to meet another where a row of large trees typical of a riparian area, where a creek or river might run. There was a man with blond hair wearing Bermuda shorts and hiking boots pointing to a surveyor's stake on the smaller hill.

"That shouldn't be too hard for an old Inde like you," she squinted at me. I woke up instantly hearing the word that sounded like "Inde." Also later I learned that the old word the Apaches use to call themselves is, "Ndee," pronounced Inde, and it means, the people.

I contacted a real estate salesperson in the area around Sedona and told him I was looking to rent for now but planned to eventually purchase a ranch where my horses could retire and I could have a foundation. I told him who I was. I believed with my determination even more fueled that I would yet meet my father and he would open a door for me to use my music for fund-raising concerts to earn the money. I wanted to offer healing with the use of horses and music to people who were suffering from neurological disease, as both had contributed to my own recent wellness. We met with the listing agent to go and see a ranch on the market that also had rental cabins on it. The agent representing the owner was wearing Bermuda shorts and had blonde hair.

I moved my horses and dog on the ranch within twenty-four hours after locating it my first day up in the Sedona area, looking for a place in the red-rock country. Harley and I would go on nature walks where everything already appeared familiar to me. Checkers, who suffered from years of painful arthritis in his knees, would begin to miraculously run again with Missy Starr in the grassy pastures that lifted his spirit.

For the rest of May and the months of June and July I rented use of a recreational building that looked down over the rest of the 70 acre ranch surrounded by thousands of wilderness acreage, and also down on a little rock house which had a small patio in the back of it. The girl who had been living there moved out and it became available. I sat with a cup of coffee at a table she left that had a gingham cloth on it, gazing out over the field to the trees where a red rock cliff rose up behind a creek. I slept my first night there on July 31st, 1997, five years from the date of that dream. Because an Apache girl's coming of age ceremony happened only once in her life, I realized I had lived at least three lives here already. I happen to believe in reincarnation, but this didn't diminish my amazement that the dream had manifested into my reality. The sign had been the right one to follow. Following the eagles north had brought me to my old home, and the first morning after I moved into the house one flew over me and whistled a greeting as I went out to feed the horses.

The ranch lay in a broad canyon where the mountains as they circled the land created a bowl of stars at night and the land itself laid in the arms of a creek flowing around the perimeter. Even though it was owned by someone else and had a different name, I called the ranch "Skywater," after the title of a song I had written even a year earlier than the dream. The reference to this place was obvious in my lyrics—"An eagle diving in my canyon, you assassinate my sadness and welcome me to the holy instant of my birth …"

Adjacent mountain ranges, as seen from a satellite photo covering several square miles layered out from the ranch in circles like petals on a rose. The little rock house, built in the late 1800's was the pin-point in the center. Although I didn't know it yet, it would be here in the heart of a rose that my father and I would connect and begin to interact with each other.

June, 1997

After Arthur Crowley's brush-off, Carol Lynn sent a letter to him on June 27th, offering me for a lie detector test and requesting that DNA testing take place to resolve this once and for all. Once again the attorney dodged the obvious, and added that Mr. Sinatra was too ill to be asked to do DNA testing and that we should respect his condition and basically go away.

Carol Lynn wrote again another letter stating clumsily that Julie didn't care if her father was ill she just wanted the chance to meet him, etc. I was very upset with her choice of words … didn't care? I was praying every day for his recovery and the chance for us to get to know one another, even a little. She hadn't meant it that way, but it could be taken as a total lack of sensitivity on my part on the other end. We had just given the opposition a rationalization with which they could justify their stonewalling.

On July 7th there was a post card in my P.O. box in Sedona from Gayle. She had been trying to contact me during a period in which I had no phone. She wrote: "I have news of your father. Not good. Call me when you get this." When I got back to the ranch I dialed Gayle's number. Her sister was taking care of her and explained Gayle had just gone through a surgery and was recovering but had left word she wanted to talk to me if I called. She came onto the phone and I don't think she even said my name.

"Your father has Alzheimer's Disease, and no short or long term memory … nothing. He is basically vegetating and Barbara has taken control of everything, and is being extremely greedy, and is excluding his children," she stated in one breath. She added that she needed to rest and hung up. I didn't get in a single word.

I don't know if it was because I didn't want to believe how ill he was or if it was my intuitive voice, but something in my gut told me something was not right about Gayle's report. The next day I had gone over to Cottonwood to the old town section where there were second hand stores. I needed a very cheap table lamp for my bedroom. I never expected that I would get a sign from my father there—one that seemed to show me that he did not want me to give up my quest.

Out of a dusty bin where some old 331/3 LP's were stacked, I pulled one out that had a picture of a very young Frank Sinatra singing next to band leader, Tommy Dorsey. "I'm Getting Sentimental Over You," was the title of the album that had stereo effect from the original monophonic one recorded by RCA. On the back of the jacket each song was listed with the date of its original recording. The song, from the Paramount film, "Holiday Inn," "Be Careful It's My Heart," was a solo recorded by my father June 9, 1942—the title was ironic enough for me, but the date was easily counted forward to my birthday February 10, 1943. It proved what I had already established in my mind that my mother was with him during this period of time when Dorsey took the band to Hollywood to make the album. It was during May and June of 1942 that Dorsey had given permission to Frank Sinatra to try a few solo recordings on his own with the band's arranger Axel Stordahl—those few songs my mother kept the sheet music for. But this particular song he did on my conception date and that date, June 9, in 1996 was when I first discovered I was his daughter by watching the mini-series. The album included as well the song, "I'll Never Smile Again, recorded by Frank Sinatra with the Pied Pipers in May 23, 1940, for the movie "Las Vegas Nights" where he was filmed singing it again in October, 1940 with my mother as his audience. I purchased the record for four dollars.

For the first time in all of this I began to consider the possibility that a spiritual element was at play, and I felt there must be some purpose beyond myself and still beyond my grasp that would be served by my learning now, so late in my life what my true identity was. I began to wonder if the discovery about who I was had been divinely orchestrated to kick in not a day before it had, and I wondered if my father was somehow leading this orchestra.

Several weeks had passed since Carol Lynn's last letter went out to Barbara's attorney. Rod thought it was interesting that I would get a call from Gayle after each letter Carol Lynn had sent out. He said not to take too seriously what had been reported about my father's health. Rod believed the message from Gayle had been a stand off for the request to do DNA.

I noticed with the copy of his previous letter that Arthur Crowley had changed to a different address on his letterhead, one I recognized was in a residential area of Los Angeles. Frustrated over being ignored while the clock was ticking in regards to my father's health was too much for me to sit still for, especially while the attorneys played cat and mouse with each other. I phoned him at his home around seven in the evening ...

"Mr. Crowley, this is Julie. I'm very worried about my father," I began, and it was apparent he knew immediately who I was.

"Mr. Sinatra is very ill, and my client Barbara does not want to meet with you."

"You have been able to see with all I have sent out, that I am for real. I want you to do everything you can to convince Barbara that I should be allowed to come out there and meet my father. Why am I being blocked from this?"

"Aren't you afraid the shock of you could give him a heart attack?" His question shuddered through me, as he must have expected it would. Clearly he had already recognized me as 'for real'.

My mind rushed back over his words. Had Arthur Crowley just spoken out of his belief that my father did not know about me? I took a deep breath and spoke next from my own experience with self healing, suspecting I could likely have this too in common with my own father.

"I think my father is a very strong man, still. I think it would be healing for both of us to meet."

"The information you shared does not serve as proof that you are his daughter. I did talk to Tina about this, and she told me the actress who played the starlet you think was portraying your mother, was somebody she just got off the street," he defended.

This conversation was not the place for me to expound on how it was that I did not believe in accidents or coincidences and I did know something about my father that Crowley would not be able to deny as I continued my plea.

"My father is known for his attention to detail. I don't believe for a second that the starlet was just an accident. He has been very hands on with anything that had to do with him. The way she looked and her mannerisms were not just coincidental. She was specifically designed to mimic my mother." Arthur Crowley, being an attorney, had a quick come back ...

"You have to agree, that your mother is an unreliable witness. Frankly, I don't understand her behavior in all this," Crowley's statement had just revealed the source of his information. None of Carol Lynn's letters ever shared that my mother was refusing to co-operate and come forward for me.

"Yes," I answered him truthfully. "She is unreliable now, but she was very clear and immediate when she confirmed Frank Sinatra was my true birth father during the phone call she made to me I told you about in my letter that Carol Lynn included to you with hers."

"Well, I have to get off the phone because I have an appointment," Mr. Crowley said escaping any more discussion. After we hung up I realized I'd gotten distracted from bringing up my proof that my mother was with my father on my conception date. I hoped at least hearing from me in person might encourage him yet to forward my appeal to his client. I wasn't counting on that, but I was holding tight to my belief that "Maggio" was still in there fighting.

Skywater

Old rock house

Julie's horses, Checkers & Missy Starr
Spring 1997

CHAPTER NINE

A firestorm …

R od wasn't counting on Arthur Crowley to encourage Barbara Sinatra to step up and do the right thing either. He had another idea up his sleeve. He made an appointment for the two of us to sit down with a Catholic priest he and Carol Lynn had known for years from the same church Gayle attended. The priest had been recently transferred to a parish in Wickenburg, Arizona, a town two hours drive away for me, and I had a somewhat harrowing drive down there in my "Z" which barely had brakes. Rod hoped this priest would agree to intervene on my behalf by talking with Gayle's brother-in-law she said was a priest, and the person who was her source for the information she was passing on to me.

The discussion took place among the three of us addressing the moral issue regarding a daughter and father being kept from each other, at moral risk, Rod pointed out, for all the parishioners involved. The priest agreed to speak on my behalf, but the brother-in-law turned out to be a reverend, so the conversation between them never took place. I phoned to thank him anyway for the time he'd given me and asked him how I could approach ever forgiving my mother— another moral issue I was coping with. He said, "Look to have peace in your heart."

I hadn't put much store in that indirect route to reach my father. Short of driving my "Z" through his gate in Beverly Hills, not practical as a solution and additionally I did not want to shock him into a heart attack, I had to cope with go-betweens. I thought about the two men Kitty Kelley had written about in her book, "His Way," that had been close to Frank Sinatra during that two year period my mother was involved with him. George Evans, the publicist had passed away, but Ms. Kelley had interviewed his two sons, Norman and Phil Evans, as part of her research. Nick Servano, once my father's personal manager might possibly still be alive. I decided to contact Kitty Kelley to see if she knew how I could get a hold of these men I hoped might be able to corroborate the facts surrounding my birth. Reading her book it was clear she mostly took an unflattering slant on my father and I felt somehow disloyal in approaching her. She had balanced her heavy take on alleged Mafia associations by pointing out as well that he had performed many acts of philanthropy, often giving quietly from behind the scenes. Still, she must have been more influenced by his locking horns with her before she even wrote her book.

In the front section Ms. Kelley shared with her readers that my father had begun a lawsuit to stop her from writing his unauthorized biography. He wanted to tell his story himself in his own time. A score of writers came forward helping to defeat the attempt they felt went against free speech as Frank Sinatra was a public figure by his own doing and therefore the public had a right to learn whatever they wanted to about him. He dropped the lawsuit a year later in September of 1984. Kitty Kelly had several lawyers who had represented her during that time. I phoned one she had listed as her attorney in Los Angeles. I must have passed his initial screening. Kitty Kelley phoned me the next day on a Saturday morning from her home.

"Hello is this Julie Alex-Rider? This is Kitty Kelley."

"Yes it is," I said.

"Julie I understand you have something about Frank Sinatra you wish to share with me."

"I'm his daughter. How did you miss me?"

She chuckled back and I told her my story as I knew it so far.

"Your story interests me," she commented back. "I would like to sit down with you and discuss it more at some time in the future. Right now I am working on my book about Princess Diana."

"It would be nice to have a chat with you," I said, and then continued on by asking her if she knew how I could reach the Evans sons and Nick Servano. She said all that information was in files in storage and possibly some time later when she had a break she would have her assistant go through it all and let me know.

"Who is your mother?" she asked just before we hung up.

"Dorothy Lyma, and I think you have a photograph of her sitting behind Ava Gardner at a party at my father's house in your book." I believe she may have been using the name Alora Gooding. Do you have any other pictures of Alora? The one I saw shows just half of my mother's face."

Kitty Kelley did not have any other photos of Alora Gooding. She gave me her home phone number and said she would like me to send things to her "from time to time" as I went along in this. It was interesting for me to have spoken with her, but she did nothing to help me. She seemed to have just glossed over my remark that I was hoping those men might help me in my need to meet my father.

I was not able to find a listing for Nick Servano in Los Angeles, where I thought he might be living, if he was living. I reached a Norman Evans listed in

New York and spoke with him briefly. He said he knew nothing personal about Frank Sinatra and he had not heard of anyone named George Evans or Phil Evans. I knew he had not been up front about that. I could feel he just avoided getting involved.

That afternoon I was out cleaning my horse corral when a blue heron suddenly flew to the branches of a not very tall juniper tree by the gate. He was too large and looked all elbows and knees as he began a harried squawking in my direction. This whole scene was way outside of the bird's normal behavior. I could hear a commotion down at the creek at the bottom of the hill from my corral. It was clear that some ravens had gotten into the heron nest down there. This bird had flown up to recruit me to go down there and chase the ravens away. He needed a go between. I shook my head no and explained as he was still looking at me with this exasperated expression, that it wasn't my place to interfere with the natural course of things … but I felt badly for him. My lessons are always immediate.

August 14, 1997

The following is what I wrote down during a phone call from Gayle at approximately 9 PM:

"Julie, I have just gotten off the phone where I had discussed the subject of you and your father with a very close friend of Frank and Barbara's," she began when I picked up the phone.

"How is my father?"

"He doesn't know anyone, is unaware of where he is, and he is being made comfortable. Barbara cannot introduce anything new to him. I want to correct what I had been told before that I shared with you about Barbara being extremely greedy. There are bad feelings between Barbara and his other children," she was running these statements as if she was reading them off a piece of paper in front of her. She finally took a breath and added, "It's true Barbara has control of everything and she feels she deserves to because she's tolerated an awful lot in 20 years of marriage, and Frank has been a very difficult person to live with." With another short breath, Gayle continued, "Barbara is combating the greed of his children, and she is not greedy. She is kind and loving, but she cannot recognize you, Julie, because it would put you in position legally to sue the estate."

So there it was—and it was all about money. "I can work with Barbara about that," I barely began speaking when she cut me off. I wanted to say that I wanted my recognition not money.

"Is it true that you still are not seeking anything material?" Gayle interjected.

"I am not." I managed.

"That's what I said about you when this came up." Gayle stated and then as though reading her next part, "There is nothing to stop you from using your real name of Sinatra, if that would help you feel better, Julie, but Barbara cannot legally recognize you."

"I would like to have my birth certificate changed to reflect my true identity, for my sake and my son's. My mother has been working hard to discredit me with him." I stated firmly back.

Gayle sighed in exasperation at this, and I went on saying, "I have kept this out of the media because I do not want a news report coming into my father's living room. I have been going about this in a way to keep everything quiet and private within the family. Barbara should be helping me to meet my father."

"You don't owe him that protection." Gayle could not have known how wrong that was to say to me as his child who wanted to protect him. Her words "he's being kept comfortable" were still scathing through my mind. Was this being done so Barbara Sinatra could "control everything"? She was still talking while I was now just half-listening to her saying that she didn't "want me to feel hurt hearing how my father would not be able to recognize me and how Alzheimer's Disease does not reverse itself" … She asked me if I wanted to hear all these facts about my father and I told her I did. What else could I have said?

"Julie, this information I'm giving you is straight from," she hesitated before continuing, "the source, I mean rather, a close friend of Barbara's. This is not gossip," she finished, and started in with her next message for me.

"Just because a man impregnates a woman doesn't make him a father. Have you considered looking into welfare to help you financially with your Multiple Sclerosis?" Without a space for me to express my indignation Gayle moved forward.

"You wouldn't want to know the bad things about your father, Julie, you should just let all this go." Apparently finished with the list she went on to say, "This next part is coming from me, Julie. Think about letting it go, and know someday you will meet him in heaven." With the same breath, "I have to hang up now I've been on the phone all evening with my cousin in San Francisco." I heard the click off the line before I could say another word.

The experience had sapped my energy and I temporarily collapsed into tears. I kept thinking why couldn't they just let him alone to self-heal? They were killing him by killing his spirit, and this whole thing was killing me.

I woke up the following morning just as the sun was rising over a bluff and seemed to explode its light so brilliantly as if a flame was igniting the hills. It was time for me to start my own fire.

I had a strong feeling that it was not Gayle's brother-in-law or a "friend" she had used for the liaison for this last call. I believed it had been Barbara Sinatra herself who constructed Gayle's messages for me. I looked up the Reverend in Rancho Mirage, California where Barbara had her center for abused children. He was listed and I phoned him. In a very brief conversation he informed me that this was the first he had heard about any of this, and said he couldn't imagine Gayle's involvement. Fifteen minutes after we hung up Gayle called me and accused me of being someone "who can't be trusted."

I then phoned my attorney, Carol Lynn and told her I had had enough of these one-sided conversations on a back-road designed to discourage me from meeting my father, a man being described as being too far gone to be able to meet me, which I still did not wholly buy into. I shared what had just transpired and asked her to compose a letter to Arthur Crowley and expose Barbara as the source of what I was being told. I wanted my frustration included about it being okay to use my name but not okay to meet my father. I asked Carol Lynn to send this letter out now and not continue to wait for Crowley's response to our last letter, which had not yet been answered. She agreed to write our letter.

My real estate work had been slow since the move from Cave Creek, and I had only one sale in an escrow that would not even close for several months. It just wasn't working anymore for me as a source of income and doing real estate sales seemed more like just hiding from who I was. Still I needed to make a living even though I could physically handle only part time hours out driving and showing properties. During the few days that Carol Lynn was composing her letter, I phoned a client who lived in California to see if he and his wife were coming to Arizona to look for a large piece of land they could build a home on. He was a stunt man in Hollywood, looking to retire with his wife one day here. When I reached him I learned his wife, a truly lovely person, had just passed away from cancer. He was devastated by his loss but reached out to try and be of help to me. I shared who I had discovered was my father with him and during our conversation Loren told me he had known Frank Sinatra for many years. He said he had been the stunt man for him when my father did the Magnum P.I. show. Loren offered to speak on my behalf saying he could easily see I was Frank's daughter from the times he and his wife had been looking at property in Arizona with me. Carol Lynn added this to her letter to Crowley. Loren also shared with me that when Frank Sinatra appeared on Magnum P.I., he had just recently undergone prostate surgery and he hadn't let that get in his way of doing the show.

September 7, 1997

Seven deer, one for each day in the month to date with the clock still ticking and still no assurance in sight that I would be allowed to go out there and meet my father. They appeared at dusk suddenly in my back yard and jumped the fence there by three at a time and collected themselves around Checkers and Missy Starr in their horse corral. That made the number "7" come up in "3's" and those mystic numbers struck a note. Additionally, horses symbolize power and the deer stand for gentleness. In Native American mythology I had read from the Lakota Tribes, that picturing the deer in your mind was a way to use great strength for overcoming negative obstacles on the "Good Red Road to Life." It seemed to me I had just witnessed this message.

Later that evening I sat down in my study and wrote a letter to Arthur Crowley. In it I shared a comparison to my struggle to come and meet my father with the old mythological tale of the deer on her journey to the Father, who encountered a monster guarding the gate who would not let her pass. Like me, the deer in the story tale expressed that she and her Father had good works to do together. I asked Mr. Crowley if he thought it was an act of loving kindness on the part of his client to position him at that gate?

In the little tale the deer succeeds in melting the monster with love and she travels on to see the Father … I would just have to wait and see. Two weeks went by with no response.

Carol Lynn mailed her letter which exposed the "back road" out on September 17. and Crowley spun back an immediate response to it denying again that the Sinatras had any prior knowledge of me, and stating that Barbara did not give her permission for me to use my real name. I got my firestorm but nothing else positive resulted on behalf—except how quickly I realized that I didn't need Barbara Sinatra to tell me if I could be Julie Sinatra or not.

Arthur Crowley also ordered my attorney not to correspond with him again. I was astonished when Carol Lynn told me she didn't see any reason to do so.

"Crowley is there to be a wall and he isn't going to come down just because we are writing letters, Julie," Carol Lynn stated this firmly to me and she had no further ideas—but I had one.

"I want you to file an order to do the DNA testing in a court out there. When my x-husband had his heart attack the doctor had blood drawn for testing, so this could be done with my father's drawn blood they already have without disturbing him. I want a judge to order it and have the chance to prove beyond any doubt who I am to the family."

"It could be considered frivolous. We only have circumstantial evidence, albeit a houseful," she advised as she ended the conversation telling me she had other clients she needed to attend to.

But Carol Lynn would write yet another letter, not to Crowley again, but to Harvey Silbert, quoted in the Wall Street Journal article published September 26,

1997, entitled, "Sinatra Family Battles Over Frank Inc.," in which my half-sister Tina had spilled the beans about our father's financial holdings estimated around $200 million. I received the cut out article in my mail, sent by my dear friend, JoAnn Braheny in Los Angeles. She had commented to me in her letter with it that she felt the in-fighting between family members was very sad. She told me that living in the beautiful place in harmony with nature and with the love I shared with Checkers, Missy Starr and Harley, made me the one who had true wealth.

Harvey Silbert was quoted saying he was Frank Sinatra's attorney—stating it in present tense. He was the lawyer my father had trusted to draw up his will which was re-written in the past five years—the contents unknown, according to him, to Barbara and the other Sinatra children reported at odds with one another in a bitter fight to control my father's record royalties, real estate holdings and a beer company in Long Beach, California with annual income of 30 million per year by itself. Because of the back road information I had been privy to, I realized that Tina had decided to "go public" to get support for her stand against Barbara having taken control of everything as I had been told—but it didn't put me in any position to judge who was in the right or wrong and I didn't have any desire to get in the middle of it and take sides. Nor did I intend to sue the estate, but it became even more clear to me why I was up against so much resistance—I must really have been looked at as a threat to all of them out there—the new kid on the block that nobody wanted to have to add to what they were already coping with between themselves. My friend Jo Ann was right. It was very sad.

The family battle was most likely also the reason why I had not heard back from my half-sister, Nancy. I had written her a letter on September 23rd, and sent it to her home address that had been given to me by another dear friend who had worked for the company who managed her royalties from the "boots" song. My friend, Dan Howell, was himself suffering from acute leukemia and we would talk once in a while about spiritual things. He had known Nancy a little and told me she was a very nice person and would have the compassion to reach out to me. I was still coping with my own dilemma over whether or not our father ever knew I was his child. It had struck me that possibly Tom Lyma had been acting as his proxy all those years while I was growing up and I based my personal introduction to Nancy upon this. I shared that I was being manipulated on a back road that was never going to lead me to my father. I was hoping and basically begged her to act as a sister just this once to help me, saying I wanted nothing else—that I had been given all I needed as a child. Nancy was quoted in the Wall Street Journal article saying that she and Tina and Frank Jr., were being kept from seeing him as well. She said Barbara was holding their father "hostage."

Patrick M. Reilly, who authored the article, supplied the contact information to me for Harvey Silbert without hesitation, but he said he didn't believe I was just someone "doing research" as I told him I was. He had that nose of a journalist I guess because he asked me several times what my relationship was to the family. I had given him my name as Julie Alex-Rider.

Our conversation caused my hopes to lift when Mr. Reilly shared that while he was talking with Barbara Sinatra, who told him she never discussed her husband's business, he could hear Frank was "up and around in the background, yelling his usual insults" for journalists. My heart leaped at this report that my father was feeling fit enough to be up and swearing at the newsman, but I stuck to my story about doing research, not completely a lie, but the way I could avoid spilling my beans before I was ready.

I obtained the phone numbers from Patrick Reilly for Nathan "Sonny" Golden reported as long term business manager for Frank Sinatra and a television producer, George Schlatter, who claimed to be a close Sinatra confidant. Then I phoned my attorney, Carol Lynn and she agreed to write to my father's attorney Harvey Silbert immediately.

In the meantime I decided to contact Sonny Golden. I was on hold listening to Frank Sinatra singing while his secretary was locating him. I had not told her who I was as Frank's daughter, but that I wished to talk with Mr. Golden about a private family matter. I was hoping again against hope that he would understand why a daughter wanted to meet her father. He was so relieved that my subject matter was not about my father having passed away, that I realized I had frightened this old friend unwittingly. He listened to my plight and kindly responded by saying he "could tell" where I was "coming from," and if he had a chance he would put a word in for me.

Harvey Silbert wasted no time in answering our letter once again stating who I was and that I wished to have a meeting with my father and no interest in litigation etc. Mr. Silbert claimed he was no longer Frank Sinatra's attorney—he was past tense. I phoned him at his office that afternoon. His secretary came to the phone and explained that he would return my call in about ten minutes and she took my number.

My phone rang in less than ten minutes and she announced him before he began speaking—and I could hear a tape recorder noising over the line. I was already riled up over his misstatement either in the Journal's article or to my attorney.

"How can I help you Julie? I've already stated to your attorney that I no longer represent Mr. Sinatra."

"I read in the Wall Street Journal that you said you were my father's attorney. I'm tired of being lied to. Where do you come off telling her you're not—which is it?"

He glossed over my rude outburst and said calmly to me, "I helped Mr. Sinatra with the writing of his original will several years ago, and I haven't heard of you before, if that helps you."

"I'm not trying to be a threat to the estate. I just want to meet my father. I'm being blocked from being able to do this. Don't you think my father and I deserve a healing together?"

"No, you're not a threat," he condescended, and added, "What makes you think this would be healing for Mr. Sinatra?"

"That is something between my father and me."

"I can't help you because I have no way of knowing what Mr. Sinatra would want because he is too ill to ask."

"I know the family is fighting with one another and I also can deduce from the news article that Frank Jr. does not participate in that. You must know him also. Would you be willing to contact him for me at least?"

"Frank Jr. is out of town on a music tour and besides he was once kidnapped."

"Mr. Silbert, do I sound like a kidnapper to you?"

Harvey Silbert agreed that I likely was not a kidnapper. He went on to say that Frank Jr. would probably not respond to a "stranger".

I wished during our conversation that I had been able to be more gracious with him, but I was so frustrated by all the stone-walling that I know I came across as the outside kid with a big chip on her shoulder. I didn't find the right words to convince him I was not seeking my father for money, but because he was the lawyer who wrote the will he must have believed it was on that basis that I contacted him. It wasn't. I knew that if my father trusted this man enough to choose him for that service, that Harvey Silbert must have been someone I would be able to trust also … But I was probably seen by him as not being trust worthy—Does anybody have a guide book for illegitimate kids—something like, "Twelve Steps For The Unknown Child's Approach To An Icon Father" …

Before we hung up I asked Mr. Silbert to pass my phone number along to Frank Jr. anyway because in spite of our never having met, he was more than a stranger—he was my half-brother—the person who might, like me, be someone who would care more about truth than about money.

CHAPTER TEN

Later in the fall of 1997

*A*s you've probably already guessed, I didn't hear anything from Frank Jr. And, you're right if you're thinking my waiting for a response from him was operating under unrealistic expectations. The article published in the Wall Street Journal had maintained a sophisticated level of reporting but had none the less painted a picture of the family members picking over the bones while the flesh was still attached and breathing—engaging in something I wondered might turn my brother's stomach as it did mine. If Harvey Silbert did in fact let him know I was out here, that report would probably have cast me in the wrong light, and without knowing his agent or personal manger or where on tour or where he lived … At least for now there didn't seem to be a way to alter this course for the better in my quest to meet my father. But there was something included in the by now infamous article that I hoped had not been eclipsed by the sensationalism over the family's squabbles—something that had made me feel very proud to be his daughter … A statement that back in April, 1997, the United States Congress had voted to award Frank Sinatra the Congressional Gold Medal.

It takes 290 votes or two thirds of the House and at least 67 members of the Senate to sponsor the Gold Medal my father was a recipient of on May 14, 1997. Since the American Revolution, the U.S. Congress has commissioned Gold Medals as it's highest expression of National appreciation for distinguished achievements and contributions by an individual or a group and after the war of 1812 the scope broadened to include awarding it to actors, authors, entertainers, musicians, pioneers in aeronautical and space explorers, life savers, notables in science and medicine, athletes, humanitarians, public servants (like Presidents) and foreign recipients.

Frank Sinatra shared the list with George Washington, Irving Berlin, Sir Winston Churchill, Jonas Salk, Walt Disney, Douglas MacArthur, Harry S. Truman, Joe Lewis, Robert Frost, Robert Kennedy, Mother Teresa of Calcutta and Nelson Mandela—just to name a few.

This high honor, it was reported in the Wall Street Journal, allied a truce among family members who shared the celebration of the Congressional award with him around a dinner table together. I could easily accept their contrasting behavior as being what I'd witnessed coming from an Italian background myself … This was not a time for war. It was a time for peace. God love them.

Just imagining my father, a man who had lived such an incredible life, now in his 80's surrounded by his family being celebrated for what that life produced … I wished I could have been there, but in my heart mind I knew that would have been inappropriate, not just because I was the illegitimate daughter, not that. In spite of the fact that it wasn't my fault, I hadn't paid my dues for that privilege …

I wasn't his little girl who cried, missing her daddy each time he went away to perform as the young crooner who pulled at the heartstrings of the gals left behind in the WWII years singing, "I'll Be Seeing You" for Victor Records with Tommy Dorsey and his orchestra in 1940—nor was I there for the Swingin' years when he recorded "Chicago," in 1957, by multi Sinatra recorded songwriters, Sammy Cahn and Jimmy Van Huesen for Capitol Records, arranged by Nelson Riddle. I didn't offer any moral support when he and "Uncle" Nelson decided to leave Capitol and risk forming my father's own record company together, Reprise.—And I wasn't in Vegas in February, 1966, when he emerged as a jazz singer joining force with the great Count Basie and his Orchestra for that very hip recording of another Cahn and Van Huesen song, "Fly Me To The Moon."— And absent from my chair on still another day as part of the small audience consisting of mostly insiders in the studio when he evolved into his own genre recording "Sinatra's Sinatra" for Reprise, the album featuring his greatest hits, including the one his fan clubs rated as his number one song of all—"I've Got You Under My Skin".

But, like the song says I could feel him closer to me the more I read and learned about the importance he gave to the principles our great country was founded upon—and our corresponding feelings toward the view that freedom and the pursuit for happiness should be available for all peoples evident by the career choices he made—like starring in movies like "The Manchurian Candidate" that exposed the ugly art of mind control used by corrupt and immoral governments to manipulate their dark agendas—or another, "The Man With The Golden Arm," made to show as he stated, "the real misery drug use causes"—closer to me as he chose for the first movie he would direct as well as act in, Warner Bros',"None But The Brave," a story about Japanese and American soldiers stranded on a Pacific island during World War II, sharing food instead of fighting each other in order to survive—my father's platform for sharing his optimism over what I believe too—that peace can be the final reality for mankind.

I wasn't beside him when he was confronted with the threat he saw to freedom even years before that he spoke out against taking considerable personal risk when Joe McCarthy presided over his un-American like committee investigating activities of fellow citizens and ruining their reputations and careers—we never knew each one of us had performed a concert to support Dr. Martin Luther King's fight for civil rights for African Americans; his I didn't attend at the Carnegie Hall in 1961; He wasn't at mine at the Long Beach Memorial Auditorium in the 1970's—yet nearer and thinking alike as we both had in common that we begun to speak out against racial and religious prejudice ahead of the times ...

In 1945, in Hollywood, California, my father's music and early movie careers were at a peak and he must have seen this as an opportunity to use his fame to speak out against the very prejudice he had experienced from boyhood and fought all his life. He got together with Albert Maltz who wrote the screenplay, and they made the movie short, "The House I Live In," produced by Frank Ross for RKO. Frank Sinatra played himself speaking out for tolerance to a group of teenagers. Here is what he said to them:

"Look fellas, religion makes no difference except to a Nazi or somebody as stupid. Why, people all over the world worship God in different ways. This wonderful country is made up of a hundred different kinds of people, and a hundred different ways of talking, and a hundred different ways of going to church. But they're all American ways. My dad came from Italy, but I'm an American. Should I hate your father 'cause he came from Ireland or France, or Russia? Wouldn't I be a first-classed fathead?"

The movie won a special Oscar from the Academy of Motion Picture Arts and Sciences. The proceeds from it went to various charities and my father had donated his work and convinced everybody who worked on the film to do the same.

I wasn't there, but I can look back into my own life and see that from behind the scenes he must have been there when I wrote and gave a speech at one of my high school assemblies in 1960, that spoke about how we must not learn hatred for people of different color and religious choice even if this is expressed by our parents in our homes—and was he possibly walking beside me when I entered a bus in Atlanta, Georgia in 1968 with my little son and sat at the back of it with people who were not allowed to sit at the front because they were Black?

But now at that moment of celebration with his family, how could I expect to be there when I wasn't when he grieved his losses, grieved the death of his father, or his fellow Rat Packers Dean and Sammy—more so the death of his mother, killed in his private plane that crashed on the way to his concert—not there that night while he waited for word of her and sang his performance in case she was already in heaven and would hear him from there. I never leant him my ear—to "talk it all away"—I never said a word when he tearfully announced his retirement and disappeared from the stage in June of 1971—I missed the "The Main Event" concert at the Madison Square Gardens in New York when he came back with the gratitude of 20,000 or more in the audience—I didn't rush to his aid when he collapsed from exhaustion on the stage where I had been conducting his orchestra—I wasn't the one who produced a mini-series for television about his life—I had never been someone who stayed with him still after living with him wasn't easy for twenty years or more—I never said "yes" to him, or "no"—I never whispered how proud I was when he won the Jean Hersholt Humanitarian Award in 1971 in Los Angeles because he gave all the everyday people who did their part on their one to one basis to lift others the credit for it—I didn't see him lift up a little child in his arms who would soon benefit from his World Tour For Children concert fundraising series—I never brought his first-born grandson to him to take to a baseball game—I was absent when he anguished over the kidnapping of his son—I never acted like a daughter, showing him he was needed, asking him for his advice—I never laughed or cried or sang with him.

Yes, I was a 'stranger,' the outside child who didn't belong with the members of his family where they sat celebrating his award of the Congressional Gold Medal, but I belonged to him. He was the forklift for my ideals described and resented as too lofty to fit in with my mother's family—he was the "airs" I was putting on because I had wanted to become a singer, majored in Threatre Arts in college—rather than study to be a teacher or a secretary—he was my dynamics and why I always did better when I was doing it my way—He was the other person I was related to who also loved the color orange and preferred lemon pie. Because of him I was. I could feel him under my skin.

November 10, 1997

A bright autumn morning which began with a walk along the creek with my dog, Harley. He trotted happily beside me as I collected a few especially beautiful gold and reddish fallen leaves to decorate my dining table with. I never suspected it would turn out to be such a magical day.

I wrote the date down on the yellow-lined paper in a tablet after I finished the song that had sprung up seemingly from no where while I was rehearsing with my guitar for an upcoming event in Sedona I had been asked by the town cultural committee to perform my music for.

While practicing one of my original songs I thought I had just made a mistake as my fingers switched to a different three-finger arpeggio. But before I corrected myself a new melody began to emerge. I played the little riff a few times and suddenly I started singing the words … "I know it's late but could I sit with you awhile … I've thought a lot on what I'd say. The time has passed for getting to the heart of things. Let's not get lost in the remembering …" Then another verse and a chorus melody lift and words … "Everybody says I've got your famous eyes blue as the sky. and from your best I want to thank you for my song and the rest you gave me Dad, made me strong …"

The rest, three verses in all and a bridge and the repeated chorus lines came so quickly I could barely write it down. While I was singing the conversation I wanted so much to have for real with my father I kept hearing a cello playing in my head. It seemed to be coming in and out with little musical lines that could be used in an arrangement for the song—I had never thought to use a cello in my music before …

A week later I was in a title company in Sedona where I had an escrow closing on a lot sale and picked up a copy of Newsweek magazine. There was an article about Bob Dylan that had been published a month earlier, in October, 1997, authored by David Gates. In the first paragraph Dylan was quoted, "… Or Sinatra: The tone of his voice. It's like a cello. We wanted to record him doing Hank Williams songs. I don't know, for some reason or other it never got off the ground." I was astounded. I felt too close to my father to ever refer to him in the formal text any longer—From that moment on he was my dad.

I wrote our song titled, "Made Me Strong"—composed on the same day a year after the first time I ever tried to contact him when I began to compose that letter I sent to Tina to pass along to him. That letter mailed just in time for his birthday in 1996 … this song was to be my first gift I would ever give him … that is if I could find a way to get it to him in time for his birthday on December 12, 1997.

The first time I performed, "Made Me Strong," was at an outdoor festival held in Sedona during that same month of November for awareness of the Native American and Spanish American cultures. It was the closing song for my set and while I was singing it a couple approached the stage and waited looking up at me after I finished. The woman spoke first …

"We are visiting here from Florida and we know who you were just singing about," she stated with a compassionate expression in her eyes.

"Yes," I answered the question she had not exactly asked. "I am his daughter and I want so badly to meet him. I just recently found out about it."

She nodded and turned toward the man with her who had stepped to the side of the stage. I was aware he seemed to be studying my profile.

"This is my husband, Eliot Weisman," she stated giving me a knowing look, but I didn't know why.

"I'm happy to meet you sir," I said as I turned toward him while I picked up my guitar to put it away in the case.

His face was full of irritated frustration as he announced, walking over to join his wife again, "Oh I'm sure we will be meeting again, young lady!" in a tone of authority he somehow seemed to feel was justified. Then he motioned to his wife and they turned around and walked away without another word.

I remember thinking to myself, "They seemed to have some personal basis with my dad, not just fans." The incident was mysterious.

In a conversation with Rod a day or so later, I shared this strange happening with the couple at the festival and also that I had written a song I wanted to send to my dad. Rod saw it as a gesture to get the family's attention on me again, missing the point of my gift, but when he offered to take me to a music studio to record it I was grateful.

Rod seemed amused that I reached out again on my own to have those brief conversations with Harvey Silbert and Sonny Golden and suggested I should also try contacting George Schlatter who I hadn't talked to, who had produced the television special tribute to Frank Sinatra a few years back. I read his remarks again from the Wall Street Journal article, and he did strike me as being a sensible and fair-minded person.

I crossed my fingers when I dialed the number in Los Angeles for George Schlatter's office and hoped he would turn out to be the person who would take my song for my dad to him for his upcoming birthday. Maybe this man who was welcome in the inner circle might intervene to help me meet my dad—a "close confidant" would be within the boundaries of universal law—maybe little blue heron … maybe.

"Mr. Schlatter's office, this is Paula. How can I help you?" She explained she was his assistant and that George Schlatter would want to know why I was calling before she could connect me with him. I told her only that it was a private matter having to do with Frank Sinatra. She took my number and said she'd give him my message.

Later on that afternoon Paula phoned me and insisted on my telling her who I was and the specifics regarding my earlier call to them. I protested once more about wanting to speak about it only with Mr. Schlatter, but she convinced me my conversation with her would remain confidential. He phoned me that evening.

"This is a surprise to me. How is it that you came to believe you are Frank's daughter?" His tone was pleasant. I brought him up to date beginning with my discovery of the portrayal of my mother in the mini-series. I told him I had been trying daily to reach my dad because I wanted so badly to meet him in person, and asked George Schlatter if he had a daughter and didn't know it or know what had become of her, wouldn't he want to?

"Yes I would," he stated warmly, "I live right next door to Frank Sinatra. I'll do this much for you … Gather some photographs of yourself and your mother and send them out to my office … if I see something there I think the family should see I'll take it over."

"Thank you! I have pictures to send. I also want to send a copy of a video that was done while I was playing my guitar and singing a song I wrote for my dad along with a letter to him. I've been hoping he could get it in time for his birthday."

"Mr. Sinatra isn't watching TV or movies at all now and isn't doing any reading … I'm afraid he is too ill for that now, but get all your things you want to send out together and as I said, I'll see if there's something I can do."

"Thank you, Mr. Schlatter. You are the first person who has been able to see that my wanting to meet my dad is for him as well as me. Please consider yourself hugged."

I was doing my best to try and ignore that quiet inner voice that was vying for my attention while I excitedly mailed my package out. I wanted to feel only a sense of celebration at this man's kindness and the opportunity that had so far been denied. But George Schlatter had nothing to gain by telling the truth about the progressive state of my dad's illness … His message was clear … It's midnight.

CHAPTER ELEVEN

Cracked eggs and hats …

C hristmas went by very quietly. I spent a good part of the season in intro-
spection, partly because I had not heard anything back from my dad or the
family as his birthday passed. Paula at George Schlatter's office had confirmed
with me that he had taken everything I sent out, "over to the family." She didn't
say to my dad personally. Additionally, my son, Dan had not called on Christmas
eve or Christmas day. He had visited my mother in the fall and confronted her
with "doing the right thing" about Frank Sinatra and me, and told me that she
had laughed in his face. I knew my son well enough to understand this whole situation was something he wanted to escape from. I couldn't blame him but I
hoped I wasn't losing him. I don't remember ever feeling so alone. Once again,
Harley and Checkers and Missy Starr gave me the sense of family during a
sparkling moment of holiday cheer when I pulled doggy biscuits and carrot treats
from stockings filled by old Saint Nick.

The weekend after Christmas my friend Dan Howell lost his battle with cancer. His wife had given me his phone number for reaching him in the hospital
and he and I had had a chance to share some thoughts about what it meant to be
spiritual beings as well as physical ones. He asked me whether or not I sent that
letter out to Nancy Sinatra and if she answered it. He told me upon hearing that
she had not, that I shouldn't give up trying to meet my dad. I was touched very
deeply that he offered this moral support as his own life was ending. I didn't have
the finances to travel to Los Angeles for the funeral.

My good friends, John and JoAnn Braheny also knew Dan Howell, and JoAnn
agreed to go to the services in my place. A short time later in the month they
came in for a visit with me from California. I shared the song I'd written for my
dad with them and how I had come to be on the ranch. They had known me for
years and were not surprised I'd had yet another close encounter with eagles. I
asked John, who had always struck me as a person who possessed deep insights
into life, what he thought about past lives in regards to any impact that might
have on the present identity of someone. He said, "We're all of it."

As our afternoon continued with shared music and wonderful long philosophical talks I confessed that I was now just approaching a true sense of myself because of learning about my true father. John said he could understand why I had always felt like the ugly duckling among my mother's relatives. His son also mainly took after him, bearing seemingly nothing at all coming from his mother. But my dear friends were both silent when I brought up how I was still determined to convince the family I should be allowed to go out there and meet my dad ... The look on JoAnn's face said it all ... The swans would never welcome me.

I thought for some time after they left about the extent of control my mother had been able to exercise over my identity. I always had to use the last name of her current husband as I grew up. Even when I had my son I included the name Hunter, her third husband's, for his middle name. Daniel Francis would have been my ultimate choice, but I didn't know it of course. I wished that I would have at least used Harold, to stand for the step-daddy I had loved so much as a child. My son's grandfather on his father's side had the name Harold also ... I really missed the boat there.

But I wasn't that lost anymore, thanks to my real dad. He was the one I took after, never having much likeness to my mother. In spite of her tactics to keep me housed within the identity she created for me, there were times when that shell began to crack. She fought it every time it surfaced.

I remembered being in my early 30's and returning to college once again and majoring in theatre arts. The head of the department and another professor saw my potential and asked me to help them launch a children's theatre project ... I directed it and got a full page accolade in the Long Beach Press Telegram, the major newspaper. My mother saw the review and phoned me about it. She seemed proud and surprised when she first began speaking to me and then she began raging at me, telling me I was a "bad mother" because she knew the long hours it took to do a play saying, "that was too long to be away from my son." I recall wondering at the time how she knew about the long hours involved in a production. During that call she ordered me to drop out of college and become a real estate salesperson, she elaborated, "because Tom Lyma was a good salesman," indicating that was the father I was supposed to be acting like. Again, I had no idea what had been going on behind the scenes as I played out that stage of my life, and soon after I divorced from my second dysfunctional marriage and couldn't afford college ... I hurried to patch up those cracks, casting aside the recognition of my talents and began a career selling real estate.

A large portion of America was watching when a time came that my dad felt the cracks in a shell that had been put around him too ...

After Frank Sinatra separated from Tommy Dorsey in 1943 and George Evans became his publicist for his solo singing career, Evans astutely wrapped him up in a sellable image as the boy next door. Astute because the other men, you might remember, were away fighting a war and my dad was home. But all the floppy bow ties his first wife, Nancy sewed for him and all the photos taken of him with her and little Nancy at their home could not endure the changing face of America when the fighting men returned home. The shell began to crack as it must always have been destined to, because the enormous appetite for life and his high energy could not realistically be contained. But, ironically, my dad's first response had been like my own, to try and patch it up. After all, his career was in the hands of an expert, and this image had worked very well for him so far—and he was still not ready to self-realize and present his true persona as a performer as late as 1948, when he recorded the song, "Why Try To Change Me Now?" at Columbia Records … his last one there. The difference between my dad and me was that he did successfully break out of his shell—That Fedora cocked slightly to one side appeared in the mid-fifty's … I needed to put my own hat on now.

Harley

I was grateful that Harley and I had taken a walk on the unseasonably warm January morning the day before he died. We were down at the creek and he actually put one of his paws in the water. He looked up at me with his doggy smile and I said, "It's always spring on Harley's ranch." He was hit by a truck the following morning in the road in front of the rock house and was killed instantly. I fell completely apart. He'd been with me almost twelve years, a long old age for a German Shepherd. I was too attached to him to face the truth that his prostate cancer had been progressing … God stepped in.

When I was out in the corral feeding Checkers and Missy, "Chex," as I usually call him, gave me a definite nudge on my shoulder with his huge nose. The expression in his eyes as he looked right at me said: "buckle up." … he knew.

During the day there were wisps of angels in the house. I wasn't surprised totally. I am someone who believes there is just a thin veil between the worlds of dimensions … separate realities. I saw Harley that night while I was asleep. He came into a gray space where I was already sitting and we got to say goodbye. I had seen that place once before years ago in a dream that didn't seem just a dream …

An angel approached me and gave me a message to love myself. It was delivered telepathically I guess … I had just sent the paramedics away after what seemed to have been a mild heart attack, and I was lying down on my bed when I must have fallen asleep. I seemed to have woken up having trouble breathing again when this paranormal moment took place. I had not agreed to go to the hospital because MS often includes having muscle spasms and the heart is a muscle. It had released when the paramedics were there so I sent them away.

I think that gray place is some kind of neutral ground. I'm not a quantum physicist. I experienced this, but I couldn't explain it. I was grateful for the gift of seeing Harley one more time.

February 21, 1998

An announcement was made on the morning news show on NPR(National Public Radio) that Frank Sinatra had gone into the hospital. I phoned George Schlatter's office and Paula talked to me. She assured me that everything was all right, that it had been for a check-up only and he was already back home. George had told her about it when she came into the office. I felt a little better for a while but by evening I began to worry. I phoned Arthur Crowley the next morning.

"Mr. Crowley, it's Julie. I've talked with Paula in George Schlatter's office and was told my dad is already back home. I feel strongly that you or someone from the family should notify me when he goes into the hospital—I shouldn't have to just hear it announced on the radio."

"Barbara, Tina, Nancy and Frank Jr., the family, still do not believe you are Frank's daughter," he said coldly back.

"That is why my attorney and I have written to you about doing DNA testing … it could be done from previous blood tests, like the one that was likely done yesterday in the hospital." I was too frustrated to breathe as Crowley continued.

"He is seriously ill, and should not be put through it—and you don't have the proof to require it."

"I don't believe the family does not recognize who I am, and there is something more than just legal questions for them to be thinking about. My dad and I deserve this chance to meet each other. I am not seeking litigation as both my attorney and I have made it clear in numerous letters sent to you. Don't you think it would be good for my dad to know about me—how I have grown up strong— Don't you think he deserves peace of mind about this as well as me?"

"This is all a tragedy," Crowley said quietly and added more briskly once more, "I can't do anything because my client, Barbara has told me she does not wish to talk with you or meet with you." He switched to a question about my mother.

"I can't understand your mother's behavior in all this. I don't want to sound harsh, but my hands are tied about helping you with the family."

"Money is not the reason motivating me," I stated calmly back, and he said:

"A man like that can find private means for taking care of that."

"I'm not concerned about the money aspects—my dad probably has done something quiet about me. I just want to meet him now before it is too late … Please. We deserve this healing moment together."

"The family does not agree with that," he said firmly and we hung up.

Within five minutes I dialed my mother's number. My half-sister Lisa answered and what seemed like an eternity passed until my mother came on the phone.

"I have heard from close confidants of his that my dad is sometimes almost in a coma state with his illness," I began. "I need you to tell me and even better, write down the facts surrounding my birth so that I can present them to the family and be allowed to meet him."

"Julie?"

"Yes, it's me, mother, did you hear what I just said?"

"I was a bad person when I was young. I did bad things. I'm a good person now so I can't come forward for you now—I can't formally confirm this for you. I'm sorry." She had just confirmed it again but would still deny me her statement for anyone else's ears … tears of frustration, anger, to put it honestly began pouring down my face.

"Mother, illegitimacy doesn't matter in today's culture …" She cut me off in a sudden rage.

"You only want to meet him because he is wealthy. I don't have to do anything. I never benefited by knowing him and I don't want you to either. Think of him as a ditch-digger!"

"I'm not after his money. He is my father. I deserve to meet my own father …" I was cut off again but this time by the click on the other end of the phone. She had hung up on me.

That night I had a dream that I was knocking on a house door. It opened and my mother appeared blocking my entrance. She was shrunken to almost half of her normal height—With no arms or legs—just a torso of her looking very rigid. Her head was turned to one side and she was clenching her teeth. I interpreted it to mean she was paralyzed in her resistance to helping me. The only thing that consoled me over the next few days I spent off and on in tears, was that Harley no longer had to see me doing that.

I spent the morning of my birthday, on February 10th, 1998, gathering up the stakes stuck in the ground by a group of developers who had tried to purchase the ranch. My present was they had fallen out of escrow and maybe there would still be a way for me to have my foundation there. I used their intended markers for dividing and scraping off that beautiful still mostly pristine land for fire wood in the old stone fireplace in my living room that had been constructed in the late 1800's. But while I was outside earlier that day I noticed a poignant cloud formation in the sky. It looked like my dad's face alongside of his mother's face, my Grandmother Dolly Sinatra's face who had died years before. My son did call to wish me a happy birthday. I shared the cloud images with him and said I was worried it meant my dad would be passing away soon. He said: "I don't know what to say, Mom." The tone he used left other words unsaid that I could feel made it clear he did not still believe Frank Sinatra was my father. It was as if he would have added something like, "so that's what you get for having this fantasy Mom …" My mother had gotten to him apparently, or maybe he just saw my desire to meet my dad as unrealistic. I didn't know for sure what he thought, but I didn't try to press my case for the truth with him then, and he cut our conversation very short. I had to trust in my heart there would be a day when he would understand his full identity also, something he had been robbed of as well by the secret.

My attorney Carol Lynn wrote to my mother asking her to come forward with just the facts about the circumstances of my birth, assuring her nothing else from her past need be brought out. Spring was in full bloom and the letter still had not been answered.

Just before dawn on May 14, 1998, I heard a man's voice start to speak to me in my head … I guessed in a dream, although it seemed I was also waking up as I heard it …: "My heart and my voice will be there with you. I will be with you." I got up quickly and wrote the words down. Often during the day I found myself talking out loud to my dad … saying things like: "It's okay, Dad. Whatever you have to do now will be okay. We'll be all right if you have to go." I knew what this meant but I couldn't face it … I hoped my behavior in talking to myself. talking to him, was just exhaustion. But I knew better. I knew I was being prepared for what was coming. At intervals during the same day I would start crying like a woman does when her period begins, mewing softly over what I really still hoped I did not have an actual reason for.

CHAPTER TWELVE

May 15th, 1998 at 7:05 AM

I got out of bed quickly as though I'd received a jolt of energy. Unlike my usual habit of first making a pot of coffee, I rushed across my living room and turned on the radio tuned to NPR. Their "Morning Edition" program was on and the announcement was made just as I stepped back from the radio: "Ol' Blue Eyes, The Chairman of the Board, passed away at his home in Beverly Hills, California, last night."

I didn't hear anything else. My mind closed off it seemed and I could feel myself screaming inside of my whole body as I bolted outside. Nothing, not screams, not crying, came out of me. I felt like I was falling through space when I heard my phone ringing and went back inside the house to answer it. Split second thought fragments … "Maybe it was a false report. Maybe they jumped the gun and he's just in the hospital again. Maybe that's someone from the family on my phone now …

"Julie, this is Shawn," the voice on the other end said and I thought, "Shawn? Why is this a business acquaintance? What can he want?"

"I got up early to come into my office to call you. I heard the announcement that Frank Sinatra passed away very late last night and I was afraid you would have to learn of it on TV or the radio. So I'm calling you so you'll at least hear about it from a friend."

"Thank you, Shawn." I managed to vocalize. "I don't have a TV that works, I just heard about it on NPR's news a few minutes ago." I started to cry.

"I'm so sorry, Julie. I believe you are his daughter, especially as I once told you, after seeing you perform your songs and with your blue eyes, it's unmistakable." His voice suddenly changed to a directive tone as he continued: "You need to gather yourself up and contact the family. Your truth is self-evident."

I ran the words and their odd delivery over again in my mind after we got off the phone. It seemed in some way I couldn't explain that my dad had spoken to me through Shawn. And those specific words: "Your truth is self-evident," blared out. I calmed down somewhat and had a cup of coffee on my patio. I used to be an avid reader of philosophy and I remembered it was Schopenhauer where I first became aware of that phrase. I began to paraphrase his analysis of truth through my mind … something close to: "Every truth passes through three stages before it is recognized. The first, it is ridiculed. Secondly, it is opposed. In the third, it is considered self-evident." I had already experienced the first two stages … Had the family's resistance to me affected my own resolve … I somehow had missed that I was "self-evident".

A little while after I fed Checkers and Missy I managed to realize that I wasn't really going to collapse or anything. I believed that I had indeed gotten a message from my dad and that was overshadowing the shock and making me feel strong. I could only think of George Schlatter in regards to the directive to "contact the family."

Paula came on the phone and said immediately and consolingly, when she realized it was me,

"Julie, oh I am so sorry, so sorry."

She explained that George was at home and wouldn't be coming into the office. I told her that I wanted her to ask him if he would not be willing to allow me to accompany him and his wife to my dad's funeral service.

"I could just stand at the back, Paula, no one would have to know I was there. Please ask him to call me and let me know, okay?"

"I'll tell Mr. Schlatter of your call. Again, I'm so sorry, Julie."

Later that evening a neighbor who lived in one of the other cabins on the ranch came down and invited me to come over and watch the memorials on TV that were airing on every major network and would be ongoing through-out the night. I was amazed to see this magnitude of outpouring for my dad. I felt like I was the only person in the world who still did not fully comprehend just how famous a person he actually was.

They ran a collage of clips from his movies and concerts. all I had missed, but people who knew him personally and professionally and avid fans were interviewed and concurred the accolades coming in from all over the country and the world. Even Kitty Kelly said something like he was a great entertainer. But when they ran a clip with my half-sister, Nancy singing with him when she was on his TV show and I couldn't help bursting into tears. I would have loved doing that with him too. I was too emotional to stay and watch any longer so I went back to my house.

I just wanted to be alone. I went to bed and wondered why every program had used the song, "My Way," to salute him. I would have chosen, "One For My Baby"(And one more for the road).

I wasn't asleep when my phone rang, but I let my answering machine pick it up. This was a short time after 11:30 PM. I could hear my half-sister Lisa leaving her message for me. She was explaining how she had had to wait until our mother was asleep before she called me. She was afraid if she appeared to be on my side that mother would throw her out of the house. She said she felt real bad about Frank Sinatra dying and apologized for not giving me any support the past year or so where mother's behavior was concerned. Lying there in bed just listening, the tears were creeping down my face and I just felt numb and very very sad.

Saturday, May 16th, my mother phoned me several times through out the day—eleven as I counted them, and left the same message on my answering machine. I was still crying quite a bit and didn't want to talk with anyone, so I wasn't answering my phone each time it rang. She was in full rage, I guessed maybe she'd been hitting the bottle, and she was accusing me of owing her lots of money and shouting she would "get me for this" over and over each call she made. It was so bizarre because I didn't owe her money. It made me think of the mad queen in "Alice And The Looking Glass," screaming: "Off With Her Head!"

On the following Monday, I got a beautiful sympathy card from Rod and Carol Lynn, my attorney. A few more cards came in from close friends over the next few days, but not one from my son, Dan, not a call either from him. Is this just too much for him, I wondered—Or does it mean he really does believe his grandmother instead of me?

I hadn't heard back from George Schlatter and there had been an announcement of the date for the funeral on the news. I called and Paula talked with me once more. I told her by not hearing from Mr. Schlatter that I realized I had put my dad's friend in an awkward position where I was concerned. I told Paula that everything would be okay, for him not to worry about it—it was all right if I didn't go to the services, I would hold my own here.

On the day of my dad's funeral services were held in both Los Angeles and then he was to be taken out to his beloved Palm Springs area to be buried. The morning service In Los Angeles was held at the Good Shepherd Catholic Church in Beverly Hills. He was buried at sunset in the family plot at Desert Memorial Park in Cathedral City, California, next to Jilly Rizzo, his closest pal and loyal bodyguard I had read about who had been killed in an auto accident years ago. My grandfather, Marty Sinatra and grandmother, Dolly Sinatra were also buried nearby him. In the morning I went out into one of the meadows on the ranch and collected some wild flowers, orange colored, and brought them in the house and put the bouquet on my dining table. Looking at them I simply said aloud, "Orange, Dad—be happy."

The residual sunlight, left as the sun disappeared over the old volcano peak in the west, was cascading a golden glow down the red cliffs as they joined the circle of mountains surrounding the ranch in the east late in the afternoon of his funeral services. I was walking out across the field towards the corral when I heard a man speaking inside my head—and this time with a distinct New Jersey accent—he said: "Let's go feed the hosses." No one will ever convince me otherwise that it had not been him, as I yelled out in my surprise: "You're here! You came here, Dad!"

At full sunset streaks of pink and gold had merged to form an umbrella of color over the ranch. In the heart of the rose under a sky ablaze in fiery orange I suddenly knew no one, nothing, not even death would prevent my dad and I from having a relationship together. It was electrifying.

CHAPTER THIRTEEN

Two weeks later ...

H ave I said before that I don't believe in coincidences? In addition to the magazine articles, news sheets, tabloids and otherwise, plus glossy short length hardback outcroppings of mostly photographs touting Frank Sinatra's life and career that had been poised and ready for their timely release, of which I purchased all, Rod sent me a new biography in the mail.

Do you remember my little glass duck story? Here is Nancy Jr.'s version found within the pages of Bill Zehme's "The Way You Wear Your Hat, Frank Sinatra and the Lost Art of Livin'," in a passage showing my dad in his role of disciplinarian parent:

"Once Nancy held a school party at her mother's home, and her father played host. A little girl accidentally leaned against a table where a pair of porcelain birds nested; one bird toppled to the floor and shattered. Nancy gasped: "That was one of Mother's favorite ..." Her father shot her the Look, stopping her cold. With all eyes trained, he quietly walked over to the table and flicked the other bird to the floor, smashing it to bits as well. He then draped a gentle arm around the mortified girl and said, "That's okay, kid. Accidents happen."(end quote)"

With that old childhood memory of mine now corrected back to its original source; the score is one Julie, Mom zero.

But the mystery still remained as to how I was there. not it seems as Nancy's little half-sister, and nothing in her story indicated that Frank knew I was his. It's more likely I was there just as a filler child for the party who belonged to Dorothy, a starlet at one of the studios Frank Sinatra knew. The trauma I experienced and remembered may well have been just because I witnessed the incident and was so little, not necessarily that I was the child who broke the porcelain bird. At any rate, I had to have been living with my mother in Hollywood when that happened.

In a book simply titled, "Frank Sinatra," by Jessica Hodge, mostly photographs, there was one taken at the Pasadena train station where he made his exit from the Santa Fe Chief to arrive in Southern California to make the movie,

"Higher and Higher," by RKO, in the summer of 1943. My dad was standing up on a ladder surrounded by greeting fans. My mother was standing in the background just behind the ladder. My eyes went right to her. She apparently shared that moment with him when he made his first starring role in a movie, in "Higher and Higher." I was maybe 6 months old, proving once again that their affair had continued after I was born.

Frank Sinatra publicity shot for movie "Higher and Higher," by RKO summer of 1943 at Pasadena Train Station. My mom is standing in the background, just behind the ladder—my eyes went right to her.

In, "Sinatra—Ol' Blue Eyes Remembered," by David Hanna, there was a photo of my dad with Ava Gardner when she was a blonde. Her earrings in this colored photograph were carved jade and they matched my mother's jade pendent, perfectly, as the other members of a once combined jewelry set. The pendent, you'll remember, my mother brought out to show me along with that diamond dinner ring she said was given to her by my "father." I don't think Tom Lyma gave those earrings to Ava.

In *Time Magazine, Newsweek, People Magazine,* and David Hanna's book, there were quotes upon quotes from celebrities who knew him. He was described as a person you didn't want to get in a fight with because he would fight until one of you died—the women he left reported they still loved him, the ones who had said "No" had received roses—he never apologized. he sent gifts—he carried on lifetime feuds with columnists who couldn't remember how or when it began—movie producers who worked with him talked about his having been beyond talent, a performer's performer—Dorsey once said "He's the most fascinating person in the world, but don't put your hand in the cage"—Bogie said, "He's tilting at windmills, fighting people who don't want to fight"—Shirley MacLaine revealed a confidence he shared that he heard angelic choirs in his head. Upon his dying, a woman who owned a restaurant in Hoboken said it "was like losing a member of the family"—Close friends spoke of recent last visits with him and how he went out of his way to make them feel comfortable.

They all knew they would not have him near again, this man they loved unconditionally, captured in a segment from *Going All The Way* written by Dan Wakefield: "… with his hat casually tipped back and his tie loosened Sinatra sings-and we all get a jolt of his jaunty courage, a feeling that we too, can snap our fingers in time to the music and move through our own loves and losses with style. He wasn't afraid to be "bad" or "good" Frank, as long as he was fully Frank. In him we saw the dark and the light of our own personae writ large."

He was lost to them all now and even to his enemies who had hinted at the admiration they had held for him. He was after all a hero and they all understood that heroic people have heroic flaws.

I read every word said about him during those first few weeks after he died. I read it all eagerly to know him, because I had vowed to myself I *would* know him; but painfully too, because he had always been lost to me. Somehow he must have peeked in on my feelings about this because I began to have experiences that showed he was becoming an active participant in this quest …

Some dreams come in short flashes and all I saw was my dad walking across a nondescript area where he sat down on a simple wooden stool. He was wearing an orange cardigan over a white turtle neck sweater and brown pants and shoes. That was all, but I had seen a photo of him in the orange sweater somewhere among the books and magazines I'd collected. In the morning I got up and found that picture of him on the first page of the *Life* book, "Sinatra remembering," that began with a piece about him written by Tony Bennett. I read it.

Tony Bennett said of my dad that he was, "a man full of love." He told a story of a night when he was with his mother who was dying and they watched Frank Sinatra doing the "Main Event" on TV. My dad told his audience that Tony Bennett was, "his favorite guy in the whole world." That moment of graciousness, Mr. Bennett reported had lifted his mother's spirits and made her happy.

From Tony Bennett: "He ran the gamut of emotions. Sinatra conquered every aspect of his world—the entertainment world … the comedy, the tragedy. Underneath it all, he was a very, very sensitive nice person."

In a reference to the sculptor, Benvenuto Cellini, whose father had passed down his passion for true justice for everyone he encountered, Tony Bennett compared my dad with this man who had drawn his sword to battle every hypocrite and phony who stood in the way of truth.

One of the last photographs in the Life book showed my dad tenderly holding a little spaniel puppy in his arms that he had just saved from the pound. He looked to be late 70's in age. But I was also struck by his house and compound in Malibu in the picture. I got my first car, a 59' MGA, in 1961, and I drove it from Long Beach up to Malibu. Looking for access to the ocean front. The first turn I made off HWY 101 led to a compound gate—his. I had no way of knowing who lived there, but the street didn't go through to the beach and I backed out the narrow drive and turned around. When the universe says it's time then it is. That wasn't.

Tony Bennett's words describing my dad's sensitivity towards others stayed with me all morning. I knew what I had to do. I went into Sedona and bought two blank greeting cards with pictographs of ancient Native American' origin on rocks which symbolized the continuous flow of life. I wrote condolences to Barbara in one and sent another with a little story about the old ponderosa tree that towered over the pinions and junipers and stood just outside the ranch perimeter, and sent it to Nancy, Frank Jr. and Tina at Nancy's address. I said in my note that there are those who stand above and outside the crowd, owned by no one, never fenced in … I felt my dad would have consoled when he was not himself consoled.

Next, I phoned Arthur Crowley and told him I was sorry I had referred to him as "a monster at the gate." He spoke candidly with me, saying he was sorry that he'd had no choice but to honor his client's wishes regarding me. I asked him if he could describe my dad in one sentence; he said, "Mr. Sinatra was a very kind person." Then he said he had known my dad for 40 years and shared the details of the funeral service held for him in Beverly Hills. His coffin had been draped with Gardenias, my favorite scent.

I told Mr. Crowley I still needed to be recognized as Frank's daughter because I needed to prove it to my son, Dan. He directed me to go back through Robert Finkelstein because I would have to take that up with the other kids.

I still couldn't understand why Nancy, Frank Jr., and Tina had not come forward when there had been the chance to meet my dad. I would have stepped up in a heartbeat for them if the shoe had been on the other foot. That seemed a normal response to me. In the back of the same edition of People magazine that carried its memorials for our father, I read the article titled, "Without Apology," by William Plummer and Cathy Nolan in Paris, about the illegitimate daughter of President Francois Mitterrand of France … She was embraced by her father's family. Even his wife accepted her warmly along with the other children. She was standing with them in a photograph of his funeral. To be fair, the President of France had long before acknowledged the daughter as his own. I still didn't know why I hadn't been, but whatever, I had no desire to be the object of Robert Finkelstein's dodge ball games and I didn't hold much in store that Finkelstein would ever make an effort to help me … besides, I didn't want my dad to run his sword through him.

June, 1998

Rod phoned to say Carol Lynn had sent for my dad's Last Will and Testament. My copy arrived a few days later. It began by naming his Executors who to my surprise had been the same three men I had spoken with, two I'd discovered in the Wall Street Journal article several months earlier: Eliot Weisman, who I met in Sedona and Harvey Silbert and their back-up, Sonny Goldman.

Frank Sinatra stated that he "had three children only," and named them as Nancy, Frank and Tina who were his heirs along with his wife Barbara and his former wife Nancy Barbato Sinatra, and additionally Barbara's son, his step-son, his long time assistant, and a housekeeper.

I wasn't mentioned anywhere. How could I not even exist for him? Had I done something or had my mother, to cause him not to want to acknowledge me as his daughter? In Bill Zehme's first edition I had of "The Way You Wear Your Hat," my dad was quoted in regards to his children that he loved them all equally and had treated their inheritance on that equal basis … The first few minutes all this was hitting me I burst into tears. It was just too much hurt. I felt like he had shot arrows into me. Why?

I paced around in the house most of the day and eventually phoned my friend Darrell Peterson for sympathy I guess. She and her husband, Jim both had a different take on it. Jim thought my dad had just found it easier not to include me in his life. Darrell responded with a question: "Do you think it's possible he never knew, Julie?"

Late in the evening I was asking him out loud: "Why didn't you ever come forward to me?" That night I had a dream that seemed too real to be just a dream. It was formatted with short scenes sequenced one after the other ...

My mother at a young age, maybe early 30's wearing a colorful patterned cocktail dress was sitting alone at a high gloss finish light wood grain round table in what appeared to be a fancy dinner club to the right and back a little from a curtained stage. What appeared to be a flashback then occurred as I saw a grand piano just below the stage and a man playing the piano had blonde hair and also looked to be her age. He stood up at the piano bench and announced to the audience that, "Toni" was coming on stage to perform her number. My mother then appeared with short dark curls done in an Italian style haircut, and began to sing in a husky brash voice—the voice I remembered hearing once when she sang merrily in my room when I was little—and the hairdo as a brunette that I had seen in a photo for the first time when Rod and I had gone over to interview her about Frank Sinatra. It was like I was watching the dream passage while knowing I was dreaming but acting like an observer of it all. At that moment the scene in my dream suddenly changed and a new sequence began.

This time her hair was back to blonde as she looked when the dream showed her the first time at the table in the luxurious looking dinner club, but the scene now showed a bedroom in a definite Spanish Colonial style building.

My mother, wearing only a slip suddenly jumped up out of a bed she had been sharing with my father, Frank Sinatra, and rushed over to look out of a window a few steps from the bed. The window overlooked a large courtyard or motor court and I could see tropical large leaf plants and vines draping across the surrounding tall walls. Through a wide entry where the gates were open, two men dressed in business suits were running toward the building. She looked back towards the bed and shouted:

"They have guns. They are coming to kill us." She went over and picked up a rifle that was leaning against the wall on the other side of their room.

My father quickly got up and pulled on his slacks. He also looked to be in his early 30's. He went over to a suitcase he opened and began shuffling to get under a stack of large blank paper in it. He pulled out a revolver and had not yet turned around when the door burst open to their bedroom and the men who had been running towards the building arrived in the doorway.

My mother aimed the rifle and fired and the man on her left fell to the floor. Next I heard a thunder of heavy footsteps running up the stairs behind the man still standing there, and within an instant the second gun shot rang out from behind him and he fell backwards into the hallway.

Frank Sinatra had still not yet turned around to face the doorway, and in those few seconds by the time he did, the whole thing was over. both intruders were already dead.

The scene in my dream changed abruptly again and I was shown both my mother and father standing together in a wide hallway, like one you would see in a hotel. Other men dressed in business suit pants and dress shirts were milling back and forth from the hall into the bedroom.

My mother asked my father:

"What happened? This has all been such a shock." He answered: "You killed that guy." She said: "But they had guns in their hands; they were coming to kill us!" Dad: "Those weren't guns, they were walkie-talkies in their hands." My mother collapsed to the floor and with her back against the wall in the hallway began screaming as the dream sequence switched again …

… A couple of the men who had been in the hallway were now up on the roof of the building, large, like a hotel roof. My mother looked scared to death as one of them approached her. He had a stethoscope around his neck like a doctor. This man was much older than my mother, was balding, portly, and looking very threatening. I didn't hear what he said, but it appeared he delivered his words to her with stern authority. She was crying still and began nodding her head quickly, repeatedly to indicate "Yes, yes, etc. She looked terrified as he pointed over to a large scoop shaped furnace vent on the roof. The dream changed once again to its final scene …

… My eyes traveled the length of a living room, past a southwestern designed fireplace to where large corner windows revealed tree tops, as if the house sat up on a sloping hill overlooking it's yard areas. There was a grand piano in a little from the windows where a framed photograph of Frank Sinatra sat. His face was the last image I saw in the dream.

"Whoa!" my mother had killed somebody? I got out of bed and quickly reached for my robe and fought with my mind resisting a cloak of denial. I preferred thinking she had somehow 'shot her career down,' and that the dream was only symbolic. But my first action was that I wrote out every detail within those first few moments after waking up while I could still clearly recall it.

It was already around 5 AM so I stayed up. I put some small logs and twigs in the fireplace and sat close to be warm as I let my mind wander through the dream's information.

It had been somewhere in a tropical area of the world when the shooting scenes took place, but it had begun in a dinner club and I thought I remembered where I had seen a photograph that looked like the same place. I spent about an hour looking through all the magazines that had come out just after my dad had passed away. I found what I was looking for in the Life book that had begun with that picture of my dad in the orange cardigan sweater … Is this another reason he had directed me to go back into that book?

The photo on page 85 showed Frank Sinatra clowning around a round light grained glossy wood topped table in a fancy place captioned as being in Miami. He looked to be in his early 30's, the right appearance to match with my dream. A woman was sitting at the bar in the picture with the same printed cocktail dress on that my mother wore in my dream, but I couldn't see any part of her face as my dad had pulled a table cloth from the table and it was waving in the air blocking most of her from the picture.

I remembered that when Rod and I had gone to Vista, California to interview her, she had let it slip that she was "once considered for singing, because they thought all Italians could sing." That must have been where she had sung.

Still clinging to denial that the dream had been about real events, I thought maybe the images I'd seen had just been leftovers that had slipped into my subconscious. But the Spanish Colonial styled building in its tropical setting in the dream kept haunting my thoughts and the next thing that came to mind was that segment in Kitty Kelly's, "His Way" where she wrote about Frank Sinatra in Havana, Cuba, in February of 1947, definitely a tropical setting. I retrieved my copy of the book I had in a drawer in my study and located the Havana stuff.

The first time I ran into this in her book I didn't want to read about my father being associated with mobsters, so I had just scanned through it and noted that his trip down there to see Lucky Luciano coincided with my mother's trip the day before my fourth birthday when I was taken to stay at my Grandmother Bonucelli's ranch. In addition to the timing, I also knew from reading that Frank Sinatra had been repeatedly investigated by the FBI regarding their belief that he had taken money in a suitcase to the mob boss Luciano who had been exiled to Cuba from the US, so it was a short leap to connect my mother to Havana because that scary incident with the mobby guys yelling at her at that strange house took place upon her return. I already had a strong sense that something happened in Cuba that called for that "summons." … now it was time for me to read all of this stuff, every word.

Kelly reported that Frank Sinatra had purchased a hand gun before leaving Los Angeles to make the trip, first including a stop in New York the first day or so in February, 1947, then one in Miami before flying to Havana on February 11th,

(I noted a day after my fourth birthday) to check into the Hotel Nacional where exiled from the US,

Charles Lucky Luciano was staying and other mob bosses were also trickling in for a summons called for by the boss of bosses.

Frank was fingerprinted in Los Angeles in 1947,
as he applied for a gun permit.

In one of the magazines I'd collected I had seen a photograph of the Hotel Nacional—it fit the building with the large flat roof in my dream.

In Miami, Frank Sinatra went to the Colonial Inn in Hallendale, Florida, Kelly described, was "a luxurious casino owned by mob members, Joe Adonis and Myer Lansky." He went there with Joe Fischetti who had been the one to deliver the invitation to join Luciano in Cuba. The FBI had taken a photograph of my dad walking from the plane in Havana, carrying a suitcase they suspected held large sums of money for the exiled boss. But I had seen a stack of blank paper, not money in it, like someone would draw or paint on in my dream. Could these "G"men have been the ones to burst into their hotel room?

The list of names, I had previously just ignored, that Kitty Kelly produced on these pages for the other mob bosses who were summoned to attend the meeting with Charles Lucky Luciano in Havana, would include the name of one that would show me the dream had been real. Any denial of the events I witnessed was eclipsed as I read the name of mobster Joseph Stacher—nicknamed, "Doc".

"Oh my God! The guy on the roof with the stethoscope!" I said aloud and stopped reading.

With a chill running through me I recalled from the dream the look of horror on my mother's face when my dad told her those men had "walkie-talkies, not guns in their hands." The magnitude of the tragic accidental shooting sank into me. Worse, it had taken place where it was covered up by the Mob—happened where the motivation of self-defense as she had believed she had acted in, could never become purged through the courts. If the events in this dream actually happened, then my mother was also a victim of this tragedy, and consequently, so was I.

Frank Sinatra denied that he had any close relationship with those mobsters. He said he was vacationing down there and was asked to sing. He said when asked each time in the repeated investigations that spanned over 30 years following his trip to Cuba, that he had, "met Luciano there but did not know him." My father never once gave up my mother's name. He had protected her and endured the repeated pressure put on him for all those years.

None of the investigations ever resulted in their indicting him for anything.

I was beginning to see what he hadn't admitted to—I suspected the invitation he got to go down there had actually been a summons for his appearance, and he had been the recipient of one of those cliché invitations he couldn't refuse. Lucky Luciano had need for Frank Sinatra to be there. How better to impress the other gang bosses than to show that he, Lucky, was still the top guy—that Sinatra would come down there and sing for free for him—that being exiled from the US hadn't diminished his power. My father, it seemed was obligated to show this form of loyalty, it was an unspoken order because they had backed him, hired him to sing when no one else would. With what I understood about his personality, I could see my dad's response as he saved face and defined the trip and his agreement to go as "needing a vacation." But both he and my mother knew they were vacationing in dangerous territory, and that explained the hand gun he bought and the rifle leaning against the wall in their room in my dream.

I couldn't help but be somewhat amused as I read that during the same period of time Lucky Luciano was arrested by Cuban police and quickly deported to Italy. They must have blamed Lucky for the shootings, one at least he was innocent of. A friend of mine I later shared some of this with, who had been in the Navy following World War II and went on leave in Havana, described the town as booming with American mobby owned gambling casinos during the late 1940's. He told me it was common knowledge that Batista "looked the other way," in regards to the Mob and as well the FBI who were down there out of their jurisdiction to keep an eye on all this activity ... Batista liked the money coming into Cuba.

Frank Sinatra made a trip to see Lucky Luciano when he returned to Italy from Cuba. It looked like my dad had also been summoned for a private meeting with the old boss while my mother received her orders that she was to erase any trace between herself and Sinatra—her life in Hollywood would have to disappear from her history—her little girl would go with her into permanent exile in Sacramento—I was the link that connected them, and the secret about who I was had just become a life-threatening. I was buried alive when I was four.

And now that same four year old was protesting inside of me. "How could you just leave me there? Why didn't you ask her who my father was enough times to get her to tell you? How long do I have to stay lost because they made that stupid trip?"

I put all of the notes I made about the dream aside as the sun came up. It had been just a dream, I thought again in another attempt to refuse the horrible reality that their vacation in Havana had cost me my father ... but the last image of my dream floated up again and I saw my dad's face framed in the picture on his piano. I could feel the weight of his sadness all around me. If he had sent me this truth, the truth I'd asked for, he had trusted me to be tough enough, adult enough to take it.

With my balance regained a little later that morning, I considered that this information wasn't meant to be the ending to my story. I believe he felt I deserved to know what happened so I would be able to understand my story, and more; he knew I could use it to transform my story. In a painful correlation I knew we both understood that in wanting to lift one's life up, hope can only ride on truth.

With this dream my mother's rage was understood because her torture was revealed. My father's presence, always there throughout my life, but never actually being there, was felt. My desire to belong that had so often flickered up only to be abruptly snuffed out, got a long overdue explanation. In this dream, that was no dream, I was allowed to walk on the edge of time and experience a little flash of knowledge about the workings of what the Native Americans call "the Great Mystery."

Beyond mere fate, God, more likely was the one who had authored this play in which my mother and my father and myself had acted so far, it seemed in predetermined roles, and He was the one who knew the hows, whys, and the what fors. Perhaps my learning about who I was had always been the intention to surface only now in my '50's. It could have been left buried forever, so was this a message, a clue about a perfect plan I still could not see? The one thing I knew was that my own imagination even in its deepest profundity could not have conjured this up.

CHAPTER FOURTEEN

A head's up for a phone call ...

*H*i Julie, it's Rod. Carol Lynn has talked with an attorney in California in regards to the wording in your father's will, because she is not licensed there." "Before we talk about that I want to share some information I received about my mom and dad in a dream I had a few nights ago. I believe what I saw explains why the secret about who I am had been cemented in 1947." After hearing the details from the dream, Rod said:

"I think there could be something to that. I've always believed your mother had a reason besides trying to punish you, her daughter, for being born, to keep her secret so guarded all these years. Carol Lynn strongly believes as I do, that Frank was never told you were his. In legal jargon that translates into your being what is called a "pretermitted heir." This gives you the same rights and privileges the other children have."

"If he really did not know I was his he would never have been able to plan for me? Is that what you mean?"

"Yes, basically."

"If my dad knew I was his daughter and made the decision not to leave me in his will, then that's his business. After all, Rod, he was the one to earn his money. He has the right to do with it as he pleases."

"The law doesn't look at it that way, if indeed he did not know about you. The attorney in California is preparing a letter for Carol Lynn as we speak to explain the language in the probate statutes regarding this. I'll send you a copy of it when it arrives for your information."

I was listening just half-way to what Rod was explaining. He had let the information that came in my dream mostly wash over him. But it wasn't his responsibility to grasp the tragedy of it. It was mine.

After we hung up I couldn't help wanting to be included in my dad's estate along with his other children, but it wasn't that simple for me. I still had not become convinced that my dad didn't know ... I couldn't trust my self to jump once again at that because I knew I wanted it to be true too badly. This wasn't because of money I might end up inheriting. It was because I wanted to believe he really was a man, as Arthur Crowley had described him to me, "who would have found a private way" to have a relationship with me while he was alive. I already had a big hint that was true because a man who had been known to stand up for justice as Tony Bennett said he knew him to be, would not consider leaving one of his own children out of his will. I felt a tug in my gut that this was real about my dad, and I would be looking in that direction, crossing my fingers, but I promised myself I would stay open to whatever I found as I continued to search for the man behind the mystique who was my father.

Within that week I had a small escrow from a lot sale close. With monies for a few rents ahead covered, I decided to treat myself to at least a couple of cassette albums of my dad singing.

Mostly everything the music store had of him was sold out, but I was able to buy a copy of "In The Wee Small Hours," put out by Capitol Records from the original recordings done in February and March of 1955, with Nelson Riddle as arranger.

There was another cassette I bought also; one recorded by Frank Sinatra Jr., "How I Remember It," a collection of our famous father's signature songs sung by his son with shared comments from personal memories. I played both albums several times that night on my little cassette player. I sang along with my dad, playing the cassette over several times. I was very moved by Frank Jr.'s memorial in song to him. The only way I could say thank you to my dad and honor what he had given me, was by doing my music too. Going into a studio, hiring musicians and recording engineers was what was needed to put an album out. I didn't have a fraction to cover the cost of that.

A few days later when I was coming back in from the pasture where I'd given Checkers and Missy each a carrot treat, I heard my dad say in my head: "Contact Junior."

"How?"

It took another day or so before it dawned on me there would likely be a producer's name on the credits on my half-brother's album. Eliot Weisman had produced it and his company was named. I looked it up through phone company information and called him. A receptionist forwarded the call to his assistant in his office. When she asked who was calling I said:

"This is Julie Alex-Rider Speelman Sinatra. I need a business phone number for my brother." I didn't know which name they would recognize me by so I used the name I had been singing by, and my x-husband's; but I had surprised myself by using "Sinatra" for the first time to anyone in my dad's camp. I realized I should never hesitate to use my real maiden name.

"One second. Are you ready?—here it is," she quickly supplied me with the name Andrea Kaufman and the phone number for her and told me she was Frank Sinatra Jr.'s personal manager.

I reached Ms. Kaufman that afternoon. I introduced myself over the phone as 'Julie Sinatra,' and explained I had gotten her number from Eliot's office and was told this was where I could contact my brother.

"Many people have been phoning to become recognized, Julie, don't you think it would be better for you if you waited until the crowd dispersed? You wouldn't want to be counted among the phonies would you?"

"No, not after what I've been through this past year and a half trying so hard to meet my dad. I was blocked from getting to do that, I realize partly because he was too ill and in and out of a coma state."

"He was never in a coma. I took a walk myself with him recently in Malibu before he died."

"Andrea, you have just told me you got to take that walk on the beach with my dad I wanted to do so badly. Did everyone lie to me about his condition?"

"I'm sorry Julie, I really am, but why contact his son, Frank now?"

"Over fifty years have gone by, Andrea. Frank Jr. and I are way overdue in contacting each other."

"He prefers to be called just "Frank." Why don't you write a letter to him to begin with. I'll give you my fax number so you can send it and then I'll pass it along. I'll do that much for you. He can decide if he wants to answer you or not."

I wrote and faxed a letter on June 18th, giving a brief synopsis of what I knew to date about my recent history after discovering I was his sister. I also asked Frank (Jr.) if he would consider helping me to put my songs together on an album for commercial release. Almost two weeks went by with no response. On July 1st, I spoke again with Andrea Kaufman, asking her if she had in fact sent my letter over to him.

"Frank said you were full of shit." Here we go I thought, but I stood my ground.

"What made him think that, Andrea?"

"When Frank talked with Bob Finkelstein about this he told him you never sent any proof out there. You had been asked to send a blood test and you didn't send one.

"Bob Finkelstein's statement about this is an untruth and he knows it. Repeated letters from my attorney went out to Arthur Crowley who Bob Finkelstein sent us to where I offered to do blood testing, including DNA. Bob Finkelstein never asked for a blood test to be sent, and Arthur Crowley just ignored my offer to do so. I will fax you proof of that today."

July 1, 1998

FAX to: Frank Sinatra Jr.
        c/o Andrew Kaufman
        (800) 266-5551

Dear Frank,

Enclosed are a letter I received from Bob Finkelstein where-in he states he is the attorney for the "Sinatra Family". His first untruth, which eventually during a phone call with my attorney, he admitted he was only the attorney for you, and Tina, and Nancy.

In addition are letters from my attorney to Bob Finkelstein which will show that it is evident that he did not respond at all, let alone request proofs of blood tests, etc. from me. He never wrote back to my attorney and it wasn't until the phone conversation she finally had with him that he sent us on to Arthur Crowley.

If Bob Finkelstein had done his job in the first place, you would be in a much better position to make the correct determination about who I am.

It appears he is covering his hiney at my expense now, and he knows it.

The letter from my attorney to Arthur Crowley proves I have offered to do blood tests, etc. It received no answer.

My word and reputation mean something to me. I hope these enclosures will give you a clearer more accurate picture of what has taken place.

P.O. Box 3918
Sedona, AZ 86340-3918
(520) 639-2348

"If Arthur Crowley has anything to add to this he should contact Bob and Frank will get back to you at a more appropriate time." We hung up.

I made copies of the letters Carol Lynn had sent to Crowley and faxed them to Andrea that afternoon, adding a note that all my letters had been ignored. Then I called a lab in the Sedona area who could test and determine my blood type and made an appointment. Next I phoned Robert Finkelstein's office and raised all holy hell about his lying to my brother about me.

His secretary told me that he said I should "contact Arthur Crowley, that he was handling everything for the kids." Then I phoned Arthur Crowley to see if he would speak on my behalf to Frank Jr.

July 2, 1998:

"Bob Finkelstein saying I'm the one handling things for the kids is news to me, and totally untrue." Arthur Crowley began impatiently when we started talking, and added, "I have never met Frank Jr. I only represent Barbara Sinatra. I don't think much of Bob Finkelstein and I'm not going to call him to speak for you."

"I don't want you to call Bob, I'm asking you to phone Frank Jr. You know enough about me and we both know you recognize me as Frank's daughter even if you are not in a position to say so."

"I have to stick with what I said in my letters. You'll have to go back through Finkelstein. I want to be left out of the loop. Tell him that."

Two weeks later I faxed a copy of the lab report stating my blood type to Andrea Kaufman, noting that it was extremely rare that someone could have this blood type and it was not the same as my mother's. The following day I was in the house when I heard my dad speak in my head once again. He said, "Frank Sinatra Jr. will phone you Sunday at four o'clock." That was three days away.

Sunday, July 19, 1998 at 4:11 PM, I answered my phone in my study. He introduced himself and I was immediately struck by how much his voice sounded the same as my son Dan's voice.

"Is this Julie Alex, uh, Alexander? This is Frank Sinatra Jr. calling."

"Hello Frank. You're trying to say Julie Alex-Rider, a name I used for a while to avoid having to go by my x-husband's name. Alex is for a cat and Rider is for my horses …"

"Now that you have me on your phone, you are going to spend this time talking to me about your animals?"

"No. I just wanted to explain the name you used."

"I am sorry to sound harsh because you are a woman, but I want you to stop contacting the family. You are driving everyone crazy. You have upset my personal manager and everyone at the attorney's office. My family does not even feel safe in their homes."

"What on earth? Why would that be, that they wouldn't feel safe where I'm concerned? How can I be the one to be driving everybody crazy when all I did was try to contact you, my brother."

"I can't understand why you've waited to do that until Frank Sr. had passed away".

"I didn't wait. I talked with Harvey Silbert last year and asked him to convey the message that I wanted to speak with you. He told me you were out on tour and couldn't be reached."

"I've been keeping an eye on all this behind the scenes for the past year or so to see where it was going." I wanted to shout back at him, 'so why didn't you ever come forward to help me meet our father?' but I said nothing. Frank continued.

"I just buried my father two months ago."

"That was my father you buried also," I said softly back.

"You are among a handful from many more people who have contacted me and wanted to become recognized. I am calling you, and just those other few who seem to have some basis for this. If you are genetically related, it makes no difference personally to me or the rest of the family."

"I was hoping since you must also know that I write and perform my own songs, that you could spec a project with me to help me record them with good musicians, to be able to put out a quality album," I managed to say in spite of the coldness of his previous remark.

"If I did that I would have to have a social relationship with you, and I don't want that. If you do not interfere with us, I won't interfere and the rest of the family won't either, regarding the use of your name or doing whatever you want to be doing in your life."

"By the 'family' do you mean Nancy and Tina?

"Yes".

"Okay, I will respect that of course, but my door will remain open to all three of you. I couldn't feel otherwise." At that point I had started crying and was trying to control my voice so it wouldn't show over the phone.

"I can hear all this is causing you a lot of pain," he said softly.

"What choice do I have? What would you do in my shoes?"

"I think I would just walk away," he said almost as a question.

"Whom would I be walking away as?"

"What is it you base being Frank Sinatra's daughter on anyway?"

"My mother confirmed it and then spent the year I was trying so hard to meet him by attempting to put her cat back in the box."

"Why did she do that?"

"You tell me."

"I can hear your frustration with her," he said more softly back. Then spoke about another possible brother.

"I got a call from someone claiming to be his son," Frank said next and I could tell this upset him.

"This isn't your fault, Frank. You are not responsible for me or any other kids that might be out there. But, go easy in case they are hurting like this."

"Your birthday is February 10th, a year and a month before mine," he said softly, almost sadly, "We are the closest in age."

"That's true," I answered quietly. It's funny my having to approach you with this because he was my dad before you were even born on January 10th, 1944."

"We've already lived over 50 years of our lives not knowing each other. What's the point now? And I'm hard pressed to understand why you call him 'Dad,' when you never even knew him?"

"It's in a person, I don't know what else to say. What happened with all the photographs and the videos I sent out to him?"

"I can guarantee you that nothing you ever sent out there was put in front of him." I thought to myself he must be referring to Crowley and Barbara stonewalling me, but I didn't want to get into that or try to take sides if he brought up the infighting going on out there. Frank spoke again:

"What is all this about your wanting to have a foundation anyway? Nancy is planning the Frank Sinatra Foundation."

"I want to do healing work with the use of horses. Mine would be the Julie Sinatra Foundation."

"Humph."

"I need to tell you that I am not looking for a penny out of your pocket Frank, I only wanted help with my music. I can earn my own millions if that's what is needed."

"What is it you do want?" he asked, and I answered simply and truthfully:

"My identity. Would you be willing to do DNA testing with me?"

"I couldn't get involved in that," he said firmly back. Then

Frank Jr. wished me luck with "this identity thing," and we hung up.

My emotions were flipping back and forth between feeling exhilarated that I'd finally gotten some recognition of who I was from a member of my blood family, and the pain in my heart facing the fact I would likely never know my sibling "born closest in age to me."

I needed to re-center myself out in nature. I didn't have to wait more than a few seconds for that to begin. The moment I stepped out of my house a bald eagle flew low over my head sounding a triumphant whistle.

"Hoya!" I called out using a Hopi word that roughly translates to: "Teach me to fly!"

August 1998

There was a letter package in my mailbox in Sedona from Carol Lynn. The attorney in California, Ray Meline, had sent her photocopies of past cases regarding pretermitted heirs in the probate courts in California. Her note simply said, "For your information, Julie." Mr. Meline's letter she included as a copy for me, stated that the statues out there prohibited a judge from ordering DNA testing from surviving siblings—he added, the only state in the Union that did that. He said the statues also otherwise from this, were on my side, but he did not want to get involved with my case until I could bring the DNA results into the court on my own.

I read through the past cases, two of them involving small children who had not been known to their fathers when living and were now deceased. Both cases did not prevail due to their not being able to supply the court with DNA proof of paternity.

"This is wrong," I thought out loud. No child should be omitted their right to prove their identity. Ray Meline had spoken to this in his letter as well, saying that California was out of step and would eventually correct this in their probate requirements, but it would take an act of legislature to do it. He also mentioned that the current writing of these statutes had been the result of work that Andrew Garb, of Loeb and Loeb attorney firm and a Mr. White, a now deceased congressman had devised that had succeeded in becoming law. Loeb and Loeb were the attorneys handling my dad's estate.

As a nightly listener to National Public Radio, I had heard discussion over what is known as the "Mary Queen of Scott Law," that became the law of the land through the United States Supreme Court. This had been reported in following the case of the descendent of one of America's Founding Fathers, Thomas Jefferson, and the Court ordered he be dug up, to my aghast and tested for DNA., I remembered feeling to my amazement. She prevailed and was recognized and bestowed all rights in the possession of the other known descendents. Basically, this law states that: "No child is illegitimate."

By denying the ability to have DNA testing ordered by the Court, California had found a loop hole to get around this law of the land. Because, the child in question has to be able to present that he or she is "like or same" with the known children of the decedent father, and without DNA the highest proof of sameness scientifically accepted, the loophole results. Because DNA is legally accepted as that proof. I could just imagine my dad with his sword swinging on this one, knowing how he felt about unfair treatment of an underdog ... maybe he would be passing that sword down to me.

This likely was the basis for keeping my dad and I from meeting each other ... he would have done DNA testing with me I felt sure of that, and the family did not want me to be like or same. But now, I guess probably because of the old Apache in me, I would never disturb his resting place ... something I considered very sacred. I had three alive and well siblings that I felt strongly should already have come forward to do the DNA testing with me; if for no other reason that out of respect for our father.

I phoned Rod and told him how I felt about the statutes and I also shared the recent conversation I had with Frank Jr. He was pessimistic about the DNA requirement we would be challenged with and I got the impression that Carol Lynn was not still trying to locate another attorney in California. The wheels had stopped turning even before I'd had the chance to prove to myself I had the moral right to make a claim out there in the first place.

Rod was glad to hear that Frank Jr. contacted me though, and his take on that conversation was he said he believed I had just received recognition from my half-brother. Carol Lynn, he added, was sending me a form to be filed that would require the Court to send me copies of all legal documents that would be filed in my dad's probate. She was going to call me soon to explain it.

I was required to file the formal Notice under her instructions myself, because I did not have a California licensed attorney to do so for me. This took place sometime in September, 1998. Carol Lynn insisted, when I protested that I still did not think I should go against what my dad had written in his will until I knew for sure he had not known about me, that I file the document anyway because that information could still come and I would not be able to go into the court at some later date unless I had previously filed

Within a couple of weeks, I got a letter from Mr. Andrew Garb of Loeb & Loeb.

He wanted to know on what basis I had filed my formal Notice document. I wrote him just a sentence back a couple of days later and mailed it to him. I simply said the reason was because I was the daughter of Francis Albert Sinatra.

I didn't hear anything else back from Mr. Garb, or anyone at Loeb and Loeb. That didn't surprise me.

Towards the end of the month of September, I got something special in the mail from Rod. It was a clipping he had taken from the Arizona Republic newspaper published in Phoenix during the first week after my dad passed over. A note shared he had been meaning to send this to me. I already had sensed that he and Carol Lynn were not going to be on board with me, my case was no longer appealing without having my DNA proof. Whatever I decided to do about being a pretermitted heir, I would likely be on my own. I felt the clipping was a way to finish up his end with at least something of sentimental significance for me. And it was.

LOEB&LOEBLLP
A LIMITED LIABILITY PARTNERSHIP
INCLUDING PROFESSIONAL CORPORATIONS

ATTORNEYS AT LAW
1000 WILSHIRE BOULEVARD
SUITE 1800
LOS ANGELES, CA 90017-2475

TELEPHONE: 213-688-3400
FACSIMILE: 213-688-3460

DIRECT DIAL NO. 213-688-3406
e-mail: agarb@loeb.com

CENTURY CITY
10100 SANTA MONICA
BOULEVARD
SUITE 2200
LOS ANGELES, CA
90067-4164
TEL: 310-282-2000
FAX: 310-282-2192

NEW YORK
345 PARK AVENUE
NEW YORK, NY
10154-0037
TEL: 212-407-4000
FAX: 212-407-4990

NASHVILLE
49 MUSIC SQUARE WEST
NASHVILLE, TN
37203-3290
TEL: 615-749-8300
FAX: 615-749-8308

WASHINGTON, D.C.
2100 M STREET, N.W.
SUITE 801
WASHINGTON, D.C.
20037-1207
TEL: 202-223-3700
FAX: 202-223-5704

ROME
PIAZZA DIGIONE, 1
00187-ROME
ITALY
TEL: 011-390-806-0459
FAX: 011-396-974-8823

September 9, 1998

Ms. Julie Speelman
Post Office Box 3918
Sedona, Arizona 86340

Re: **Estate of Sinatra, deceased**

Dear Ms. Speelman:

I have received a copy of your Request for Special Notice in which you state that you are a person interested in this proceeding. In order for us to determine whether you are entitled to notice, I need to have you tell me exactly what the nature of your interest is in this proceeding.

I will look forward to hearing from you at your earliest convenience.

Cordially,

Andrew S. Garb
of Loeb & Loeb LLP

ASG:sv2
792717195
GAA18653.L01

September 18, 1998

Andrew S. Garb
of Loeb & Loeb LLP
1000 Wilshire Blvd. Suite 1800
Los Angeles, California 90017-2475

    RE: Sinatra, deceased

Dear Mr. Garb:

    The exact nature of my interest in this proceeding is
that I am the daughter of Francis Albert Sinatra.

Very truly yours,

Julie Speelman
Julie Speelman
P.O. Box 3918
Sedona, Arizona 86340-3918

Rod had cut out a photo the newspaper had put in color on the first page, which is unusual for them to do, of an outpouring of respect at a star placed in the sidewalk at my dad's birthplace in Hoboken. There had been a picture of something like this I saw in one of those magazines, where people had placed flowers on his star on the Hollywood Walk of Fame. But this was different, much more homey and grass roots. Unlike the sophisticated commercially assembled bouquets in Hollywood, these people in my dad's hometown had brought flowers picked apparently from their own gardens, wrapped simply with rubber banded paper towels or with tinfoil. I was very moved by this. Clearly these people had loved him.

I was compelled to phone the newspaper and got a number for the Associated Press photographer who was credited for the picture and called out there to learn more about how the photograph had come to be. He told me he was moved also about the outpouring he saw at my dad's birthplace and that's why he took the picture. Then he connected me with a reporter saying she knew the history about the star at the birthplace.

It took some graceful moves on my part to avoid giving her my story she was excited to hear of. I told her I was just following up on what I had seen, hoping it would lead me to learn more about my dad. I explained I was not ready to "go public." She gave me the phone number for the man she told me had paid to have the star made in Hoboken. Ed Shirak Jr., she said was a devoted fan of Frank Sinatra's and he knew quite a bit about the history of him growing up in Hoboken.

I phoned Mr. Shirak that afternoon at the number I had been given from the reporter in Newark, for Lepore's Chocolates in Hoboken. His mother came to the phone and I introduced myself as the "unheard of kid." She was very nice and said her son would be excited to talk with me when he returned from vacationing. She took my phone number.

A week or so later Ed Shirak phoned me and we talked for a while. He had written a book, "Our Way," as a rebuttal to Kitty Kelly's, "His Way." He said the people of Hoboken had been outraged about the misquotes Ms. Kelly made about them in her book. He said he wanted to write the book to show my father how much the people there in Hoboken respected and loved him. That is why, he explained, he had that memorial star made—to honor Frank Sinatra at the location where he had been born. Listening to him, I began to long to visit there.

"I'll send you a copy of my book if you would like that, Julie," Ed offered. I said I would love to read it and gave him my address. "Your timing in contacting me is good, because there is going to be a conference held on Long Island soon to honor your father."

"What is that all about?" I asked very intrigued.

"It's a three day conference that will happen at Hofstra University in Hempstead, New York, in November. I have been asked to be one of the speakers to represent Hoboken there."

"Can you send me the information about this? I would love to know more and possibly attend."

"You should go to this, Julie, you would be able to learn a lot about him during those three days. And if you can come out, I would like to invite you to come to Hoboken and spend a few days too. I could show you around to all the places that had to do with Frank and his parents, Marty and Dolly Sinatra too. I have a collection of photographs here that my Uncle took of your father and grandparents. He and Frank palled around when they were teenagers. My mother has a guest room you could stay in. There are not any hotels here, but I have an idea for one that has to do with your father … I'll share more about that with you when you're here."

"I am so excited hearing about the conference and a chance to travel to Hoboken where my dad had begun his life. This is a miracle I am going to work very hard at being able to follow through with, Ed."

"Good. Let me know your plans. My associate Mario and I would like very much to show you Hoboken. I believe you must be who you say you are or you would have had no other reason to contact me. I'll put the conference information in the mail today for you, Julie. You'll have to act fast on it because there is a deadline on registering your name to attend."

"Thank you Ed. I'll call you soon."

"Call him soon??? I had about 13 cents to my name! How was I going to raise enough monies to make a trip like that? How was I going to ever live with myself if I didn't go?"

When the application for the Sinatra Conference, "The Man, The Music, The Legend," arrived, I saw that paying the registration fee in addition to the cost to travel and hotel expenses amounted to almost $900.00, but I still kept saying to myself that this has to happen; it must happen.

Remember how I don't believe in coincidences? I had been accepted earlier in that summer to begin teaching songwriting classes for the Sedona Arts Center that would begin in January the coming year. Real estate work had been fading away, and I needed to supplement my meager income. The Arts Center phoned the day after I spoke with Ed Shirak. They were having a special speaker in for all the teachers, someone who would be talking about the role of grants for the arts. I went to it. I talked with the woman speaker and she connected me with yet another gal who knew her way around in writing grant proposals. This led to getting a grant from the State of Arizona to help pay for going to the Sinatra Conference. Their grant would go up to $200.00, enough to cover the Conference registration fee.

I phoned the Arizona Commission On The Arts and told them I was the unheard of daughter and not one of the wealthy Beverly Hills kids and why it was so important for me to go as Frank's daughter in addition to being able to learn how he handled his music as a songwriter and singer myself. The gal there bent over backwards to instruct me as to how to fill out an application she sent me for their grant program. In a unheard of short period of time, and on time to make the Conference Registration deadline, their check arrived for $200.00. My only obligation would be that I write a report when I got back showing what I got out of attending the conference.

I phoned Rod and Carol Lynn and told them about my invitation to Hoboken and the Hofstra Sinatra Conference. Rod agreed that my going to my dad's home town might afford a chance to locate something which had his DNA on it. They put up the monies to cover my round-trip air fare.

Next, I phoned my friend, and the President of the Arizona Songwriters Association, Jon Iger. He agreed this was something the Association should sponsor and got two more members to send me money also. I now had the hotel expense covered. All I needed was money to pay for the airport parking and hopefully a little more for food costs there. My son, Dan, agreed to cover the parking fees. A couple of people who lived on the ranch said they would pay me if I would do their laundry. I had just under $20.00 for food and cups of coffee, and everything else was covered, including that I had hay and feed in my barn for the horses. Another gal from the ranch agreed to feed them in my absence, and I also thought it would be nice if they had someone around who could also enjoy vacationing at my little rock house. My trusted friends, John and Jo Ann Braheny agreed to come from Los Angeles.

It was going to happen. It was as if someone, and I'll bet you can guess who at this point, had rolled out a red carpet and covered every detail that was needed for my trip. I had already been able to phone Ed Shirak before the end of October to tell him I was going to attend the conference, and more than that ... I was coming to Hoboken!

CHAPTER FIFTEEN

November 10, 1998

*W*aking up minutes before the radio's clock alarm went off, a quiet excitement stirred inside the little guest house on Orillo Oeste Road, in Cave Creek, Arizona, where the early morning glow had turned its white adobe brick walls to a pale gold. In a couple of hours I would be boarding the plane in Phoenix that would take me to the Sinatra Conference, and in less than a week I would actually be in my dad's birthplace of Hoboken, New Jersey. I got out of bed knowing the desert sky had something special going on that created this glow. I went over to the east window and looked out. The dawning sun was blazing through some wisps of clouds shaping a golden horse that seemed to be galloping over the cactus covered hills with a gypsy rider on its back, adorned with colorful long cloud scarves mostly orange in color with a touch of turquoise and lavender flowing out on a soft morning wind ... A sign, glorious and optimistic that my journey across the country to the "source" would be a powerful experience.

I was already tucked in a little pig-skin chair smoking a cigarette on the patio when my hostess, Darrell Peterson arrived with a fresh mug of steaming coffee, and a smile typical of her gracious demeanor, in spite of the early hour. Her husband, Jimmie, had made me a hot bowl of soup when I'd gotten in late the night before driving from Sedona. Because of the MS, I knew I wouldn't be alert enough neurologically to attempt making the early flight with a three hour drive from the ranch, and my friends allowed me to break up this first leg of my journey by staying the night with them.

"Isn't the sky spectacular," Darrell chirped. "What a greeting for the new day!" She added.

"See that orange streak across the sky? ... my dad's favorite color. I think it means he is blessing my trip." I chirped back, feeling so happy.

I quickly showered and brushed out the little braids in my hair I had done in order to have a head full of curls to hide the fact I badly needed a hair trim I couldn't afford. I loaded my over packed zipper bag with clothing to accommodate mild to freezing weather, as I didn't know what to expect, into my "Z" as Darrell waved from her porch with a look in her eyes that said, "You're running late."

Missing the correct turn for the east budget parking lot at the airport I missed the shuttle I needed. I would have to wait ten minutes for the next one going into the terminal at Sky Harbor, in Phoenix. I arrived at the baggage check-in counter and presented my round trip tickets. The girl looked at them and shook her head, frowning up at me.

"You've missed the luggage loading for your plane. You must travel with your luggage, so you are not going on that plane. I'll check to see what the next flight going into JFK is that can be available for you."

"What? I have to go on that plane. There are people I have never even met yet who will be expecting to meet me at our designated time this evening." I was wasting my breath. She shook her head again in the negative.

"No. You're going on this flight," she said handing me a new updated computer sheet she had been typing up during my protest."

"I have hotel reservations that are good only until 6 PM!," I stated back as firmly as I could.

"You can use the courtesy phone upstairs to phone your hotel. Relax. Your flight doesn't leave until 2:15 today. Go into one of the café's," she smiled.

Accepting my defeat, I took the new flight sheet and went up on the upper level. The hotel in Hempstead agreed to hold my reservation and I also left a message for Ed Shirak that I would be coming in too late for the dinner invitation he had proposed, and to go ahead without me. I was so disgusted with myself. Just an hour into my journey I had already screwed up by arriving four minutes late to check in my baggage. I spent the following few hours sipping a large paper cup of coffee and greedily smoked cigarettes I knew I would miss having on the seven-hour flight into JFK. My feeling of excitement returned in a flash when the announcement came to begin boarding the plane.

I got in line and could hear grumbling coming from three older gentlemen who had just come to stand behind me to board the flight. One of them was saying something about how they never had to stand in lines before. I couldn't hold back from wanting to spread the joyous feelings engulfing me.

"What's all this complaining I'm hearing. It's a beautiful day and we are all getting to go someplace." I announced turning fully around and facing the closest of the three men.

"Yes. You're right," he brightly retorted. "We're going out to the Sinatra Conference on Long Island."

"Small world," I grinned back at him, and I was already getting a strong feeling in my gut that something was up. "I'm Julie Sinatra, Frank's daughter. I'm going out to the Conference to learn more about my dad … Who are you guys?"

"My God! She looks just like him," exclaimed Chuck Berghofer, as he introduced himself as having been Frank Sinatra's bass player for 25 years of his career.

"Al Viola," the next man who was standing with a guitar case at his feet, stated introducing himself. "I played guitar for him for 30 years. I was in Egypt with him. Maybe you've read something about it?"

"No, I haven't gotten to reading and learning everything yet … there's so much," I trailed off as the third gentleman, who was white haired and looked at me intently as Al Viola introduced him as, "Bill Miller, who has been with your father for 40 years at the piano."

"I do know who you are, Sir. NPR aired a special about my dad and included a taped rehearsal of just him and you together. You were accompanying him on the piano as he sang, "One For My Baby." It was just wonderful, magical. I'm so glad to have this chance to meet you in person." I said all that in one wind. "Yes," he said pleasantly. "I remember something about that."

"I taped it off the radio. It's my favorite keepsake of my dad." He smiled.

"Who was your mother?"

"Dorothy Lyma," I answered and saw the recognition that flashed quickly across his face.

Bill Miller suddenly looked very uncomfortable so I pretended not to have caught on that he must have known my mother. I didn't press him for anything about that. I just smiled and shook his hand and told him again how much I enjoyed meeting him. Then I shook hands with the other two and a moment later, they stepped away from the line, it seemed to catch their breath.

"I guess he must know something, Dad," I thought to myself. "I don't want to spoil this magic moment you likely orchestrated when I took that wrong turn into the airport this morning … looks like you will be my guide for this journey. Welcome aboard!"

My seat on the plane was not nearby where my dad's old musicians were, but I did see them again just after the flight arrived. I was waiting as directed for the hotel shuttle arranged to meet and pick me up at JFK. Chuck Berghofer stepped away from the other two as they passed by me to board their shuttle for a different hotel. He was concerned about my standing alone there. He trotted up to his driver and then came back to me.

"It's not safe for you to be waiting here all by yourself. My driver can take you to your hotel if you like." He graciously offered. Al Viola was walking back towards me as well and Bill Miller, obviously the elder to the other two, was sprightly hanging on the open door to their bus, leaning out with one leg swinging, ready to jump down, when I said, "Thank you. But I'm okay waiting. My driver should be here any minute. Your driver could get in trouble. Go on ahead. I'm really alright."

Chuck said, "We're performing on Saturday night at the Conference."

"I'll be sure to be there," I said back, thinking, "They're wonderful, Dad."

I watched their bus leave and wondered if it was possible I could be in any danger standing where I was. A car slowed on the street in front of me and the driver called out to learn what flight I had just arrived on.

"What town is this? Where am I exactly?" I shouted out to him.

"Lady, you're in Queens!"

Hempstead, New York ...

Huge glass doors opened onto a spectacle of glitz where oversized crystal chandeliers hung down and reflected on the mirrored walls in the small lobby of the Best Western Hotel, giving it more size and grandeur. Up on the seventh floor my room overlooked a busy boulevard, commercial buildings on one side were dark, but there were lights glowing from the windows of the steeped roofed houses that lined the other side of the street. The traffic noise was a strong contrast to the solitary cries of the loons on Oak Creek I was used to being lulled to sleep by on the ranch. It struck me how far away that was now.

It was around 9 PM when my phone rang in my room. Ed Shirak and his associate, Mario would enjoy having me meet them for dinner in the hotel dining room ... In New York, Ed had explained, dinner often isn't until ten PM.

"How was your flight?" Ed greeted me wearing a brightly colored Hawaiian print shirt, and I mused to myself how I had made it a point to wear a gray sweater with black pants to look more keeping with New York style.

"It was magical from the start," and I went on to tell he and Mario what took place with my dad's musicians."

"That's how Mr. S. works," Ed piped back as Mario reached out for a folded t-shirt on a chair next to him and held it out for me.

"This is for you," Mario announced brightly, adding, "It's too big. We didn't know your size." The shirt was printed with the words: "Hoboken's Brightest Star," with a youthful Frank Sinatra face in the center and his name below.

"It's great. Thank you. I love having it guys."

We laughed a little over how Ed had worn his brightly colored shirt to make me feel more comfortable as a Westerner coming to the East; and I admitted I had borrowed the gray sweater to look more appropriate. Our conversation moved easily into a discussion about symbols and signs and the synchronicities that allow the perfect thing to happen perfect places. Ed shared his otherwise inexplicable experience in a restaurant sitting close by where Frank Sinatra was dining, that led him to write his book, "Our Way".

"Mr. S. delivered a monologue from his table looking right at me," Ed stated with the amazement he felt when it had taken place still with him.

"What did my dad say to you?"

"It happened at I' Medici at the Sands, in Las Vegas. He was there with his family having dinner before he performed that night. I had spoken with Tina Sinatra earlier that day. I just phoned the hotel and asked to be connected to her suite. I was surprised she answered the phone. I wanted to tell her about an idea I had for a hotel in Hoboken I named after him, "From Here To Eternity." I told her I was having a bronze star made to go in the sidewalk at his birthplace and wanted to have the hotel built there. She was very polite and seemed moved by someone from Hoboken caring that much about her father. I had no idea they would be dining when Mario and I went to dinner that night. They were originally sitting on the other side of the room, and too far way to hear them talking with one another, when Mr. S. suddenly shouted out to his son who had been hanging back from their table. "Frankie, don't be a schmuck! Join us." A few minutes later his family left and he got up and came over to a table just across from ours. He began speaking, out of the blue with a glass of Jack Daniels in his hand. The room became silent. He talked about the days with Dean Martin and Sammy Davis Jr. He said Sammy "gave everything away." He said how Doris Day was a "challenge to work with." He looked at us and said that he "calls Dean's house everyday but he refuses to come out of his house." He spoke about music, life and wisdom and he lit a Camel cigarette and directed the rest of his words to me personally: "You know," he began, "I'm from the streets of Hoboken. That's where I come from. That's where I was born. I'm just a regular guy born in a small city."

"I knew I had to write a book and tell the truth about Mr. S. and the people from Hoboken. I sent him a copy of it and got a thank you letter back. I want to believe he typed that letter personally to me. I'll show it to you when we're in Hoboken in a few days from now," Ed finished and looked over at me.

"Wow, Ed. I came here to learn about my father and you have just shared a poignant insight with me. I read your book and it is wonderfully sincere. I'm sure it did move my dad deeply."

"Julie, Mario and I both understand how much it means to you to make this trip, and also about how hard it was for you to pull it together. We are hoping to buy you dinner each night here at the hotel during the conference if you'll let us contribute that. We would be honored to have that company with you. It's like dining with Anastasia."

"Thanks. Ed. But, I think that woman turned out not to be actually related to her royal father.

Talking about special timings, yesterday, November tenth, is an anniversary for me. It was November tenth of 1996 when I first wrote my first letter ever to my dad. It was the first day of my journey to come here to explore my roots as his daughter."

"That date is more significant than even that," Ed said back looking very serious suddenly. "It was on November tenth last year that Frank Sinatra went into the hospital with a serious heart attack he wasn't expected to recover from. The world almost lost him then. The reporter you spoke with who gave you my phone number even woke me up in the middle of the night to tell me what was happening with him, and I knew I had to get the star ready at his birthplace right away. It was finished but not yet installed in the sidewalk. The press, nationwide was alerted and ready to release the announcement that he'd passed away. Miraculously, he recovered, proving he wasn't giving up yet."

"This was in 1997?" I asked.

"Yes."

"I keep notes on my calendar at home in my study; it's like keeping a journal. I wrote a song on that day, November tenth, 1997, that is a musical treatment of a conversation my dad and I have together, one I was being blocked from having by the attorneys representing his family."

"Again, Julie. That is how Mr. S. works."

I listened to Ed's comment, the second time he'd made this reference to my dad. I didn't miss the mystical implications.

Before we parted to go to our rooms, Ed handed me a reprint of something my dad had written in the Magazine Digest, published in 1947. It was titled, "Let's Not Forget We're All Foreigners." I read it before I went to sleep.

"This is our job ... your job and my job, and the job of the generations growing up ... to stamp out the prejudices that are separating one group of American citizens from another ... "—Frank Sinatra

November 12, 1998, Hofstra University ...

Ed spoke at the first panel among the historians from Hoboken. His speech made it very clear how much he admired and honored Frank Sinatra. There was another young man who spoke and then sang, not very well, and he had made it clear that he felt it was unfair that as he put it, "Sinatra got all the breaks." I was amused over the contrast and remembered reading something about my dad having been booed by several people from his home town when he had once returned for a singing engagement there after he was very famous. He had vowed never to return to Hoboken because of it. But Ed Shirak was bent on bringing him home now, as he had spoken about Frank Sinatra who was, "an honest man who lived his truth and had respect for all peoples." It had made me tearful just to witness this tribute along with others in the room from all over the country and the world.

When the panel was over, Ed and Mario came up to me and pointed out a man with his wife there to represent Barbara Sinatra. Mario suggested I go over and introduce myself to them. Dr. Bruce Wooding, as he explained was the Executive Director for Barbara Sinatra's Children Center, at the Eisenhower Medical Center, in Rancho Mirage, California.

"I'm proud to meet you," I said extending my hand. "I have heard about the wonderful work going on there to help abused children. I know my father cared very deeply about this."

Dr. Wooding extended a shaking hand back and just nodded without a word. His face went suddenly white.

"He probably thought he was seeing a ghost.," Mario grinned at me after observing the encounter.

Ed talked with me before we all parted to go to the next panels we'd chosen to attend, saying he hoped I would understand if he and Mario left me on my own during the conference. He explained that there were things going on in Hoboken where he hoped to become Mayor and I was "controversial." It hurt a little, because I didn't see myself that way, but I told him I understood.

"Thank you, Julie. I am planning to make sure you see everything in Hoboken that will give you information about how your father grew up here".

"I trust you, Ed, and I'm very grateful for that. I would be no longer controversial if I could have DNA to test with. Would you help me in finding an article with my dad's DNA on it in Hoboken, if you know of one? I'm not planning to explode his Will, but I need it for my identity."

"Yes, I can help you with that … just between us though, okay?"

I caught a few minutes of the Psychology panel only, as it had been going on while I was in the Biography one. A Professor of Education at UCLA in Los Angeles, James E. Bruno, described my father as, "A man who crossed rivers in his life." He also said of Frank Sinatra that he was, "An artist whose creative expression amplified the whispers of the American collective unconscious."

Ed and Mario had caught up with me as I was about to go in to the auditorium where the opening Conference Ceremonial was to take place around noon.

"Julie, there will be a lot of reporters around during this ceremony, so be aware if you don't want to get caught up in going public yet." Ed warned. "You could be approached because of your obvious likeness, and you have that nametag on to confirm it," Mario added.

The nametag was the only nod I received from the Conference staff. As Frank Sinatra's daughter attending, because Ed made sure I hadn't had to stand in line with the other visitors to get it. It was waiting for me at a staff table separate from where the lines were formed. Everyone attending the conference was required to wear a nametag.

Ed and Mario went in and sat somewhere away from me. I sat down in the center of the first row of seats closest to the stage behind a ribboned off row off limits to underdogs.

The President of Hofstra University opened and Sid Mark who had a nationally syndicated radio show out of Philadelphia that played mostly Frank Sinatra songs, was the Master of Ceremonies.

They were followed by my half-sister, Tina Sinatra, who took the stage for "Greetings" to the packed full audience. She spoke easily, intelligently, and I felt proud of her until with my aghast she included a remark about being sure she came so she could "see what all these strangers were saying about Daddy." Looking down into the audience where I was seated, she also added an incongruent remark about Dad becoming "impotent," as she put it, "at one stage of his life."

"Good God," I thought, "Doesn't she know I was born at least five years before she came into this world?"

Skitch Henderson spoke about my father's music; and Will Friedwald got up and talked about his biography, "Sinatra, The Song Is You." Gay Talese commented as to a "writer's view," but I didn't hear most of their words, all eloquently delivered I guessed, because they had followed Alan King, the comedian who had stated in stone seriousness from the depths of his soul that, "Frank Sinatra had been, not just a man, but an event." I began sobbing uncontrollably after that remark and was searching for tissues to bury my face in from my purse. I hung back when the ceremonial was over to allow almost all the people to exit the auditorium while I pulled myself back together. I had just walked down the steps at the exit when I was confronted.

"Fill me in here. I'm ignorant about this. What's your story?" I looked up astonished and a reporter from the New York Times was standing in front of me holding out a microphone. Another man, a photographer was at one side of me already filming the scene.

I looked at the reporters name tag. "Peter Townsend, you are too early in my story to get one from me. I have simply come here to learn more about my father. I don't even know enough about my story as his daughter to share it with you in a public platform. I'm sorry."

"Fill me in here," he repeated his order aggressively. "Are you really Frank Sinatra's daughter?"

I looked around for Ed and Mario in hopes to become rescued. They had disappeared. I realized this guy wasn't going away without something from me.

"Do you have your note tablet ready?" I asked him. He stepped up putting the microphone near me. "Write this. I am Frank Sinatra's daughter and have come to attend this special conference not only in his honor but to learn as much as I can about my father while I'm here."

Peter Townsend looked disappointed, and I added once again. "I'm sorry but I am still learning my story myself and there isn't anything I can add to this at this time." He relented and I walked away.

"Whew." I felt relieved. I had been considering writing a book and when I knew I was ready to, I would share my story, my whole story with the world one day. but not that day.

I needed a break and took my refuge in the campus student center snack shop. I bought a large blueberry muffin and a cup of coffee, affordable on what I had budgeted for each day's lunch meal, and sat down at one of the tables. A moment later a young woman came over and said she had noticed my name tag. She explained she had brought her elderly mother to the conference because she had been a fan of my father's for sixty years.

"I would love to say hello to your mother. Would you both like to join me?" They sat down with me and introduced themselves. Diane was the daughter. Her mother, who had one of those faces that symbolized all humanity, Carla Faggio, humbled me at once as she began to speak about the love she'd had all her adult life for Frank Sinatra.

"Thank you for inviting me to sit with you, Julie—may I call you that? I already feel like you are one of my kids, because I loved your father so much."

"My mother would have left my father who she was married to for fifty years in a snap for Frank Sinatra." Diane laughed. "She has every record he ever made."

"Your father saved my life." Carla stated, surprising me. "I had cancer. real bad. I was in the hospital and I played your father's songs on a tape recorder as I wore earphones there. His voice, him singing in my ears, healed my cancer, Julie."

"I think you're talking about the special energy in his voice. I've been listening to him sing only for a year or so. I was kept a secret by my mother all my life. I just recently found out I am his daughter ... but I think it's love that comes through him when he sings." I said, allowing the words to flow from me, more, through me. I knew my dad was there with us. I felt compelled to say what I said next to her. "Carla, my dad believed that creativity was the key to life. I think he would want you to know that you created your own wellness, inspired from the love you feel for him maybe." I continued and shared a children's book story that had always stayed with me from when I was very little. "It's like the theme of "Dumbo, the Flying Elephant. First he is given a feather to carry in his little trunk at the circus he belongs to, in order to fly across the top of the tent. But eventually the feather falls from him and he sees that he is flying on his own. We all need to find our own wings."

"Yes, Julie. That is the truth, but I will always give your father credit. I wrote a poem about him I have with me. I would like you to have a copy of it if you want."

I read the poem titled, "Just Only To Me," by Anna Carla Faggio, penned, August, 1998. It was about how when he sang it felt he sang directly to the person listening.

"I'm thinking about writing a book about my journey to know my father. May I use this poem for it someday. I would like very much to include it, Carla."

"Yes you may use it, Julie," she said before we shared a hug and they left. I truly did feel honored to have met her.

That evening at the hotel …

Ed and Mario and I were having dinner in the dining room. I'd ordered a pasta dish with red sauce just as I had the night before. There hadn't been any Parmesan cheese, as the restaurant didn't use it, as the previous night's waitress had apologized for. This night she arrived at our table with the cheese in a soup bowl.

"It's fresh grated for you, Ms. Sinatra," she beamed. "Courtesy of the chef."

November 13, the second day at Hofstra …

There were numerous panels to choose to go to. Unfortunately, there were so many that had to be missed because they were scheduled in different classrooms but at the same time as others. There were five for instance just on discussing my father's psychology, I didn't want to hear about that from "strangers," as Tina had also surmised. There were three on musicals and dance;

Five again on the cultural meaning presented in his films; there was even a heading called "Iconography"; but I was drawn to go into the panel regarding his philanthropy.

Dr. Wooding and Mrs. Wooding passed by me going in and they gave me a silent nod of their heads in my direction. This must be the appropriate protocol, I mused to myself. A moment later I was knocked off my righteous perch as my dad's speaking voice suddenly came out of a monitor I hadn't noticed when I chose my seat. I was right in front of it, just a few inches away. I had only heard his voice when he spoke inside my head, and when he was playing a role in a movie I watched. This was the first time to ever hear his voice speaking just as himself in the physical world for me. I burst out crying. I could have died at doing this in this small room with now, all eyes trained on me. I stepped outside for a few minutes and then I returned more collected.

Frank Sinatra, I learned in that panel, had given regularly for many years, $400,000.00 from his own pocket each year to the Variety Club International in Los Angeles. It was the largest fund-raising activity in the world for handicapped children. Additionally, he had given large sums to other charitable activities and as well had helped to raise multi-millions of dollars for them. This was not just an act to improve his personal image … this repeated, devoted giving was from a sincere desire to help others in need.

I was sorry to not have heard much of his words through that speaker that morning because of my emotional outburst, but I did recognize his was the same voice I had been hearing lately in my head. Learning about his philanthropy, I felt that if he had known about the way I had struggled with MS and even earlier in my life when I was trying to pay my way through college and at the same time provide for my baby son and myself, he would have expected me to work hard. But when my wings faltered, there would have been a safety net … that is if he had ever known about me.

I walked over to a smoking area set up outside the student center. A man walked up and lit a cigarette and noticed my name tag and looked up at my face.

"You look just like Frank Sinatra," he said.

"He was my father," I said back and smiled.

"I met your father when he came to IBM some years ago. I was his security guard and showed him around. He wanted to see the computers he'd invested in, in person."

"That sounds like him."

"I have a story about that time if you would like to hear it," he offered.

"Yes. I would. That's why I'm here. to learn about him."

"He was going to sing at the Westchester Theatre that night of the day I showed him around at IBM. I told him I was working security for the concert and my father who had just gotten out of the hospital from having triple Bi-Pass heart surgery, was insisting that I take him to it, in spite of the fact he'd be there in a wheel chair, not recovered enough to walk well yet.

Your father asked me what my dad's name was and told me to bring him around back stage. to make up some kind of story that I had to check on security or something. Then he told me to knock on the stage door and he, your father Frank Sinatra, would take care of the rest."

"What happened?"

"I took my dad around and I knocked on the door and your father stepped out with his hand outstretched to shake hands with my dad and greeted him saying: "Hello Bill, It's great to meet you." Then we had our picture taken with him and he put my dad in the middle. That's how gracious your father was. That was Frank Sinatra.

"What is your name?"

"Tom."

"It's wonderful to meet you Tom, thank you so much for sharing that with me," I said reaching for and shaking his hand. Were you there when he also had his photograph taken with Carlo Gambino and those other members of the underworld at the Westchester Theatre that night? I've read how he was accused of associating with them."

Tom said there were some guys who had been cleared by the owner to go back stage because they wanted to meet Frank Sinatra. That was enough for me to see that my dad had not known those gangsters personally. I've been back stage at some concerts, mostly folk-rockers like me, and had witnessed celebrities having their pictures taken with total strangers myself."

My dad, by the way, put himself in the middle of that infamous photograph.

"Are you planning to attend the Entertainment Law Panel this afternoon?" he asked me.

"Yes I am. I'm a singer songwriter. I'm hoping I'll pick up some information about how my dad handled his music."

"I'll see you there," we exchanged before he walked away. I felt good about the way my dad had treated Tom's father. I wondered why in the biographies I'd read about my dad, the authors had been so bent on pinning mobby association on him every chance they thought they could. In an interview I read one biographer did with him on the subject of the criminal mind, my dad said something to the effect that he could not understand why someone would work so hard to think up a criminal act when that much thinking could also lead to success in a legiti-mate field. I knew that he was genuine in saying that because it was one more time I got to see how he and I think alike. I've often said something like that myself and wondered at how anyone could actually become a criminal. Frank Sinatra said his response to choose which life path from the two was simply as he put it: "Me, I grabbed a song."

Later on that afternoon I went into the Entertainment Law panel. The pan-elists included, Robert Finkelstein, my favorite attorney ... I sat down in the 2nd row from the front in a center seat. The men I guessed must be the panelists were milling about talking with one another on the stage in the amphitheatre and had not yet taken their seats. A moment later, Tina Sinatra walked in and went up to one of the men on stage. Because the sound lifts up from front to the progressively higher seats all the way back I could overhear what they were saying and so could the entire seated audience.

"Your sister's here," the panelist I realized must be Finkelstein said in a loud whispery voice to her as he took hold of her shoulders and looked directly into eyes covered by her sunglasses.

"Oh my God!" she said, and turned to stare at me. He brought her attention back to him and said to her: "Don't say a word. Not a word," as Tina stood there nodding yes.

The tension thickened the air as the panelists, including Tina, took their seats. Bob Finkelstein sat in one that put him directly in front of me.

The woman heading up the panel discussion standing at the podium on stage glared sternly in my direction. Her face asked me, "What could you be thinking of by coming in here?" "Oh my God is right," I thought to myself.

Suddenly the amphitheatre filled with the sound of my dad singing. Tina burst into tears and said she should have been warned they were planning to do this. She said she still could not stand to hear him sing without crying. I knew how she felt too, but I controlled myself this time.

Tina spoke about how our father had "learned the hard way" of the importance in keeping the copyright control on his music, keeping ownership of the masters of the recordings. I made a note on the tablet I had brought, because, I really had gone in there to learn about these very things. Tina and I said nothing to each other while she was there. We both couldn't help from staring several times at one another. At some point before the panel had been opened for discussions, Tina left.

I wanted to ask the experts there about the right way to handle my ownership of my songs when I was in a studio recording with an arranger. I knew sometimes the line could get fuzzy as to who and what had been contributed to the song. I raised my hand after several other people had done the same to ask their questions. This activity was being controlled by the woman at the podium, and she was ignoring my raised hand. Eventually, there was no one else to call on from the audience and she acknowledged me and I asked my question about if the arranger got credit as well or was the copyright for the song just on the melody line you could whistle and the words you sang?

"Who are you and what do you want to know this for?," she as much growled at me.

I began to answer and she interrupted me saying she couldn't hear me, so I stood up.

"I'll project," I said in a loud clear voice and the room rippled with chuckles.

"I'm a singer/songwriter and sometimes I run into this in the studio. On what basis would a producer or arranger claim any ownership in a song?"

The woman who was at the podium and who had said she was with a large music publishing company, was about to answer me herself when Bob Finkelstein suddenly piped up and cut her off. He proceeded to tell me with a smile on his face, that I was correct, that the tune and words alone created the copyright.

"All you need to do is pay them for their service and get a receipt," he said, adding, "There, I've just given you something for free."

My only option as a one time old Apache was to take "coup" on him, a way of defeating the enemy by not touching them but showing them your power to do so if you have to. I stared down this arrogant "little shot" who had inserted himself between two sisters, preventing a chance they could have had to get to know each other, until his face got blushed and he shifted uneasily in his chair. Then I dropped my gaze. A moment later I got up, put on my sunglasses and made my exit, taking note first of the expressions of my earned admiration from the other panelists and as well that woman publisher at the podium. "How's that Dad?"

I sat down at a table in a far corner of the student center snack shop to re-center myself from the experience I'd just had. In spite of my appearing triumph there, I was feeling very hurt inside about Tina's reaction to me. Within an instant a man came over and sat down across from me.

"Is it true you are Frank Sinatra's daughter?" he asked.

"Are you a reporter? I'm not going to give my story out at this time," I breathed in deeply to prepare for this confrontation I hadn't invited.

"No," he said putting a brochure on the table in front of me. "I have something for you," and saying that, he got up to leave adding, "The artist wanted you to have it."

It was a pamphlet that showed a picture of a sculpted bronze head, my father's. I recognized the name of the sculptor, Domenico Mazzone, as he had been introduced from the audience who attended the Entertainment Law panel along with me. There were other pictures of his sculptures, mostly famous people, I noticed one I admired greatly, Eleanor Roosevelt.

The head and neck bust of my dad had been finished in gold. I couldn't help thinking from the Sufi spiritual philosophies I had read in the past and personally related to, about what the Sufi Masters called, "Making a head." This stood for a person who had become a master himself, had mastered his life on both physical and spiritual levels and had thereby derived himself into gold alchemically. I suspected the artist used the color gold symbolically to represent this concept where my father was concerned. I was very deeply moved, and because of the means by which my dad was participating in our relationship thus far, I already had some keen insights that there was much more about who Frank Sinatra was than what most people thought of him as. I wondered if I would ever come close to mastering my own life.

"Excuse me Ms. Sinatra. Would it be okay to get your autograph?" I turned around to face the gentleman who had come up to me while I was leaving the snack shop.

"You can ... but do you think I'm Nancy?"

"No, but you look like her. I know you are a daughter we haven't heard of before this. I loved your father's music and admired him all my life."

"He was the celebrity, not me," I said wondering why he wanted my autograph.

"You're the closest I've ever been to royalty," he said, astounding me.

I signed his Conference program book writing a thank you to him and his wife for honoring my father enough to come to the conference, and told him my father believed we are all equal.

I went into a couple more panels but only stayed a few minutes in each one. The psychology panel seemed way off the beam to me, and I ran into Ed and Mario on the way into one about my dad's music. They wanted to meet me where the shuttle from the hotel would pick us up in another fifteen minutes to go back to the hotel.

As I stepped out of the shuttle van, the driver spoke to me.

"I topped the driver from the Marriot who was boasting about driving Tina Sinatra from her hotel to the campus each morning. I told him I have the blue-eyed daughter." He was grinning at me broadly. Then he got serious and told me how he had admired my father because he had "given so much to the poor." "Frank Sinatra was a good man," he said to me. I told him I was grateful he had taken the time to share this with me, and I shook his hand.

"It's been an honor to drive you to the conference each morning, Ms. Sinatra." He had no way of knowing his timing had helped heal the wound I still carried from my experience earlier at the Entertainment Law panel." Thank you for your kindness," I said to him and went inside the hotel. "Thanks dad," I said silently to myself.

During dinner, Ed explained that Mario needed to get back to Lepore's Chocolates in the morning instead of staying the final day of the conference. I would have to go with them then if I still wanted to visit Hoboken. This meant I would miss the Saturday night performance by my dad's old musicians I'd met at the airport, but it would just have to be. Here on Long Island I learned he had been more than an event … He was a universe. Now it was time to see where it all began—all roads lead to Hoboken.

"LET'S NOT FORGET
WE'RE *ALL* FOREIGNERS"

Reprinted from Magazine Digest
July, 1945

WELCOME TO
HOFSTRA UNIVERSITY

JULIE SINATRA

SEDONA, AZ

I haven't forgotten the things that happened to me during my school days. I was getting pushed around and didn't even know why. Me—the brain. But now I know why, when I was going to school over in Jersey, a bunch of guys threw rocks at me and called me a little Dago. I know now why they used to call the Jewish kids in the neighborhood "kikes" and "sheenies," and the colored kids "niggers."

Let's take it right from the top. Ever hear that corny old saying: "Sticks and stones will break my bones but names will never hurt me?" Want to know something? That's not only corny—it's wrong. Names *can* hurt you. They can hurt you even more than sticks and stones. I'll show you what I mean.

Once there was a little guy named Dick who had lived all ten of his years in a neighborhood where there weren't any Negroes. He'd never even seen a colored person, and had never heard the word "Negro."

Then one evening his dad came home tired, hot, and upset—and told about some trouble he'd had downtown with a "dirty nigger." Now, Dick's dad sounded sore, so naturally Dick got the impression that "a dirty nigger" is something to get sore about. Dick didn't understand what "nigger" meant, but he needed no explanation for "dirty." Any youngster knows what *dirty* means, because he hears plenty of gum beating when he comes to the table with dirty hands. So to Dick, "dirty" is something that'll cause him trouble. See how this thing's building up in that little guy's mind?

Of course Dick loves his dad, and anything his dad is against, he's against . . . whether it's right or wrong! So quick as a flash he's against colored people—a whole race of people he's never even seen . . . people who've never done a thing to him.

So you see how a name can really hurt. But it may not always be "dirty nigger." Sometimes a kid hears his father running down a "big dumb mick," or a "greasy wop," or a "stingy Jew."

Let's take the Nazis. They were brought up to hate everybody . . . they even hate one another, now. First, they picked on the Jews—who are a cultured and wonderful people—peace-loving, home-loving, and industrious. But the Nazis hated culture, peace, and love. Everything that was wrong with Germany, wrong with the whole world, the Nazis blamed on the Jews—even after they'd killed most of them off!

And while they weren't brazenly blaming the Jews, they were secretly blaming the Catholics, setting neighbor against neighbor. That's how the Nazis used racial and religious prejudice to weaken the people they wanted to defeat and enslave. And that's exactly how racial and religious prejudice can undermine a nation.

To excuse these atrocities, the Nazis called themselves the master race, and wanted to rule the world by eliminating all other races. The trouble is that the German people aren't a race. And after the way they've had their ears slapped down recently, they aren't master, either. The word "Aryan" is the name of one of the more obscure languages spoken in India. There is no "Aryan" race. The only three existing races are Caucasian—that's the so-called white race; the Negroid—or the colored race; and the Mongoloid—or yellow race. There's no essential difference between any two people of any of these races.

No scientist in the world can examine blood and tell from which race of man it came. Take a brain from any man's head and no one can tell you positively from what race it came. Every race produces men with big brains and men with small brains; men with big strong muscles, and men like me. All human beings, from whatever race, have exactly 27 bones in their hands, and 26 bones in their feet. The lungs, liver, intestines, and other parts of all human beings are exactly alike.

Now that gets us back to this prejudice thing. How can we be prejudiced against people who are exactly the same as we are? The chief difference between a Chinaman and an Englishman is the color of the skin. Find an Englishman with jaundice and there is little difference, except that the Englishman doesn't feel well.

It would be a fine thing, wouldn't it, if people chose their associates by the color of their skin? Brothers wouldn't be talking to brothers, and in some families the father and mother wouldn't speak to each other. Imagine a guy with dark hair like me not talking to blondes!

Kids normally like other kids. They get along pretty well together until some misguided parent finds out her little boy is playing with another little boy with the name, maybe, of Sammy Levine. So a couple of days later her little boy tells Sammy they can't play together any more, because his mother won't let him play with Jews. This is a terrible thing. What's pathetic about it is that it breaks up a kid's friendship. Nobody has any right to do that, because that's the kind of friendship that's important to the future development of this country—one child's fondness for another.

Look. The next time you hear any one say there's no room in this country for foreigners, tell him you've got a big piece of news for him: tell him that *everybody* in the United States is a foreigner. And that includes the American Indian, who originally came here from somewhere else!

This is our job—your job and my job, and the job of the generation growing up—to stamp out the prejudices that are separating one group of American citizens from another.

Remember what Abraham Lincoln said: "Our fathers brought forth on this continent a new nation, conceived in liberty and dedicated to the proposition that all men are created equal." Get that—*created equal*. As they grow up, some have advantages of education and environment. These are generally the ones who don't become the subjects of prejudice and hatred. Prejudice can't conquer you if you're determined not to let it.

It's up to us to lay aside our unfounded prejudices and to make the most of this wonderful country—this country that's been built by many people, creeds, nationalities, and races in such a way that it can never be divided—that it will always remain the *United* States—one nation indivisible, with liberty and justice for all.

JUST ONLY TO ME

I remember the swooning, the mesmerized fans
When you first held that microphone in your hand
And from those lips flowed the sweetest songs
As you captured the world with your voice like a storm
Though "The Voice" is now silenced, you will always live on
For the spell of your magic still echoes from beyond
No one can ever even dare to compare or replace
Your fabulous voice, your eloquent style, your wonderful grace
You are now embraced in the heavens with love
While leading a chorus of angels above

You entered my heart through a song
And thrilled me since you came along
I felt your joy and your pain, in every refrain
As you sang just only to me

You made me happy and sad
You made me cry and felt real bad
But soon it would all disappear
For you were just singing to me

How can this world now go on
With this lonely emptiness since you have gone
Although from afar-you were my shinning star
As you sang just only to me

In the still of the night as I gaze at the stars
From the heavens those twinkling "Ol Blue Eyes" appear from afar
Then a soft whisper of song soon is heard in my ear
As your vision appears-you seem ever so near
Singing tenderly just only to me

And as you sing each and every refrain
The song in my heart is now you

Anna Carla Faggio
████████████████████
████████████████████
████████████████

August 1998

Carla Faggio. Photo courtesy of Diane Faggio.

From the red cliffs ...

to the high bluffs ...

going my way.

CHAPTER SIXTEEN

From the red cliffs to the high bluffs ...

C oming down the ramp off the New Jersey Turnpike, a road sign on my right read, "Welcome to Hoboken, The Home of Baseball and Frank Sinatra." It was painted without any real fanfare and looked a little faded from the weathering of many yearsEd and Mario were grumbling in the front seat of the car about never being able to find a parking place. As we drove up and down the narrow streets, I marveled at the vintage turn of the century Victorian brownstones. Except for the absence of cobbles on the streets, the town looked very much like it had in the photographs I'd looked at in Ed's book that had been taken in the 1920's. As we approached the corner where Lepore's Homemade Chocolates sat, someone pulled out in front of us vacating our place to park right in front of the store.

The first thing I noticed as we entered the building was the blown up photograph of my dad filling up most of the front window. As I entered I saw an entire wall had been dedicated to pictures of him. Ed led me to where some framed letters and their corresponding envelopes hung in frames.

"Julie, I think your dad typed this one to me himself. What do you think?" It was a loaded question. I certainly didn't want to be the one to say a secretary probably typed it. Ed had told me before that is was common knowledge when my dad was living that, "No one gets to Sinatra."

I looked closely and saw little dots were used to separate the thoughts being expressed in the letter. Also, it seemed to have been typed on an old manual typewriter. It was signed by my dad,—basically a thank you to Ed for the star at his birthplace and also for writing his book, "Our Way".

"It looks very personally created Ed. A secretary would have a much more modern machine to type a Sinatra letter to someone on. It doesn't look professional or slick, it looks like he just sat at his own typewriter and wrote this to you. Also, I tend not to use semi-colons as I switch thoughts or add them in a sentence. I use these same little dot dot dots to accomplish that ... maybe it's a trait."

Ed was beaming as I noticed two ladies who were standing quietly behind the candy counter waiting for us to acknowledge them. Ed introduced me to his mother and his aunt. I apologized for not having dressed up to meet them. I was in jeans and a sweater, a relief from dressing up each day of the conference. His mother put me at ease saying she wanted me to feel comfortable.

The two women went into join Ed's father and Mario in the small factory section of the store where they made the candy. They were facing a deadline for a very large order to be ready by Thanksgiving. I was amazed when I learned Ed's elderly parents had already individually wrapped and packed most of the 5,000 pieces required.

"Like the town, my parents have been well preserved," Ed commented to me after I told him how young they looked for their age. He continued, "In Hoboken, people work hard but they own their own businesses. They live never more than a few blocks away from their stores and they don't experience traffic gridlock or stress of losing their jobs. They are their own bosses."

"I admire that kind of independence," I said, as he continued to talk about how he wanted to become mayor to help preserve this kind of lifestyle in the town.

"The star is at the birthplace and there is a park, "Sinatra Park," now named after your father. There is need to expand the museum. And, there is a tour set up for when people come to see the birthplace through the museum. I think Hoboken could be saved by just being the home of Frank Sinatra."

"Maybe when I finally am legally recognized, I can come back here and speak to that, Ed."

"You will be recognized, Julie, I am going to help you as I said I would about the DNA you need. There is a woman who had a cigarette butt your dad had smoked and then threw down on the stage during a performance. She retrieved it and I think she might still have it even after all these years."

"I hope that's true, because from what I know, DNA would still be on that cigarette Ed."

I didn't even think about the envelope that could have been sealed by licking it that was in the frame with the letter Ed believed my dad sent personally to him as we were talking. My attention turned to the hunger pangs in my stomach.

"Mario, Is it okay if I take a raspberry chocolate cream?"

"Second case from your left. Help yourself."

"Julie, I'm going to take you up the street to your dad's high school, and then I'll point the way for you to walk down to his birthplace at 415 Monroe. It would be a good idea for you to see the places you will go to on the museum tour tomorrow, before you have to be in the midst of all the other people on it."

"I do need to walk this on my own, Ed. Thank you for your sensitivity."

As we approached Demarest High School at 4th and Garden Streets, my insides went suddenly topsy turvy and I began sobbing uncontrollably. Ed looked at me in sheer horror. I had lost it, drowning in my burst of emotion. Ed took my arm and led me over to sit down on the steps in front of the school's entry doors. He tried to capture my attention by telling me how my dad once had a school picture taken on these steps. He had a copy to show me later and more photographs of my dad and my grandparents that his Uncle Frank Sirocka had taken when he had been a school chum of my dad's.

"I'm sorry Ed," I managed after another few deep breaths. I felt like an idiot.

"Are you going to be okay now?" Ed looked at a loss.

"I'm fine. You go on back to Lepore's. I'm going to sit here for a minute and then I'll start walking toward Monroe Street.

I was thinking about how my dad had dropped out of high school, just as my own son had, in the tenth grade. I had read somewhere that he'd said they couldn't teach him anything. I wondered if he meant they couldn't teach him anything about becoming what he wanted to in his life—a singer. He spoke up right away in my head: "This is just half of it kid."

"Half of what? What's the other half?" I got it. My own story gives an example of total repression of natural gifts and talents ... Maybe, I thought, my dad wanted me to find a way I can inspire changes in education.

A couple of blocks down towards Monroe Street, I noticed an Italian deli just to the left of the corner I was on. There were loafs of bread and twists of Mozzarella in the front window. I stood in line with a small loaf of coal baked bread they sold there from Dom's Bakery—like I'd read my dad had shipped to him in California.

I turned smiling to a woman standing behind me and said: "There is the most wonderful smell in this place." She didn't say a word back. As I left and walked back to the corner I heard in a voice loud enough for me to hear: "Smell! Fiores has never had a smell!"

I walked back to her and apologized for my poor choice of wording. "I'm so sorry, I meant to say what a wonderful aroma."

"Oh aroma! That's different!" she brightened a smile and a nod of approval she extended to the man walking with her I supposed was her husband.

I had just learned a clear lesson in linguistics, Hoboken style.

Unlike the sidewalks lined with Maples in front of the upscale brownstones near Lepore's, not a single tree stood the length of the block on Monroe Street. The buildings and houses were very plain and needy of new paint.

Monroe Street was in this section of town I had read had been on the wrong side of the demarcation line that separated the middle classed Irish from the impoverished Italian immigrants in Hoboken. In this place that had been called, "the sewer," my dad's birthplace was the second number from the corner.

The house wasn't there. It had burned down some years ago. The front of the property had locked wooden gates across it. There was an attractive newly constructed brick arch over them.

The bronzed backdrop for the "Star" was a deep blue and the star itself was gold with his name, Francis Albert Sinatra, The Voice, born here, and it gave the address of 415 Monroe and the date of his birth. There was a blue circle inside the star with a microphone, styled from the 1940's. The star had been set in the sidewalk a few feet to the left of the gates. It was beautiful but badly in need of cleaning. Leaning against the wall behind it, was an almost man size cardboard backed photo of him in his "Pal Joey" suit and hat. I lit a cigarette and leaned against one side of the arch next to the picture of him.

"I'm here Dad. I followed this star."

Ed had mentioned I should go next door on Monroe into the Sinatra memorabilia store and ask for Pinky, the owner. I did that next. I wanted to see if she had a rag and some cleaner I could use to brighten up the star before the tour bus crowd would visit it the next day.

"There's one in the bathroom you can use. I just have water there to rinse it with. My husband, John Spano will come in the morning early and I'll ask him to bring some brass cleaner for it," Pinky assured me, standing behind a counter where I noticed the entire wall was covered with photographs of my father. I went back outside to clean the star. I needed this activity to keep from crying again and it gave me time to think about what I knew about my father's birth, here in a "manger".

All the biographies began the same about this. My father came into this world on December 12, 1915, upside down, injured and as silent as this lonely star in front of his birthplace. The doctor's forceps and the fact that the baby weighed more than thirteen pounds and came in a breech birth combined to injure both mother and son. My grandmother, Dolly Sinatra because of this would never be able to have any more children—and this one was not breathing. "I raised an only child too, Grandma," I whispered, feeling she might hear me. "I had a bad time in childbirth too. My Dan was fine, but my tailbone shattered as he came into this world."

I could almost see inside that cold water flat and watch the quick thinking of my great grandmother, Rosa Sinatra, as she grabbed the baby and put him into the kitchen sink filled with the icy winter water. My father cried loud and clear into the destiny a torn eardrum, leaving him partially deaf in one ear, had just moments earlier designed. He would grow up but stay home during the War— He would echo the longings and the endearments of the fighting men—He would become Frank Sinatra, the singer, eventually the greatest entertainer of the country and the world … "from humble beginnings," as he had put it himself."

"I was an only child too, Dad, at least until I was grown enough to leave home for college," I whispered to him. "Maybe that's why you sang … maybe why I love doing it on stage too when I can … being there, not alone, but with all those people embracing you. It fills something as you give something."

"Nancy came in when she was here when the park was dedicated and told me there was another daughter who had been, "very well cared for," Pinky said, calling me back from another world I'd slipped into. She was looking at me expecting me to comment.

"Yes," I said simply back. I knew I had been the one to give Nancy that impression from the letter I'd written when I wanted her to help me meet our father. I believed then it was plausible that Tom Lyma had acted as a proxy … now, I knew that wasn't it. But I was still debating whether or not my dad had not known I was his, so I didn't want to say anything more about it. Nancy, I noted from Pinky's comment, apparently was not in any doubt about my being her sister however.

When I got back to Lepore's, Mario was washing his hands in the back sink and Ed was standing in the doorway between the factory and the store sections. Ed grinned a welcome.

"I told Mario how you almost passed out on me at Demarest High," he greeted.

"I said you would do that at the first sight of a place that had to do with your father," Mario delivered with an all knowing confidence.

"I just couldn't help it. But there's more to it I think than it just being the first place. I think my dad wants me to help change or at least inspire changes in the way we educate children," I said but their attention was already involved in a discussion of boxing that large candy order for shipping. It was time to lock up the store and drive out to the Jersey Shores area where Ed's parents owned a house with the guest quarters I would be staying in.

"Let's go eat!" Mario announced and my first day in Hoboken came to an end.

After a charming dinner of pasta cooked "al dente" the way they told me my dad always liked it, prepared perfectly by Mario, Ed called me into the living room where he had put my dad's "Trilogy" album on.

The first part, "The Past," I recognized the songs my mother had those song sheets for. My favorite section was, "The Future," probably because I'm an Aquarian … we live in the future.

I listened as he sang about the time to come when there would be, "World War None," and how the people of the world would join together to "build a fire that could be seen across the seas" as all prejudice and hatred would be burned away. It hinted strongly of a new spiritual world order. When I heard him singing with the chorus behind him singing out his name, I realized that this wasn't done out of vanity as I had read criticism of him for; he was imagining himself in the midst of that celestial music he reported to Shirley MacLaine he heard in his head. He sang about how he would, "return, coming down a mountain where trees overlooked a quiet pool." He had just described my thinking place on the ranch in Sedona … as well as his own home in the desert of California, but he first made contact with me at my quiet pool. I heard it as a message, subtle, but I got it. My dad and I shared the same belief that civilization could, would lift if enough people believed it.

I felt humbled and yet empowered somehow by him to use my famous name in efforts for this to happen. Maybe this was the "other half" he didn't state at Demarest High School on the steps there. I think he could see ahead of his own life how precarious the survival of humanity would become. Maybe, this was one and part of the agreement we might have made in heaven … that I would some-how kick in where he left off at the time of the coming millennium.

Ed handed me a Kleenex after looking at my face.

"I'm going to need a lot of guidance entering the world as his daughter," I said to him.

"Julie this football was a gift originally made to your dad. He autographed it and sent to me on his birthday," Ed said picking up the ball and tossing it to me. "It was a tradition Mr. S. had of giving someone else a gift on that day."

I tossed the football back to Ed and he sent it back to me again saying, "East coast. West coast."

He next showed me a photograph his Uncle Sirocka had taken of my dad sitting on a dock on the Hudson River gazing across the water to the sky soaring buildings of Manhattan. His uncle and my dad had both been teenagers at the time when the picture was taken. My dad looked to be deep in thought. "Your father was a dreamer, Julie, from the start," Ed said looking down at the old photograph.

"I got in a lot of trouble with my mother's family for being that way when I was young," I said. "I've always managed to find an out of the way place to sit alone with myself like that."

"The dreamers are the movers and shakers of the world," Mario contributed.

"Dolly Sinatra shook up her world," Ed added in. "Your grandmother could speak all the dialects among the Italian immigrants who arrived in Hoboken and needed to find jobs, just like my grandmother could," Ed beamed.

"I read about your grandmother and your aunt and Dolly in your book, Ed," I said.

"Dolly, Cookie and Maime were all the same," Ed continued. Those ladies were tough and they were known to talk tough too, "Son of a bitch bastard, and worse came out of them if they were riled. But they were all good, the best. They all helped people poorer than themselves. But Dolly wasn't afraid to clock someone who got out of line."

"Clock' someone?"

"She was at a fundraising your father was going to come and sing for. Somebody at the tables yelled out, "Sure Sinatra will sing tonight if he gets paid." Dolly got up and went over and hit him, clocked him good." Frank Sinatra sang for free that night as she knew her son planned to do," Ed announced proudly.

"Tell me more about how she operated in the town politics?" I asked.

"Dolly would take the men who had just arrived and who couldn't speak English, which she could fluently, over to the Irish politicians and promise them votes in exchange for employing the newcomers. She did this in-between the hours she put in working at a candy factory. Dolly could pass for Irish herself because she was so fair and that service she provided lifted her status in town and that's how she was able to get your grandfather, Marty a job as Fire Chief," he continued. "She did that and at the same time she worked in their bar, her power had allowed her to obtain a business license for, "Marty O'Brien's." In those days Italians could not get business licenses, but Dolly did." The thought flashed through my mind that my father had learned at a painful early age about the cruelties of prejudice and he never forgot it—fought against it always.

"For her, it was a cinch," I said brightly back. "That's also one of my mother's expressions, along with her too common use of "son of a bitch bastard." I grinned again at him. "My dad was quoted using the expression "It's a cinch" when he expected something to go his way easily. My mother must have picked it up from him. I can remember hearing her say that when she was in an up mood over something," I finished and Ed nodded, eager to continue with more information for me.

"Dolly was very ambitious and away from home working three jobs at once at times. Your father was alone a lot of the time because your grandmother was a woman ahead of her time. She became the first woman and the first Italian to hold the position of head of her ward," Ed explained.

"It sounds like Dolly was the source of our Sinatra grit," I shared, and both Ed and Mario agreed it was a Sinatra trait.

"When we go on the museum tour tomorrow I'll point out to you where "Marty O'Brien's" used to be. Your grandmother was known to have danced on the tables there, and your father would sit on the bar and sing as a little boy. You'll have time in the morning in Hoboken to take pictures of your grandparent's other houses before the tour starts. Dolly moved the family up into the top neighborhood in town on Hudson Street eventually," Ed told me.

At Lepore's in the morning I looked at the collection of photographs Ed had of my grandparents. I would have loved copies, but he didn't offer that, so I didn't ask. I could see the intelligence and sparkle in Dolly. I noticed my dad and I actually got our eyes from Marty, because of the shape of his blue eyes even though Dolly's eyes were blue too.

I took a walk to see her home on Hudson Street, just a block down from the edge of the river where a college was that I'd read my dad's parents had wanted him to attend and become an engineer. Imagine that. Then I walked down and over a few blocks to the ball park where he played on a baseball team as a boy. "Your grandson played first base in a t-shirt team, Dad."

On the tour bus I overheard a couple of women comment they had just been to one of Frank Sinatra Jr.'s concerts in Atlantic City. One of them was telling the other how good he sang. It made me happy he was getting the notice he deserved.

The bus stopped at the "star" and Ed took a picture of me. Mr. Spano came up to meet me and said I had cheekbones like my dad's. I thanked him for his efforts because the star was gleaming with new brass polish rubbed and shined.

Our last stop on the tour was at the newly christened, "Frank Sinatra Park." It was on a bluff overlooking the skyline of Manhattan on the other side of the Hudson. Ed pointed to a partially sunken pier at the docks below us. He told me that was where his uncle had taken the picture of my dad as a teenager imported on his gaze as if he could already hear himself immersed in the lyric of his famous signature song ... "New York, New York ... If I can make it there. I'll Make it anywhere ..." "I can see you sitting there, Dad," I said silently, as Ed snapped a photo of me with the pier in the background, "Could you ever have imagined that one day they would bathe the Empire State Building in blue for Ol' Blue Eyes, and across the country the Capitol Building in Hollywood where you would record some of your best music albums, would be draped in black to honor you when you crossed your last river?"

There was time before going back to the house to stop by and meet someone Ed said knew my dad well and they had stayed in touch with one another over the years.

Mr. Joe "Gigi" Lissa welcomed me warmly and seemed ready for my visit. He showed me the famous photograph taken by his late wife at the Paramount Theatre in New York. My dad was being shielded by my grandfather dressed in his fireman's suit coming through a throng of screaming reaching bobby-soxers. Mr. Lissa's grandson was learning to play the piano. The family owned the restaurant next door to the house and we went in where I saw once again walls filled with pictures of my dad. Ed had decided to introduce me to Mr. Lissa as "a distant relative of Frank Sinatra's." A protocol I didn't quite understand, but it was very clear that Mr. "Gigi" Lissa knew immediately who I was.

It had gotten dark outside when we left. I was very anxious to get over to the St. Francis church where my dad had been baptized. It was closed but we got out of the car and I walked over to the statue of the great Saint I personally admired, although I wasn't a Catholic. I had learned about his life as a student of philosophy and came across him reading about the Sufis, mystics that had preceeded all the major religions in the world today. They counted him among their Masters. Saint Francis of Assisi, because he was a mystic, had always been controversial among the Catholics. My father, before he re-joined the Catholic Church after my grandmother died, had related closely with the mystics in the belief that you can go one on one with God with no one in between. That is my way too. I felt a bond that somehow linked my father and I to Saint Francis. I can't really explain it, other than to say it was like sensing a linear spirituality.

As Ed opened the car door for me when we were getting ready to leave I suddenly felt a warmth coming through my jacket sleeve and pressure on my upper arm like someone had taken hold there with their hand.

"Ed! Come feel my arm here," I called back at him. He looked quizzically at me as he touched my jacket where I indicated.

"It feels warm, doesn't it?' I implored him.

"Yes," he said, I can feel that. It's odd."

We were driving over to yet another church for me to see where my grandmother had volunteered to help the poor people of Hoboken for many years. She continued to send them money, Ed told me, when she had moved up in the world. Before that, she had given her time in addition to all her other activities in Hoboken. We parked and Ed exclaimed:

"Julie, look at the license number of the car we just parked behind. It equals a grand slam if we were in Vegas."

"I guess my grandmother wants me to remember if I ever come into any money how I should spend it." Ed took my picture with a flash on the camera at the top of the steps at St. Joe's.

That night we all stayed up late to talk. Ed said he and Mario had sent for and gotten a copy of my dad's Will. He told me to look at the filing number for it and how it contained the numbers in my birthdate. He also pointed out that in the Hofstra Sinatra Conference Program it was stated that Frank Sinatra signed his agreement for the Conference to take place on February tenth, the month and day of my birthday. "Do you see now too, Julie, how Mr. S. works?"

"You know, the Sufi's who go back before the time of formal religions, used numbers to symbolize spiritual meanings translating the numbers to letters to spell it out among themselves. They always kept their knowledge on the "Path," as it's referred to hidden that way in order to preserve it through centuries of emperors and kings who preferred to have people conformed and controlled. I don't think it's an accident that Frank Sinatra became famous enough to have been in front of millions of people in his lifetime. Even our name, "Sinatra" has a sufic base. "Sinat" stands for bat, the Sufi symbol for head down in spiritual contemplation; and "Tra" represents the letters to express example of the Path. My dad seems to have embodied all this special energy and it's still around after his passing."

"Like I said at the panel, Julie," Ed answered. "Frank Sinatra didn't die."

In the wee small hours I shared the dreams that had been clairvoyant I'd had, and told him I thought my brain's difficulty in making its usual nerve connections because of the MS had somehow plugged into new avenues to carry information on ... ones that were intended maybe for paranormal deliveries. Mario agreed that that was more to the human mind. Then I shared the dream I had about the trip my dad and mother took to Havana in 1947. Mario told me I would need to gather up all I had learned and lay it out on the table in front of my mother.

"It's time for her, not just you, to have all the truth come up to the surface Julie," Mario said to me. "You need to free your mother of this awful burden she has carried all her life."

"I know. That is my next journey, to go back over to California and meet with her again."

"You will have to be very careful how you handle it ... so you don't kill her. But you can't let her die, which she will do sometime not too far away from now because of her age ... You have to set her free first before that happens."

The next morning I met them for breakfast. Ed gave me a prayer card with my dad's picture on one side and a picture of St. Francis of Assisi on the other.

"Mario and I both believe you are Frank's daughter, Julie. We want you to have this because we can see you have his heart. It's from the Memorial Mass at

St. Francis on May 18, 1998, held for your father here in Hoboken, Julie." My hosts could not have honored their guest any better.

Ed drove me to the airport and said again in parting: "East coast. West coast."

On the flight back to Phoenix I thought about how my visit to Hoboken had seemed like a mystical journey. I thought about my grandmother, Dolly, so full of life and how she could be seen in so much of my dad's and even my own behavior in life. And I thought about Marty Sinatra, my grandfather who let Dolly have her way, the gentle boxer who must have been the source of the sensitivity I was grateful I had inherited down through my father.

The town was a preserved melting pot. I had never heard so many different languages spoken in one place before. In Hoboken, I learned what it meant to be an immigrant, but now it seemed the old lines of demarcation had disappeared, and Hoboken had become that mystical America my dad had dreamed of where people had respect for each other and simply accepted one another's differences. A Polish family owned the drapery store—A Greek had a fish market—Russians sold furniture—Italians baked bread, owned a deli—A photography store had been passed down in an Irish family—Romanians owned a fruit market—It seemed they possessed an unspoken understanding that their interdependency created their survival. My father could not have come from anywhere but Hoboken, New Jersey.

My mother's family had been immigrants also, and during the WWII, the Italians had to keep a very low profile because they were suspected of not being patriots. I thought how my mother had once told me that the Bonucelli's had always enough food to eat during the depression years when she grew up, because they were farmers and raised their food; but she didn't have shoes to wear to school. Who could blame that pretty young girl for seeking a "glamorous life".

I stopped by the Peterson's to have a driving break and a cup of coffee before driving the rest of the way to Sedona. Jimmy and I talked a little about my struggle to find forgiveness for my mother.

"It's not for her as much as it is for you, Julie," he said. "It's for your soul."

It was just before midnight when I came down the mountain forest road and entered the ranch over the bridge at the creek. I drove past the barn and saw the welcoming porch light on as my neighbor Nancy had told me she would do for me. I pulled my too heavy travel bag out of the 'Z' and put it down on the ground before going in. I just wanted to take in the amazing sight of my little rock house where it sat, bathing in an ocean of starlight.

"Thank you, God. I love you Dad."

At Sinatra Park overlooking the Hudson River and the Pier where Dad sat as a boy and dreamed of Manhattan

Grandma Dolly's fancy brownstone on Hudson Street, Hoboken

Demerest High School steps…lots of tears

Julie at the "Star"

Ed Shirak Jr. and Joe "Gigi" Lissa

Mr. John Spano

Pinky's Sinatrabilia store at 417 Monroe Street, next to the, "Star", in Hoboken. (Location is now the museum, "From Here To Eternity", honoring Frank Sinatra.)

Dad perched on this fire hydrant as a boy

St. Francis Church, Hoboken, New Jersey

St. Joe's in Hoboken where Grandma Dolly gave her time to charity

and...That's what a Grand Slam is for.

CHAPTER SEVENTEEN

"Within your mind ... Within your heart ... You've got it right there."

—*Apache*

T he second evening back home I was looking through the photographs that traced my steps in Hoboken. An aroma of gardenias suddenly permeated the kitchen where I was sitting. My dad was close by. I thought about the stories I'd heard at the Hofstra conference, testimonials to what a good and caring person he was. When he was doing concerts across the country he was known to cruise the local newspapers, and when a story popped up about someone in need, he took action.

He paid for a woman's cancer treatments, for example. There had been a little piece about it in the hometown paper; how her husband was hoping to raise funds locally to save his wife's life. My father paid for this and in addition covered all the hospital costs. He didn't leave his name. The man shocked when he discovered the bill had been paid insisted over and over that he be told who paid it for him until, eventually, he learned it had been Frank Sinatra.

Another story was about a little boy who had Leukemia. My dad showed up at his house and held the child in his arms ... like Saint Francis, his chosen personal Saint ... perhaps, healing with love.

"Okay, Dad," I whispered, I already know from all the testimonials I learned of, that you are not someone who would likely have turned your back on me. I guess I've just been too afraid to ask you directly, the question I need to have answered.

As I was falling asleep later on I found myself in that special dream place, that gray place where I had once seen an angel and where my dog Harley had met me to say goodbye after he died. A moment later my dad walked in, dressed in a dark blue suit. I stood up to greet him. He looked to be in his seventy's, hair white and a bit portly. He walked briskly over to me and put his arms around me.

164

We shared that hug that I had wanted to so badly while he had been alive. He spoke to me first:

"I'm sorry, Honey, I'm so sorry."

"It's okay, Dad, we'll be okay," I said to him and then I stepped back and asked:

"Is it true you never knew I was your daughter?" He looked at me very intently and said:

"I've been trying to show you that," then he disappeared and I didn't dream any further that night.

A few days later, I phoned the woman who had helped me learn about obtaining the grant from Arizona that contributed my being able to go to the Sinatra Conference. I told her that I was convinced that my dad never knew I was his child, but I still felt torn about making a claim into his estate regarding this. She had a brother in law who was a retired judge and living in Beverly Hills. She gave me his phone number saying she would call ahead to let them know I wanted to talk with him. I asked him if he thought man's law reflected in any way Divine law? He said he liked to believe that the law had been created to reflect that.

The law said I should be included and my dad had shown me he wanted me to be. Whatever I would decide about this I knew I needed to have DNA testing done. My first concern was being able to prove the truth to my son, Dan.

I phoned Ed Shirak and asked him if he had spoken to that woman who had the cigarette butt my dad had thrown down on the stage during one of his performances. He said he thought she did not want to be involved. I remembered the letters he'd shown me that were from my dad and asked him if he wouldn't let me have the envelopes tested for DNA from possible residual saliva. He really balked at this. Ed was talking about his running for mayor again and I felt he had decided I was some kind of political risk to him.

After we hung up I became frustrated with all of this I had to somehow cope with. I was frustrated over my dad having died before this had been resolved, leaving me to cope on my own. I accused him of giving up too soon in my mind. I was already ashamed of myself for feeling this way, and he must have caught it because within another night there he was in a dream with me again.

"I didn't give up. I did keep fighting," he said as he walked across a sandy area with some tropical plants around. I called out to him that I was sorry, I knew it wasn't his fault.

He was wearing a bright tropical design shirt, mostly orange with some pale green and cream colors that sharply tied in with some light colored cotton slacks. He looked much younger and refreshed, maybe to be in his fifty's.

He was grinning as he said next, "Before I left I used to dream and come to this island, and you would always show up. I kept asking myself, "Who is this gal?"

I just stood there gaping at him as he walked over to me. I think I was doing lucid dreaming, where you can watch yourself having the dream. He took hold of my shoulders and looked very seriously into my face and said, "Go for it Honey … the music, life, all of it … Don't wait." Then he turned me around and I could see a picnic table near by.

My dad's first wife, Nancy Barbato Sinatra was sitting there but as I looked at her she changed into Barbara Sinatra. Nancy Jr., was also sitting at the table and Tina was approaching to sit down. Frank Jr. was standing just a few feet away from it. My dad pointed his finger toward them and said to me, "You're included, Honey. Don't forget that."

The dream ended there. He had just told me he wanted me to be recognized as his heir. He came all the way from heaven or where ever to deliver these messages … just for me, and I promised there would never be another moment I would doubt that he really was with me.

"I'm sorry I've been such a hard case, Dad," I said silently the following morning. Figuring he probably already knew I would be required to bring DNA proof into the court I asked him to give Ed Shirak a sign of some kind if that was allowed in universal law—something that would let Ed know my dad wanted him to help me.

Three days later, Ed Shirak phoned me from Hoboken. He said just before he went to sleep a few nights earlier he was sure he saw a blue star in mid air … just for a flash second. He told me my dad had shown him he must let me test those coveted envelopes.

I spent the next day locating a lab in Texas that was the only one I could find in the country that could determine paternity by testing for DNA from an article of some kind, instead of having to use a blood test. I called Ed and he packaged the envelopes as the lab instructed him to do, including the tracking information about how he came to have them in his possession, etc.

I talked next with Rod on the phone and gave him an update regarding this. He and Carol Lynn were hesitant in putting out the money to cover the cost of the test. He told me he would get back to me. I had no idea this would take another two months.

The other thing my dad had encouraged me about during our last dream-time spent together, was my music. While I felt totally abandoned by my attorney during this period of time, I knew I needed to find some way, some place to sing, if for no other reason than to keep my sanity. It came up to my surprise when I was in town during the Christmas holidays.

I couldn't go shopping because of no money, but I wanted to walk around and enjoy the Christmas decorations in a effort to feel some holiday spirit. From out in a patio area in an open air mall I could see a Navajo rug hanging in a carpet store. The main color used for its design was bright orange. Naturally I couldn't resist taking a closer look at it.

The two salesmen there and I started talking and they said in the late spring and summer the store was turned into a music club on week end nights. I told them who I was and that I would love to perform my songs if they wanted me to. It would even pay a little. Stefan, one of the salesmen and I became friends. He was a big fan of Frank Sinatra and he seemed to appoint himself as a Quixote wanting to right the wrong he could see where I was concerned.

It was Stefan who convinced me I should begin now to write a book about my story in discovering I was the hidden child of my icon father. And, it was Stefan who paid the train fare for me to go over to California to have that meeting with my mother I needed to have.

The trip was scheduled for the day of my upcoming birthday on February 10th. I gathered all the bits and pieces of what I'd been able to put together that I planned to lay out in front of her and organized it into a folder. I also had been keeping a box of Lepore's Homemade Chocolates fresh and unopened in my refrigerator ... Mario wanted me to give them to her when I saw her.

I wanted to go there with a take charge attitude. True, I had put together quite a lot to feel confident about my discoveries, but I still didn't know exactly what had taken place when I was born in 1943. I suspected my dad's publicist was involved in the cover up of my birth, but I had no facts yet. Stefan suggested we go into the Sedona library and see if there were any more books about my dad. He was as surprised as I was that there was only one on the shelf. I checked it out, hoping, "Sinatra, A Complete Life," by Randy Taraborelli, would include possibly more about my mother's relationship with my father and maybe something about me that none of the other Sinatra biographers had uncovered. What I was looking for was in the latter section of the book.

The author had interviewed a woman who had been a close friend to Nancy Barbato Sinatra, my dad's first wife, when they had their home in Hasbrouck Heights, New Jersey.

The woman, a neighbor, told him a story about a starlet, Alora Gooding (the name I had suspected my mother had used in Hollywood) who had phoned the Sinatra residence late in the year of 1942. This woman who Taraborelli interviewed, explained she wanted to finally come forward about something she had been sworn secret to all those years ago.

Nancy Barbato had told her that Gooding had wanted to speak with Frank, but he wasn't home. She talked instead to Nancy and told her she was going to have Frank's baby, due a few months away, in February, 1943. Nancy told this woman about Alora Goodings phone call and in another conversation a few days later when she asked Nancy what she was going to do about Frank having fathered someone else's child, Nancy told her: "It's all been taken care of."

The author did not disclose this woman's name. He wrote she wanted to help right a wrong about Frank's child because she knew he deserved to know about it all those years. He wrote that she felt better now at least from the telling of it, but she would not allow him to say who she was in his book.

I had enough. I already knew the minute I read the quote from Nancy Sr., that she had contacted her ally, George Evans—the publicist that had as much to lose about Frank Sinatra fathering a baby with his girlfriend as she did. I now had, in time for my trip to see my mother, the last missing piece of the puzzle … I just needed was to take hold of the reins.

I should say here, that I don't judge Nancy Sr. for how she handled it when she learned I was coming into the world. Who could blame her for doing all she could to keep her world from being shattered—to hold her family together—to protect what was hers. When I surfaced 54 years later, I'm guessing she might have been told about it. I can't guess what she said or left unsaid all these years later. The author Taraborelli did reach her about this however, and he wrote that she essentially told him she was at an age when she didn't have to talk about the past anymore.

The attorney in California that Carol Lynn had been in touch with, told me over the phone that he would not consider taking my case for two reasons, and would not agree to meet me at my mother's. His first was again I didn't have my DNA proof. Secondly, he said he was put out somewhat about Carol Lynn's idea of what his split would be if a claim was successful. He didn't feel he should be the one to go up against the powerful firm representing my dad's estate and then not be proportionately compensated. It's all about the money to them I resolved in my frustration.

After spending several days contacting more probate attorneys in California, I finally found one who thought it would be worth a trip down to the San Diego area. He picked me up from the train depot in San Juan Capistrano, and we drove south to my mother's house in Vista. Before we went in together I told him I needed time alone with her to discuss another personal matter that would not be something he would include in taping the interview with her. He dropped me off and said he'd be back in an hour.

It was twelve o'clock when I walked into her house … high noon, I mused to myself. I knew what the attorney had no business in hearing was the Havana trip stuff in 1947. I took a deep breath and asked my angels and hers as well to guide me through this. I needed that higher sensitivity to protect her while I hoped what I would be doing would finally free her from a lifetime of undeserved torment.

"Oh, Julie," she greeted me and smiled. She was sitting at her dining table. I sat down across from her and pulled my folder of photos, notes, etc. from it.

"Hi Mom," I smiled back. "How are you?"

I continued as she glanced at the stuff on the table. "I brought you this box of candy all the way from Hoboken, where my dad was born and raised."

"Yes?" she looked at me and frowned a little.

"I have learned much since we last talked, Mother. I want to clear the air between us about it."

"What have you learned?" She delivered with a sarcastic tone and I immediately took out a photograph of my dad with George Evans I had from a book and pushed it in front of her.

"You told Rod about a man, George or Frank when we were here a year or so ago. This is George Evans who was my dad's publicist and the person Nancy Sr. called to have talk to you after you told her you were having Frank's baby."

Mother's face changed, she glanced a shameful look in my direction and then she got up from the table and went into the kitchen. I continued.

"You used a starlet name, Alora Gooding when you talked with Nancy Sr., and George Evans made you agree to tell my dad that Tom Lyma, your husband at the time was the father, and that way you would still be able to have a chance at becoming an actress in Hollywood … that's the truth, including using the name Gooding, isn't it."

She turned and looked at me. Her face was very pained and she nodded "yes" and whispered it as she looked away from me again. "I read somewhere that my dad referred to a winning in Vegas as a "gooding." That comment got her attention and she looked back again at me, this time with a Cheshire cat smile.

"To be clear, it's also true you told Frank Sinatra Tom Lyma was the father."

"Yes," she said impatiently.

"In those days the decision was likely the only one available without ruining both your lives, and his career as well as yours, Mom, so I understand," I said softening my tone. She nodded painfully but didn't add anything like the, "I'm sorry or something and she seemed to be aware I was waiting for. She just looked down avoiding eye contact with me as she came back to sit down across from me.

"It's also true that your affair took up again with him after I was born. I found a photograph of you sitting behind Ava Gardner at a New Year's Eve party at his home in Los Angeles in 1946, when I was three years old." I opened the memorial book penned by David Hanna, "Ol' Blue Eyes Remembered," and showed her the colored picture of Ava Gardner sitting in a restaurant with Frank Sinatra, wearing the matching jade earrings to mother's jade pennant necklace, and at the same time I put the photo showing her sitting on a stairway just above Ava Gardner at the Sinatra home New Year's Eve party from Kitty Kelly's book in front of her. She just seemed to home in on Ava in the picture with those earrings on.

She stood up and turned the book around to the edge of the table. She retrieved her glasses from the desk in the living room and walked back and looked down at the picture and went into a silent rage, huffing and puffing about it. I was amazed watching her. It was as if she was back in that time and felt every bit as jealous of Ava as she must have when my dad began that affair in the late forties.

I wanted to lift the mood of our conversation up, so the next thing I shared with her was having seen her as the telephone operator in "Anchors Aweigh." She chucked, when I reminded her of the time she had told me she'd once worked a switchboard.

"You looked great as a redhead, Mom ... I guess you were required to change your hair color a lot in those days." She smiled, a little uncomfortably. Then I knew what was next.

"I'm sorry about that incident that happened back in 1947, Mom ... that caused you to leave your promising career in Hollywood," I began. She searched my face.

"In February when I was turning four, you took me to my Grandmother Bonucelli's ranch while you were away. I have learned you did some singing at a club in Miami where you went under the name, "Toni," for that and wore your hair as a brunette with curls."

She looked amazed when she heard the name, "Toni." I went on quickly adding, "My dad met you there before you both flew to Havana where he saw Lucky Luciano." Mother had turned her head and was facing the window away from me.

"I know about what happened, Mom, I know there was a tragic shooting, that you had killed someone you thought was threatening your life and my dad's too." She erupted like a volcano.

"I don't have to talk about that, Julie! Are you recording this?"

"No, mom. I'm not recording anything." I emptied my purse out to show her I had no tape recorder as I continued speaking,

"You believed the walkie-talkies those men who burst into your room with my dad had in their hands were guns. they were coming to kill both of you. Mom, that is self-defense, not a crime. You need to see how natural it was for you to think they had guns. You and Dad were in the company of gangsters down there ... of course you were alert to possible dangers."

She loathed at me like I was her enemy, and said nothing.

"After you picked me up from Grandma's, a few days later I think it was, we went over to that house where those awful men yelled at you. Remember how I used to ask you about it?"

"She nodded yes, surprising me she'd decided to even participate again in this conversation.

"I know because you and Tom Lyma divorced when I was just over a year old, and that the incident at that house took place when I was four, that it had been in fact a mafia summons where you got your orders about the cover-up for the shooting accident in Havana. It had not been about your having to discuss your divorce from Tom, as you always said when I brought this up.

There had been two men killed and someone from the mob killed the other man. Isn't that the truth, Mom?"

She looked at me angrily and said: "I don't know."

"Did my dad shoot the other intruder?"

"No. It wasn't him."

"What made you both go down there in the first place?'

"It's none of your business," she retorted sharply.

"Oh yes it is because this was the reason why the truth about whose daughter I really am was never allowed to surface and why my dad died without ever having been told I was his, isn't it." The look of shame on her face gave me my answer."

There was a gangster there in Havana with Lucky Luciano who was nick-named "Doc." He threatened you didn't he?" Was he the one who told you to erase everything about your life in Hollywood ... everything about your relationship with Frank Sinatra and your trip to Havana?" She looked alarmed, and I added, "Mom, they can't hurt you now."

I felt like an ogre pulling all this awful stuff back up that she had buried beneath her rage all these years. I wanted so much to see her release it all and have some peace about it. I wondered if she ever knew how my dad had protected her. I searched for some more comforting words to say to her.

"Mom, you always had Dad's loyalty. He must have loved you very much. You may not know this, but he was repeatedly investigated by the FBI over thirty years or so about his trip to Havana when this tragedy happened. I don't believe the Feds cared about a suitcase they thought was filled with money enough to keep opening new investigations for that long a time. I think they wanted to know what happened to those two men who were killed. Dad understood there would not be a way to purge your action in self-defense, which it had been, through the courts. With the mob's cover up about the shootings combined with that, he knew that he would have to endure each period of questioning alone. No matter how many times he had to go through it, he protected you all those years."

She looked up at me. "How do you know all this ... who ...?" she trailed off and left her question unfinished.

"I just do. Everyone who knew about this is now dead and gone, Mother. What happened during your trip to Havana will not surface during your lifetime either. My dad was never asked about you when he was investigated. The FBI never knew about you in regards to his being in Havana. He was thought to have carried a lot of money in a suitcase for Lucky Luciano who was exiled down there." She looked at me like I was nuts and stated: "He painted".

With those two words she had just toppled an old myth that had haunted my dad for many years. She was there. She saw his suitcase was filled with art supplies, not money for an exiled mobster.

"It's time to let that pain, anger, and the feeling of injustice you must have felt all these years go. Self-defense is not a crime. That is not being a bad person, Mom. You don't deserve to suffer bad feelings about yourself from just having been a victim of the tragic circumstances you and my dad were in when it happened. If it's any consolation to you, I am very sorry that you paid the price of losing your life dream because of it. I know we both paid the price and so did my Dad; but it's time now to let it all go." She gave me that all too familiar look that said I was up on my ivory tower again.

"What price did he pay?" she sneered.

"Me," I answered, looking her square in the face.

I stood strong through all I had presented to her, but in truth I felt defeated because my goal fell short. I felt that I had been incompetent in freeing her of any of her old demons. It was as if this was what defined her, designed her fatalistic life, and she was not in the mood to give it all up just because her daughter thought she should. At this point, the attorney was knocking on the door.

"Mother, I have a lawyer with me who wants to record just the facts surrounding what happened in 1943 when I was born. Will you talk with him about this?

Is it okay? You won't be asked about any other subject regarding your times with my dad … nothing about Havana."

"Yes, he can come in," she said.

The attorney was there less than five minutes. He sat down after I introduced him to my mother and got out a tape recorder and placed it on the dining table. I had already cleared my stuff off and replaced it all in the folder.

"Mrs. Hunter," he began, can you tell me what happened when you first found out you were carrying Julie, Frank Sinatra's baby?"

"My daughter fantasizes," my mother said back to him.

I waved off the attorney and said it was time to leave. He got up from the table looking somewhat surprised.

"There's no point in your going any further. My mother is not planning to let anyone else in the world know about these facts she has confirmed with me today, apparently, only for my ears."

Mother followed us to the door.

"I can't believe you would not put just the information I need to help me become recognized legally, Mother … not to mention refusing to make a tape Dan would be able to listen to and learn that his mom wasn't crazy." I stepped through the screen door and she called to me:

"I can contrive something if you need it that bad." I realized that had been for the attorney's ears, as she said it looking at him. But, nonetheless, I had succeeded, at least for my knowledge, in having turned my gathered up truths into confirmed facts from her.

"I'll bet. You have been contriving all my life, Mom. Only putting the truth down that you confirmed with me today would be healing for both of us now. I'm sorry I bothered you." I left.

Once back again on the Southwest Special that would take me back home to Skywater, instead of celebrating that I had succeeded in unraveling the love mystery between my mother and father that she had corroborated with for me at least, I was wiping tears of frustration from my face. A few moments into the train ride I heard a woman comment from the seat behind me.

"I've never seen a sunset like that before," she said aloud. I looked out my window in time to see streaks of red and gold clouds where they had swirled together forming a gigantic orange eagle in the sky.

"Stay up, don't get bogged into the duck pond. Keep my wings high," I thought to myself. Then I thought I heard him say, "I'm with you, Honey."

"I'm okay, Dad, thanks for showing up." I said silently to myself as the woman sitting behind me on the train clicked off a picture of it with her camera.

Spring, 1999

Rod and Carol Lynn did eventually pay the $500.00 fee to the lab after I received a call they had completed the first stage of testing. The results of which would be held back until they were paid. It turned out that the DNA found on the envelope that had housed my dad's letter to Ed Shirak, thanking him for writing his book, "Our Way," was from a female. The second envelope had housed a letter sent from Barbara Sinatra thanking Ed for his contribution to her abused children's center, but my dad had added a handwritten note personally at the bottom of it. It was hoped he was the last one handling that letter and may have licked it's envelope. My attorney flatly refused to see any more investment go down the drain. Mario sent out the money to cover the test on it and also enough to pay for testing my DNA with it, should it turn out this time to show male DNA on the flap. Almost a month went by before I learned that envelope had female DNA on it as well.

The owner of the ranch's son who used to come up regularly to rent vacant cabins, etc., moved to Tucson, too far away. I was asked to take over all management duties for the ranch in lieu of paying rents. Walking one morning down to a cabin on the creek to meet with an air-conditioning repair man, a man and woman came up to me who did not live on the property. She wanted to know if it was okay if they walked around for a while. They used to live there before I came. She said someone in one of the other cabins she knew told her the manager was a gal who was a daughter of Frank Sinatra. I laughed and said something to the effect that if I wasn't able to get my DNA proof that it wouldn't matter much who I was.

"Your DNA is all over your face, Julie," she looked at me very seriously and added, "You're self-evident."

CHAPTER EIGHTEEN

August, 1999 ...

Mid-day on August 20th, the date I would perform my music for an audience using my real name for the first time ever, a few nature pals showed up to cheer me on. I was down in the pasture when Checkers was the first to acknowledge its presence and nudged me with his huge nose and looked skyward, not a usual thing for a horse interested in grassy treats on the ground to do. My eyes followed suit in time to see a golden eagle, recognizable by its seven plus foot wingspan becoming more noticeable as it spiraled down, flying closer and closer to us. Once overhead it was low enough to see the colorful red, orange, and gold feathers forming the circles on the underside of each of its wings. It almost seemed I could reach up and touch it. Golden eagles are rare in the area where mostly bald eagles nest to begin with, but when I got an unmistakable wing-wag along with the usual shrill whistle before it turned to go over the creek, I knew I had been honored with an intentional greeting. There are Native Americans who believe the Eagle, who flies the closest to the Creator, inspires us to choose our rightful path in life.

After feeding the horses a little earlier in order to have time for brighter make-up so my face wouldn't wash out under the stage lights, and making sure the outfit I chose to wear on stage really did look good, it was time to see if the two months of diligent practice on my guitar and repeated vocalizing would manifest in an evening's performance worthy of my famous father's name.

As I pulled up around the curve from the ranch onto the forest road leading to the highway into Sedona, a whirlwind swept up and bounced along in front of me. I had been nicknamed, "Whirlwind," by an Apache friend who said I would stir up the world and bring change. But first I would have to change my own world, and this concert was my first step to do that as Julie Sinatra.

Whether it was the nice write-up about me in the local newspaper in Sedona including a photo of me with my guitar that peaked the interest to attend, or the adrenalin rush I was exuding from the stage, and likely also the rolling rhythm of the talented guy on the conga along side of me, I felt, the audience, a full house, respond in sync with every note and word in my songs. I felt very blessed to be there.

Adding to the evening's magic, I was directed to go over to an elderly couple sitting in the first row during the break between my sets. The woman told me she had been in the audience in New York the first performance Frank Sinatra ever did as a solo singer. Her husband added, that she had never parted with Sinatra since that day. They were both big fans and had traveled at times just to follow his concert tours. She told me she had never heard of me before, but the moment I started to sing she knew I was his. She said my facial expressions while I sang were very like his, and when I talked with the audience in between my songs my mannerisms and warmth matched his own. They stayed for most of the second set, late in the night for them. Her husband had told me they rarely go out in the evenings at all anymore. I felt they were emissaries sent by my dad.

After the show, an artist approached me with a sketch he had done while I'd been singing. It showed me with my guitar and the conga player standing near by. Beneath it he wrote: "Julie Sinatra plays and sings, and Nancy Sinatra sings, and this beautiful world becomes again a joy in heaven and in us now and then."

It was monsoon season and the following day a late afternoon rain fell on Skywater, and just as sunset began the sky took on an orange glow surrounding a double rainbow … one for each sister. I sat down and shared in a short letter to Nancy what it was like to sing under my true identity and what the artist wrote on his sketch. He had included her, and I believed that our father had once again orchestrated this to happen. I wanted her to know Dad was proud of both of us.

Two weeks after the concert I was sitting at my desk where I keep a photo of my dad. I'd been trying to fend off the waves of melancholy, a result of wondering what I would really be able to do with my music now that I was in my 50's. Additionally, I was thinking about whether or not I would even be able to find my place in the world. I looked at Dad in the frame in front of me and said aloud: "Dad, do something!" and my phone rang.

"Is this Julie Sinatra?" the unfamiliar man's voice asked when I answered. After I said I was she, he introduced himself as Doug Haywood and explained that Hal Blaine was a friend of his and had suggested phoning me.

Doug Haywood used to play guitar for one of my favorite folk-rockers, Jackson Browne. I had actually met Doug once in a studio down in the Phoenix area many years earlier. He wanted to know if I would be interested in coming to Colorado where he had just opened his recording studio. He said he would be interested in producing my songs. I told him I would love it but I needed to put some monies together for it first. I told him I was just beginning to work on my book and I should earn monies enough hopefully when it became published. We agreed to talk again about it at a later time.

I called Hal Blaine and thanked him for thinking of me. Hal and I had met only over the phone and talked about my music hopes several months earlier. I had been given his phone number by a record company that had recorded his humorous vignettes. My good friend, Jon Iger, had received a copy of Hal's "Ba Doom," and knew he had also many times recorded with Frank Sinatra on his drums. Jon had phoned because it made him think of me and suggested I try to contact Hal Blaine. I had left a message on Mr. Blaine's answering machine and he phoned me later the same day.

During our conversation Hal learned that I had just recently found out whose kid I was and that I wanted to get my music out. He shared that he was going to play drums for Nancy who was going to be singing that night and was amazed at the timing of my call. He said he had played the drums on her "Boots" song when it was recorded. Beginning as far back as thirty years ago Hal had played the drums when my dad was in the studio recording albums. He told me that, "Sinatra was ready to go when he got to the studio. He often nailed a song on the first take, and he never wasted his time or the other musicians' time. He was on top of it and expected everyone else to be."

He seemed amused with me when I had told him I didn't do Frank Sinatra songs because I did my own, and I was a folk-rocker. Hal said when I got the money and was ready to record, he would come over and play for free on my album. He said I would need around $35,000 to cover the other musicians and engineer and studio time to put a good folk-rock recording together ... a title of one of my songs came to mind upon hearing that ... "Someday Paradise" was when I'd have that much money together that I wouldn't need for food, shelter and hay.

So the timing of Doug Haywood's phone call was intriguing. Hal was very close with Nancy, maybe she talked to him about the letter I sent her? Bottom line though, I'd called upon my dad. His message was, it seemed, that I wasn't too old yet. I vowed to keep my chops up. With Doug Haywood's guitar and Hall of Famer Hal Blaine on drums ... too exciting to even think about. "Thanks Dad."

But the year finished without much musical involvement. Not having my own sound equipment was a hang-up, the clubs in town didn't provide it. I began focusing more on writing my book. I wanted to prove I could earn my own way. The music would follow faith told me. There was a bright moment that did occur when I had an interesting visit with a person who had often worked as a body guard for my dad, and knew Frank Sinatra very well.

This came about first of all in a dream flash where I saw just the Hollywood sign on the hills next to Los Angeles and a magnifying glass. A couple of days later I got a call from Rod, surprising because I had not heard from him or Carol Lynn for several months. Rod had seen an interview on television with a Hollywood private investigator who had written about his episodes with the stars. He had included a chapter about Frank Sinatra. I looked up the name, Don Crutchfield I guessed would be listed in Los Angeles. He was on the road doing PI stuff with his partner and his wife passed along a message that I'd phoned. He called a day later saying he could take a "side trip" to stop by and see me if I would like him to. They arrived at the ranch the following afternoon.

"That's quite a road you have into this place," he said smiling and handing me a copy of, "Confessions of A Hollywood PI," which he'd signed for me.

"Your wife said you have some Frank Sinatra stories to share with me. Will you?" I grinned back and the three of us went out on my patio for our visit. I was amazed that a pal of my dad's actually was there at my ranch.

The chapter about Frank is when he went on that "wrong House Raid" with Joe Di Maggio to catch Marilyn Monroe cheating. But, you can read about it. I was there because my boss had been hired to investigate Monroe for Di Maggio, and I was just a kid who was training to be a PI then. I have another story to tell you about your dad, Julie." Don said.

"Besides my PI work, I often have been hired as a body guard for the stars. Frank hired me every time he appeared in Los Angeles, to keep my eye on things just off in the stage wings. One night I was there in the wings when he was already on stage doing his concert. Dean Martin was backstage that night, not to be part of the performance. He was just hanging around and for a few minutes he stood beside me in the wings. All of a sudden Martin bolted onto the stage, interrupting Frank in the middle of a song. Frank took it all in stride, pretended it was part of the act, which it had not been, but when he came off stage he gave me a look that shot through me and said, "This time you live, but next time you're fired."

"I thought Dean often pulled stuff when the two of them were in the Rat Pack. Why was this such a big deal to my dad?"

"Oh no! Not during a concert. Sinatra was a perfectionist. He didn't like surprises, especially when every song, every movement and orchestration had been rehearsed to go off beautifully, perfectly. I was lucky not to get fired for allowing Dean to run out on the stage like that." Don's eyes got big and he took a deep breath and leaned forward on the patio chair and looked at me very intently as he continued.

"There are a lot of phonies out in Hollywood, Julie. Frank Sinatra wasn't one of them. And I can see you are not a phony. You look just like your dad."

"Have you watched her mannerisms when she's talking?" Don's partner piped in.

"Yes, she's like his female twin," Don said. Turning back to look at me again he added,

"Frank Sinatra is the only man I would have taken a bullet for."

I gasped, "A bullet? My God!"

"There are nuts out there who would like nothing better than to be in the newspapers because they have shot or attacked one of the stars," Don stated, describing something I could never imagine. "Your father was the most gracious, most honest person I ever knew," Don continued. "He would have been worth any sacrifice. He was rare among men and a very very good man."

At this point I was teary eyed, and both of my guests gave me a supportive smile. They left soon afterwards. But before they got into their car, Don called back to me. "Frank would want what's right for you, Julie."

In December, 1999, on New Year's Eve, I wrote a letter to my three siblings. I told Nancy, Frank Jr. and Tina that I believed they knew in their hearts that we shared the same father. I said that even without knowing one another socially, without direct communication with one another, just by being his children we are having an impact on each other. I told them that I had learned much about our dad since my talk with Frank Jr., including the fact that he never knew I was his child. I asked them to consider doing DNA testing with me based on our father's commitment to fairness. I had sent each of them the letter to their home addresses and additionally I sent a copy for the executors of Dad's estate to Loeb & Loeb law offices. I signed the letter, "With heart," Julie Sinatra. No one ever answered it.

Because I had filed "notice" into my dad's probate I received copies of all the legal documents filed by the estate attorneys. Several months later I received a copy of the current account report and petition for allowance of extraordinary compensation. The accounting representing what the attorneys "prayed" for to the court to cover their fees during this period of the ongoing proceedings had listed my letter as well and they referred to it as my "claim." They had paid themselves a bundle for time spent on the phone discussing it, but not one of them had contacted me to address any resolution about it.

I was frankly surprised my letter had been identified as a claim into my dad's estate … it had been my way to appeal to and allow my siblings to choose to come forward and open discussions about doing the right thing … In my mind that meant helping me to resolve my identity. I had hoped they might have responded by agreeing to do the DNA in lieu of my making a claim for my inheritance. The copies I sent to the attorneys had been just a courtesy to keep everyone informed.

I noticed that Tina was in the process of following through on a dispute between the kids and Barbara over royalties from some of dad's later recordings. She had filed a formal claim, I gathered, "to protect what was theirs," a comment she'd made in the Entertainment Attorney panel at the Sinatra Conference. It appeared I still had time to find an attorney for myself because the family infighting meant dad's probate was in no way going to close out any time soon, and if I expected to ever become legally recognized I wouldn't be able to achieve that without one. I spent a good deal of time on the phone and writing letters to various probate lawyers over the next few months. They all turned me down. Some of them actually admitted they did not want to go up against Loeb & Loeb … others were more blunt saying to call them back with my DNA guarantee for them.

May, 2000

My mother phoned. She was moving from Vista up to Sacramento to be closer to her relatives. They would be coming soon to help pack and move her there. She said I should come over if I wanted anything from her house, like childhood photographs. I was almost finished with my book I'd been working daily on under my friend Stephan's urging and I would need photos for it. He graciously offered to drive me to California to see her …

Within just minutes after introductions, Stefan noticed toddler pictures of me together in a frame hanging over the dining table. It had never been there before, and I felt like it was a hug from my mother. She didn't usually keep pictures of me in plain sight. But his eyes went to the change of hair-do on me at age four.

"Dorothy, I see in these other pictures what Julie looked like before you started screwing with her." Mother looked at him frowning as he pointed to my straight wispy strawberry blonde hair dawned at age two as compared to the one taken some years later after 1947, with my short frizzy perm which made my hair look darker in color. I could see how this had changed my natural appearance.

"Did you dye her hair too?" he asked her and my mom, the accused, gave him a defensive glance. I think Stefan was prodding her to see if she would open up, but I waved him off. I already had the facts I needed surrounding my birth and this was to be a visit for saying goodbye to my mom.

Mother told me I should take any or all photographs I wanted and pointed me to a large family album she had out on the coffee table. While I was looking through them and choosing ones taken with my horses when I was a child in Carmichael, I heard Stefan talking with her.

"Are there any other photographs in the house besides these, Dorothy?"

To my astonishment she began to tell him of several places he would be allowed to go to and retrieve more pictures. A box was under her bed. Another was up on the shelf in her clothes closet in her bedroom and she told him to be sure and look in the dresser drawers in her bathroom. He began to bring them out into the living room, showing a few to me and asking her where and when the photos were taken. I never knew these pictures ever existed. I was now looking at them for the first time seeing myself at age one through three, and including a little house with a tile roof where we lived in the Hollywood area … remember, my official photographic history had always started only in 1947 at the beginning of the 'exile' to Sacramento after Havana.

I saw myself on a beach with my mother who was dressed in a classy pant's outfit. I recognized it was in Santa Barbara, recalling in my mind that day at the horseshow when I was around eleven that she had attacked and choked me. This was an old stomping ground she and my dad must have gone on short trips up from Los Angeles to spend a day without eyes around them. No wonder it was in Santa Barbara that she went so crazy. I was along at least that time as the photo proved, but way too little to remember it. He knew me only as her child by Tom Lyma. She had a perfectly groomed little dog on a leash as well. I must have been around two years old. There was another photo with me, maybe three years old on the beach in Santa Monica, with the old pier in the background.

"Are these pictures from when you lived in Los Angeles Dorothy?" Stefan again was doing all the talking. She said yes and then turned away indicating no further discussion.

Another picture was taken of her at the back yard area of an apartment building she said was in the Filmore district in San Francisco. It was taken before I was born, Mom said. A roommate's child she explained, simply, was in the photo also. She really looked hot in those short shorts and high heels ... Filmore was an area, I remembered once reading about where tuberculosis had been prevalent in California.

Hidden photo found—Mom wrote on the back:
On tropical, February, 1947.

There was a photograph taken somewhere in a tropical area of the world, maybe Mexico on the coast or I thought very likely, Havana. A large building was in the background up on a point of land overlooking the ocean. I could make out a large courtyard entry area with tropical plants as I had seen in my Havana dream. She looked away quickly when Stefan held it out to her and said nothing.

There were a few pictures that showed us living at a little one story house with a Spanish tile roof, taken outside in the yard. I was no more than 12 to 14 months old, and I had a little visitor, the same age with very blonde hair. A woman I had never seen before was obviously the mother visiting us with her child. I asked if this was Eleanor, mother's old friend I would hear her talk about getting a letter from every once in a while. No response. Eleanor had always been a mystery woman and would remain that way apparently.

From her lingerie drawer Stefan collected two little snapshots that at first glance I could see tied in with the statements Mother had made to Rod when he'd taped that interview in 1997 with her. "I met him in a parking lot coming out of a movie," she had said explaining how she met "the man whose name had been Frank or George …"

"What are these pictures about?" Stefan motioned my mom to walk over and see what he had in his hands. She just smiled and then shot a look at me that said, "This is it, Girl" I realized in a instant that this was why she had summoned me over to California to see her. All of the long hidden photos and especially these two little snapshots were her way of handing me the proof she'd refused to put down on record.

One picture showed her in a uniform, like a hotel bell boy would wear. She had gloves on and was opening a car door, showing she had that gig of greeting arrivals in the parking lot when they came to stay at the hotel. She looked very cute. The car was a black Buick or Oldsmobile, and reminded me of her words recorded by Rod in 1997, when she said the man's car was "not too fancy, not to plain."

The other snapshot was taken of her under a palm tree, posing without her gloves on. She had that trademark demure smile on. Mother nodded to Stefan indicating he should put the snapshots in the large envelope she handed him earlier he was using to house his collection.

Before we left, my mother brought out a copy of her newly revised Will and Testament. She had left me the Karestan carpet I had grown up with. Everything else was to be for Eric, my half-brother as I had advised she should do. Eric had a history of Autism and would need as much as would be available to support him. I didn't want the carpet and left a note saying it could be sold and money added for Eric.

I had hoped she would give me a painting that depicted a large vessel holding a spring bouquet sitting on a window looking out on an Italian countryside. I had always liked it very much and I commented to her that I was hoping she would let me have it one day. Stefan asked her about it and she shook her head, saying she wanted it with her for now. Then she told him something I never knew about it.

"It was painted from a postcard as a gift to me," she said, and suddenly I knew my dad had been the artist who created it. He had gone to Italy, summoned after the Havana incident in 1947 by Lucky Luciano, who had been deported from Cuba because of that shooting incident. This painting I had seen every day while I was growing up had been painted and sent to her from Naples, Italy where he got his "goodbye to Dorothy/Alora" orders.

"It's okay, Stefan. This should stay with her as it always has." I said. "It's time to leave," I said to my mom as she stepped over to me and put her arm around my waist.

"I don't think there will be a way for me to get up to Sacramento, Mom," I said letting her know what she likely already did, that this was the last moment we would ever see one another.

I was very quiet in the car when Stefan spoke up.

"Why didn't you take that last chance to get more facts you need, Julie? I could see she had let down a lot of her guard, but you seemed almost paralyzed in your mother's presence."

"I just wanted her to know I wished her well for the balance of her life up with her relatives, Stefan ... I have what I need now," I defended, but he was right. I still froze around her.

"There was a half-empty bottle of Jack Daniel's in her bathroom," Stefan continued, "She seemed to me to be someone who had never left that time in Hollywood with Sinatra. You know, those snapshots I found were in the drawer she would open every single morning. You know they were taken by him, don't you?" He stated his question with certainty and I nodded the affirmative.

"Looking at those pictures each morning, probably the first thing she did when she got up and went into her bathroom tells me she never got over him, you know?" Stefan's tone had softened in regards to my mom as he continued and said, "You could just see the shame and remorse on her face, Julie. I don't want to see you become a tragedy like your mother."

The compassion I had needed to feel for my mother washed over me as I listened to him. I understood her pain over losing her dream life and clearly I also saw that Frank Sinatra had been her Ava. But I was too like my dad to make that next step to forgiveness. I carried my wounds for a long time—too long.

"She wrote: October, 1940, on the back of those snapshots from her lingerie drawer. That was when my dad first arrived in Hollywood to sing in "Las Vegas Nights." I'm pretty sure they had just met when those photos in the parking lot were taken." I said.

"When we get back to Sedona we should go in the library and look for books about early Hollywood era. There might be a chance to locate that place specifically. It looks like a large hotel or resort of some kind … a hot spot for the stars back when," Stefan grinned, and added:

"Next stop Palm Springs."

Two years since my father had passed away and it was time for me to visit his gravesite. It was evening before we approached the Palm Springs area on I-10 and I couldn't remember the name of the main boulevard leading into the desert town. So instead of taking Palm Canyon Drive, I directed Stefan to pull off onto the Ramon Road exit. Little did I know we had a famous tour guide suddenly on board with us.

A few blocks down from the freeway we passed the Desert Memorial Cemetery.

"We won't have to ask where to go in the morning, Stefan," I said pointing out the car window on my right. "That's where my dad is buried. We drove right past it."

Next, another few blocks down, a large billboard with faded blue lettering announced that, "Ol' Blue Eyes was appearing at the Ingleside Inn." Catching on to the mystical guidance system at work I told Stefan that we had taken the right road into Palm Springs after all. He gave me a knowing smile.

The Inn was at the end of Ramon Road. The lobby embraced me at once with the old world ambiance in the Mexican Colonial building. I told the concierge at the desk who I was and that I followed the old billboard to get there. She looked into my face and reached for a brochure and handed it to me. At the sight of my dad's picture on it I began to cry. She handed me a tissue and said they were offering rooms at a discount if we wanted to check in and spend the night there. I did, Stefan graciously said yes. Our rooms were just off a lovely courtyard with blooming roses. My room, the one with a private patio had housed Elizabeth Taylor as a guest once, and the Inn boasted of past famed guests such as Greta Garbo in its long history.

The concierge had told us with a twinkle in her eye that we should go into the lounge on the other side of the courtyard. She apparently had called ahead that we were coming because the minute I walked in someone pointed out a stool at the far end of the bar as being the one my dad always sat on when he went there for a cocktail or two. I looked at it and imagined him sitting there for a second and then we went into where we could sit nearby a singer who was performing on stage. I chose a table close to the stage and sat down.

"You picked the most perfect place to sit." Stefan grinned and pointed up over my head. I was sitting under a large framed picture of my dad.

The singer looked over at me and smiled and began to sing the song, "My Way." We gave him a tip, Sinatra style, folded small and passed from my hand when we said hello and thank you to him.

The owner of the Ingleside Inn had written a bedside table book filled with short stories about how he came to buy the place originally and some about the famous guests. There was one about my dad. He and Barbara had held their engagement party at the Ingleside Inn and members of the press were hiding outside to catch their picture as they left. Dad almost ran over one idiot that jumped out from behind a large shrub into the driveway to the front of the car snapping off his uninvited camera.

Stefan joined me on my little private patio in the morning where we ate a continental breakfast on the house. A bunny ran past our table into some flower beds. Next, a hummingbird buzzed around our heads at the table. The night before we had seen a skunk on the lawn outside our rooms. I commented to him that all the wildlife from the ranch in Sedona was showing up … "So where's the horse?" I grinned at him.

"We have a long drive in front of us, Julie, we should leave now and go over to the cemetery," Stefan said, sobering the moment.

This meant a kind of closure for me, but I really didn't want it. I had just said Hello, not even in physical person, and with no time for us, except to say good-bye. I wanted to go for my dad's sake, I was worried that I was the one keeping him from having peace. Like I hoped I had on this trip for my mother, I wanted to give him peace where I was concerned.

When we arrived at Desert Memorial in Cathedral City, I realized we hadn't stopped for flowers. I had called ahead to find out how to find his gravesite and they put a little American flag on it to mark it for me. The little flag looked so lonely there, the only grave with one. He was buried next to my grandmother Dolly and my grandfather, Marty Sinatra. Jilly Rizzo, his best friend and body-guard was buried in the grave beside his. Each of the gravestones were simple and unadorned. I kneeled first at my grandparents' graves out of respect. I hoped they knew I was there.

My father's reads: "The Best Is Yet To Come," the title and lyric from the last song he ever sang, ending his public singing career performing a fund-raising concert for others. The gravestone also gives his full name Francis Albert Sinatra and the date of birth and death.

I had a deep knowing inside that he personally chose those words from the song to be there—his final expression of optimism yes, but more—I felt it was almost an instruction, and his announcement that the world would lift up to join hearts. In that way, his way, "The Best Is Yet To Come."

"You really are an old master, aren't you, Dad," the words were just whispered when I heard voices behind me.

"Nancy?," a woman's voice getting closer.

"That's her. It's Nancy," a man's voice. I stood up and turned around to see a couple dressed alike in Bermuda shorts and matching golf shirts. I quickly wiped the tears off my face and said weakly, "No. I'm Julie Sinatra."

"We've never heard of you, Dear?" the woman was still looking into my face for an explanation I guessed, when her husband spoke up.

"She looks a lot like him." I just said back, "I haven't been a public person. I have a different mother than Nancy and the other kids." Before I knew it, they called out to me to smile and snapped off a picture of me. I couldn't imagine how they felt it was okay just to come up to me kneeling at my father's grave.

"We're big fans," the man said as they walked away chatting merrily about their luck in finding me there.

"It goes with the territory, Honey," Dad spoke up in my head. So much for our goodbye, I thought to myself. He was still participating with me. Maybe the surprise interruption signaled he wanted it that way. "I guess I'm your loose end, Dad. I'm grateful for however it is that you are still on that bridge."

Our next stop was in the office of the cemetery where a woman there pleasantly gave me directions I could use to locate my dad's house. We drove over and found Frank Sinatra Drive, but a gardener at the neighboring Tamarisk Golf Course had to point out it was just across the street from where we were. I couldn't remember the name correctly of the Canadian businessman who had purchased the house, so I wasn't able to call ahead. Stefan parked in the driveway in front of the closed double gated entry. I got out and dialed the number for the house on the call box and a woman answered.

I introduced myself and she said she would come out.

"This is an awkward time, Julie, as there are guests here now," she said over the phone. She arrived within seconds and opened one of the gates wide enough for me to see the whole of the front and one side of the property. I recognized the little orange train caboose I had seen in an Architect Digest cover article about his home that he used as a barber shop. I could see my greeter was wearing a security police uniform and clearly she was standing there with a posture that said I couldn't come in, just look, that was all.

"I know you want to come in, but that will have to be cleared first through the channels," she said and handed me a business card for the owner's office and his assistant's phone number. I was fighting tears but I managed to thank her and returned to my allowed gazing at my dad's house.

It was a typical California ranch style not unlike one I had once owned in Vista before I moved the first time to Arizona in the late 70's. I remembered reading he had purchased it back in the 1950's. When the woman realized I was not going to charge my way in there, she stepped to the side to give me a full unblocked view. There in a circle garden just before the front door was something I never in the world could have dreamed would be there.

Rearing up off its hind legs with the wind tossing it's golden mane was a full-size sculpture of a horse! He couldn't have had a better symbol for his outsider kid to encounter there at his beloved desert home—and fitting really because didn't he after all fuel his life from his own inner power? I called back over my shoulder to Stefan waiting in the car.

"I found the horse!"

Pictures of Dorothy taken by Frank at the Garden of Allah Villas, 8150 Sunset Boulevard, Hollywood, California, 1940. Photos found in top batheroom dresser drawer at Mother's, May, 2000.

"And the man you had the affair with—you said had a black Buick in the late 30s model, 'not too flashy, not too plain,' whose name was short, like George or Frank.

She took a picture of him at the Garden of Allah where they met October, 1940.

The Garden of Allah Hotel and Apartments, Hollywood, California

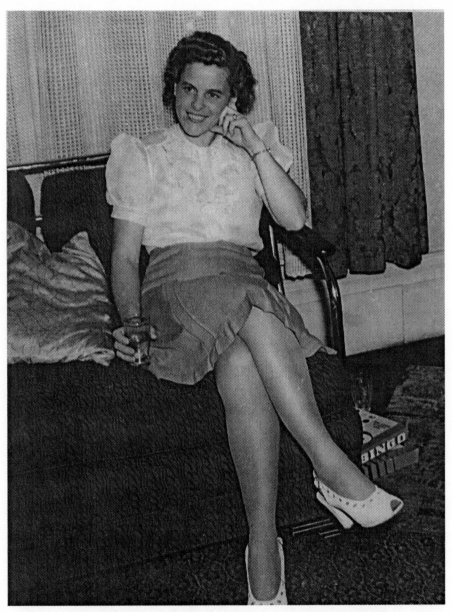

"We used to go to the Springs ...," Dorothy at the Lone Palm Hotel,
a known get-away haunt of Frank Sinatra's in Palm Springs in the 1940s.

My life during the hidden Hollywood years with my mother . . .

LAW GIVES ACCESS
TO FBI FILES

Feb. 4, 1939
Sinatra marries Nancy Barbato, the daughter of a plasterer
from Jersey City, N.J.

Related Stories:

SINATRA KIDNAPPER
FIGHTS NO-PROFIT
LAW

June 1939
Bandleader Harry James offers Sinatra a two-year contract as
a featured male vocalist for $75 a week.

SCHOLAR SAYS FEDS
SAW RED

December 1939
Sinatra leaves James to join the more popular Tommy Dorsey
Orchestra.

STILL LEGENDARY

Background:

June 7, 1940
Nancy Sandra Sinatra is born while Sinatra is away on tour.

Frank Sinatra and the
Mob

Filmography

*For "LAS Vegas lights"
by [illegible]*

October 1940
After meeting actress Alora Gooding on a movie set, Sinatra
and Gooding begin staying together at his California hotel.

The [illegible]

Discography

Bibliography

Timeline

May 1941
Sinatra is named top band vocalist by *Billboard* magazine.

EMAIL THIS STORY TO A FRIEND

G-FILES REPORTS

The Bombing That
Changed Arizona

*mother lid
Song Starts
For These 7*

Jan. 19, 1942
Sinatra makes his first studio recording, singing *Night and
Day* and *Lamplighter's Serenade*.

Tapes Show LBJ Was
Civil Rights Conciliator

Pinkerton's Papers to Go
to Library of Congress

August 1943
Tommy Dorsey releases Sinatra from his contract for $60,000
so Sinatra can pursue more records and films. Over time, this
deal becomes tainted with rumors that Sinatra used mob
strong-arm tactics against Dorsey and formed the basis for
the "make him an offer he can't refuse" scene in Francis Ford
Coppola's 1972 movie *The Godfather*.

Peter Lawford's Hard Fall
From Camelot, Rat Pack

LBJ Targeted Black Power
Radicals

Jan. 10, 1944
Frank Sinatra Jr. is born while Sinatra is away on tour.

FBI Releases Puerto
Rican Surveillance Files

FBI Just Said No to Beach
Boys

Sept. 28, 1944
Sinatra meets with President Roosevelt, who asks Sinatra
about the No. 1 song on the hit parade.

Scandals, Threats and
Creeps: Barry Goldwater's

CHAPTER NINETEEN

Sleepwalking ...

"J ulie, look at this," Stefan was holding a large coffee table book open to a double page photograph of a large hotel and apartment complex in Hollywood taken in the early 1940's. "That parking lot and the trees match with your mother's pictures," he said beaming, adding, "This is the place!"

It was named *The Garden Of Allah*, and looked to have been very upscale. Frank Sinatra was among the stars the old registry boasted of. He stayed one night in October in 1940, the same month and date my mother had written on the back of those little snapshots. Sometime later I located a photograph in Nancy's book, *Frank Sinatra, An American Legend*, of my very young and cute father standing on the grass surrounding the parking lot in front of the apartments there.

This picture was taken during the same few minutes that the two of my mom had been taken. I could see the photos all matched up in regards to the camera and the film producing the likeness. Additionally the same clouds were in the sky over his head as seen in the pictures of my mother. He had taken a picture of her. She had used his camera to take that picture of him he probably sent home to his wife.

Reading Nancy's book also tied up another loose end for me. She wrote there had been a longer original version of the mini-series about Dad that Tina had produced ... That version was the one that had aired by mistake on the local CBS station in Phoenix in 1996. That one I saw, included the segments about the little girl being born in February.

Several Sinatra biographies say that he hooked up with Alora Gooding in October of 1940 when he first came to Hollywood with Tommy Dorsey. The two of them reportedly moved in together at the Plaza Hotel where the rest of the musicians were staying ... the second night Dad was in Hollywood. The Garden of Allah Hotel and Apartments were just down the street from the Palladium, which used Dorsey's band with my father for it's grand opening.

A short time after resolving that the fancy hotel complex was where my mother and father met for the first time when he had just "come out of a movie," as Mom had put it when Rod interviewed her in 1997; if there was any doubt at all left about this and additionally any left about Dorothy and Alora being the same person, it was hammered away when Stefan presented a print out of the FBI Files from the Internet. The FBI had reported that Frank Sinatra met Alora Gooding in Hollywood in October of 1940 … again, the same dates on the back of my mom's snapshots … and dat's all.

In August, 2000, I was on a plane to Colorado. Doug Haywood had called back in the early spring and offered to produce three songs for me for free, on spec. I had spent months practicing to make the best out of this opportunity. I would be able to approach record companies and clubs that paid well enough to afford good musicians to form a band with once I had a well produced music sampling to present.

I shouldn't have been surprised when he gave me his address. He told me his studio was on the corner of Sandler and Starline Roads … of course it would be on a starline.

The recording session went well once Doug got some problems solved with his equipment. We laid down the guitar part I felt I had played better than ever before, and my vocals for the songs. He was going to put additional guitar and bring other musicians in for the rest of the arrangements.

Before I got on the plane for home to Arizona, Doug told me that Hal Blaine had talked with Frank Jr. about me. He didn't elaborate, but he had a question.

"What are you planning to do about your inheritance?" Doug asked.

"I've never been confronted with anything like this in my life, Doug, I don't know yet. What did Frank Jr. have to say to Hal?"

"I don't know what they talked about, Julie, but apparently Frank Jr. had spoken with you once on the phone."

"I was hoping he would help me get my music out there."

"You have to give him credit at least for calling you." Doug said, defending and justifying Frank Jr.'s decision I guessed.

"Yes, he did call me. I give him a lot of credit for doing that."

When I retrieved my 1939 Guild steel string guitar gingerly to keep the case with its worn clasps from falling open from the overhead baggage department, the stewardess smiled and commented to me.

"By the looks of that old case I'll bet there's a story behind your music." The moment she said it I realized that was my signal to get home and finish my manuscript for this book.

"Yes, there's a story all right." I said smiling back.

Before I went to Colorado I realized that I didn't want my book or my music to be under Julie Sinatra as just a nom de plume. I had gone to court and received my true maiden name legally as Ordered, Adjudged and Decreed.

It was already February, 2001 and I still had not received the music I recorded with Doug back in August. My good friend, Jon Iger bumped into him at a gig in Phoenix and as a result I got one of my songs, partially done, on a tape from Doug. The one he chose to work on had a fitting title: "Chasing Wild Horses In The Rain." ... what I must have been doing in Colorado, because as of writing this I still have not received the completed songs. My disappointment over it was defused somewhat by an invitation to a housewarming being held by a big fan of my dad's I met by chance in Sedona.

The date of the party was the same as my birthday, February tenth. When I arrived at Morgan Heard's home the first thing I noticed was that he had encircled a family room area with photographs of my father. In one he pointed out proudly, he had been personally invited to a Frank Sinatra party. Morgan although two generations younger than myself had an affinity for singing the popular songs of the 40's and 50's, many of them Sinatra songs. Dad had personally encouraged him to carry on this music. A few minutes after I arrived I was talking with a small group of guests when a woman behind me turned around and asked who I was, saying I sounded like Nancy Sinatra speaking. She was amazed to learn Dad had a blue-eyed daughter. She said I needed to meet her husband who had been the back-stage producer for the Frank Sinatra TV show for years ... Happy Birthday me.

Ron and Lisa Bacon invited me to come to their house a couple of weeks later. Lisa had baked the most delectable deserts and Ron had a tape to show me of the Sinatra show when my dad's guest had been Eleanor Roosevelt.

When the other teenage girls at my high school, back in the mid-fifty's were screaming their lungs out over Elvis Presley, I was home reading a biography about Eleanor Roosevelt. She was my female role model. Her personal dedication she made to human rights through her work at the United Nations, had left a lasting impression on me from that young age. So this night at a lovely home in Sedona, Arizona I would learn about the admiration my father had held for her too, followed by actually getting to see them together.

Ron told me that the shows were aired live in those days. He talked about how there was so much pressure to get the feeds right to air the show all over the nation without a hitch. That show, he shared, increased that pressure because Frank Sinatra wanted it to be the best ever for Mrs. Roosevelt.

Dad put Eleanor in the center as the cameras focused frontly on her and the audience saw him from the back as he interviewed her. Way up in her elderly years she exuded an impassable charm. Clearly she was enjoying her TV spot, but more, for me, my father, when we could see his face, was shining. They talked about peace and love for fellow human beings. Dad could not have orchestrated a better birthday present for me.

When we finished watching the taped show, Lisa told me they had watched Nancy and Tina grow up. Ron spoke up.

"It's time to put all of you girls together," he said, and Lisa added that she often talked with Tina. I told them it would be natural if the attorneys weren't blocking it.

Ron was a musician and had a home studio for recording. They wanted to hear me perform one of my original songs. I played one called, "Come Sail Love," on their grand piano and told them the last verse had taken many turns until it was resolved in its final lyric one day when my dad seemed to have joined in while I was fumbling with it.

"It's now co-written with him," I told Ron who was smiling and understood as he expressed especially after hearing how the new words ended my second verse. After my words:

"Crossing through the clouds from perils we can tell. Reaching out for stars we stretch and find ourselves," Dad's words follow: "Now and then I see an island in my dreams and wake up in a harbor that waits for you and me." And the original chorus fit perfectly with our collaboration:

"Come Sail Love and we will go to the outer bounds of ebb and flow.

Come sail love and we will be lovers sailing free, sailors coming home".

That night I had a dream, not a vision or premonition—just a dream where I met with my two Sinatra sisters. Tina picked me up in her car and along a highway she pointed to some falling down buildings, telling me, "Those have to go," symbolizing I guessed my letting go of the past. Then we arrived at where Nancy was, and Nancy upon seeing me walking a few steps behind Tina, held her hand out indicating "stop," and said: "We don't have the DNA yet".

A few evenings later I was listening to an interview show on NPR on my radio. A couple of guys, scientists who taught at a North Carolina university were on discussing what they called the, Westbrook Method for identifying sound. Based on their proven concept that no matter what instrument a musician is playing, he or she will have a distinctly unique tone because of that individual's DNA structure of the larynx. Jazz enthusiasts as well as scientists, the two men were putting together a book giving examples like comparing Charlie Parker to a contemporary of his who had a very similar sound named Frank Teschmacher. There had been controversial recordings done that record companies in order to sell more records had credited Parker when it had been Teschmacher actually playing. The two scientists with the use of what they called basically the 21st century version of an oscilloscope were able to track a graph proving when it was Charlie and when it was Frank T. My ears went wild. I called the programmer at NPR and got a phone number for these guys and called them the next day at the university.

They assured me if I sent them an example of myself singing, and one of Nancy and one of Dad, they could analyze the tones to determine the anatomical structure we would have in common based on our DNA design of it. They said it was not just that but also similar mental processes that affected the entire armature … all those factors that would create like tone and that is like having the same as a fingerprint in common; "No two are the same," they said.

A friend with a simple four track home recording unit agreed to record me singing and speaking. I was recorded singing one of my own songs and then I sang along with Dad and Nancy on their hit, "Something Stupid," doing Nancy's harmony. I included Nancy's speaking voice and also singing her "Boots" song I had recorded off the radio from when she had been interviewed By Terry Gross on NPR shortly after Dad had passed away, and then I spoke a few sentences into the mike for my example. I sang along with my dad on his recording of the song, "I Have Dreamed" as well. When it was all played back for me to hear I was surprised when I couldn't tell my own voice from that of Nancy's on the singing parts. Dad and I became obscured together on some of the lower notes in his song too. This had been recorded by putting their voices on one track and I sang along with them on another track in one take only and then both tracks were combined on a third track to produce the vocals together on each song.

It was interesting to me that our phrasing was similar. His had been credited to his having trained himself to do what he did in this regard by imitating Tommy Dorsey's long breathes to connect the notes smoothly on his instrument. But I never did that, so I think it was what these scientists were talking about … our common anatomy and our thinking alike in specifically how we felt about each word of the song created the similarity.

After a couple of weeks after sending out the taped material for their method to be applied, I talked with one of the guys. He told me when I sang with Nancy and Dad that it formed a rope on the oscilloscope … isn't that what a picture of DNA looks like?

They had been excited about the idea of including this as one of their chapters, but when I pressed them to send me documented results they balked and backed away from me. They didn't want to be involved should it come up in possible legal proceedings regarding my paternity. I tried to assure them because their Westbrook method for voice imprinting was too new and not established in the courts yet as fingerprinting is, that wasn't likely to happen. That's what I'd learned from talking with another attorney who had recently turned down my case at any rate, I was amazed and happy that I had accomplished scientific proof about whose daughter I was just by singing

NPR(National Public Radio) had another special insight on the subject of identity for me. I listened to an interview on their show, "Fresh Air" featuring author, Evan Imber-Black. Her book was titled, "The Secret Life of Families," and she was discussing what she described as, "the falling dominos affect that happens to invite negative experience when keeping something private keeps someone else from approaching decisions in their life with a full deck. She went further to say that she was, "referring especially to blocking information about conception that a child had a right to know, i.e., keeping true identity a secret." She also discussed how a young person who has been purposely sabotaged in regards to talents and abilities that would otherwise surface naturally, but have been repressed to protect the secret, goes into the world as a lost person. It was Ms. Imber-Black's opinion that this produced little success in life. Looking back over the ruins in my life I could not argue with that. During my conversation with Evan Imber-Black she nailed something else for me while we were on the phone. I told her that I regretted those first few months when I had discovered Frank Sinatra was my father in June of 1996, that he might have been well enough for us to have had a visit if I had been aggressive in trying to make contact with him then, instead of sleepwalking with the secret.

"You acted in the classical manner, Julie," she told me. "All these kids do the same thing. When they find out, they follow the behavior of the secretive parent. They take over keeping the secret themselves." I was both amazed and saddened upon hearing her answer.

Morgan phoned me in March. He had located a shirt that was being advertised on E-Bay as once belonging to Frank Sinatra—and it allegedly had blood stains on it. My good friend Stefan purchased it and it was sent to Morgan at his address while I contacted the genetic testing lab in Texas once more. It was a lovely lavender blue dress shirt that had been given to another singer by Barbara Sinatra who was cleaning out a closet of Dad's clothes. It had been especially tailored for him and the label read, made for Frank Sinatra. It did appear to have two little faded blood stains on the tails that would have tucked into his pants. I noticed the shirt also smelled of Lavender, his favorite cologne. It was wrapped in paper and put into a box without my so much as touching it, and sent off to the lab.

After waiting with my fingers crossed for five weeks, the disappointing news arrived. Those had been rust stains, not blood. Apparently the shirt must have been hanging in a closet that suffered a water leak of some origin in my dad's house. I noted with some wondering that it also no longer had any trace of laven-der aroma. The shirt also did not have any of the powdery stage make-up residue on the inside of its collar it had when it was mailed to the lab … maybe it was a victim of a second leaky closet?

I had my dad's beautiful shirt mailed back to me at my Sedona post office address. When it came the postal clerk, Rosie, was very curious. She knew who I was because there had been a few local newspaper write-ups about me and she was a big fan of my dad's. I opened up the box and took out the shirt to show it to her. It was clear she wanted to touch it. I handed it to her and she hugged it … he was truly loved by his fans.

A new club opened in Sedona and a friend who had sound equipment invited me to sit in on his gig and do a song or two. I wore Dad's shirt which fit me per-fectly except for the long tails I had to tuck all the way into the pant legs of my jeans. Maybe I was just on that night or maybe there was magic in that shirt, but I never sang better.

September 8th I received a phone call from Eliot Weisman. It came five months after a letter I had written him asking if he would be willing to help me produce my music. By this time I didn't expect to ever hear from him. I had expressed the hope in my letter that he would act as my father would have if he'd known about me and my songwriting. Eliot had been my dad's personal manager, had handled setting the dates and places for his performances for many years, I wanted him to put aside his role as executor of Dad's will and just help me as a manager too. I realized when I wrote it that it was a stretch. Anyway, now here he was on my phone.

"I like to answer all my correspondence," he began, "I'm sorry it has taken so long for me to get back to you, Julie." I asked him at once about my music and told him I was also finishing a book I wanted to have published, and I wanted his advice and help.

"My songs follow my story line quite a bit," I said to him. "What if I included a CD in with my book?"

"First get the book published then everyone will want your music. I'm sorry I cannot get involved with you about this now. Maybe down the line," he said, and his words sounded sincere.

"I want to prove I can make it on my own just like my dad did, Eliot. I'm not trying to be a threat to his estate." I stated firmly to him.

"I'm not in opposition to you. Frank Jr. whom you've talked with stays out of it. He doesn't like being involved. Barbara and Nancy oppose you and Tina does Nancy's bidding," he said, surprising me with his openness. Before I could say anything more Eliot added: "You need your DNA. Think about that over the weekend." Then we hung up.

The following Monday morning, September 11, 2001, along with everybody else in our country, all I thought about were the terrorist's attacks. Additionally, I really had not caught on to the meaning of Eliot's remark about the DNA. Was it supposed to mean he knew I needed it, which I already did know? Or, because he mainly stood in Barbara's camp, had actually come on board as a personal manager to my dad through his contact with Barbara Sinatra, was he implying she would make some kind of deal to provide me with something of Dad's that had DNA material if I didn't interfere with her part of the estate? On the emotional level, I wanted to feel like I belonged. I didn't want to alienate myself with the other kids forever in order to make some deal with Barbara who wasn't my own flesh and blood. At any rate, without a lawyer of my own I felt too out on a limb to contact Eliot again.

The following Thursday morning Missy Starr died suddenly from a heart attack. She was wobbly as I served both horses their hay and moments later she fell. Checkers went temporarily insane, whirling out of the corral running and screaming for her up and down the pastures—blanking out the scene of her lying there where he had watched her go down; it was as if he believed that by calling for her she would come back to him. His grief broke my heart as much as the loss of Missy did. They had been closely bonded for more than seventeen years together.

I learned a lesson about love from Checkers during the following weeks. I expect that he would want to just roll as horses in grief do thereby twisting an intestine and committing knowing suicide, not uncommon to see when a bonded partner horse dies. But he kept his eyes on me and I told him if he would stay I would find another pal. Horses are grazing animals and typically they do not survive long alone … like most people who need people. I was racing against the odds I knew, but he hung in there with me. He did what horses don't do in those circumstances … he loved me, a mere human being enough to fight his primordial instincts. Checkers, already very elderly at age 30, decided to live.

After making some calls around I located a lovely black Morgan mare. Pepper was also up in years and needed a home to retire at. She bounded into the pasture upon her arrival and he perked up instantly. Within the first hour they were together he was already happier. I didn't have a clue that she was bringing a gift especially for me too—one that would support and move me forward in establishing my identity in the not too long future. But isn't that how God works—hitting two birds with one stone—and especially when love is involved?

Around Thanksgiving I received something to be grateful for that added addi-tional information about my mother's relationship to Frank Sinatra. Dan Kubota, a Sinatra historian and devoted fan, after spending days of his time looking through the Film Institute Archives and other archive sources for me over in Los Angeles, came upon Alora Gooding listed in the credits as an extra in the movie, "Around The World In Eighty Days," filmed in 1956. Finding this would put my last missing puzzle piece left over from my teenage years into place. Stefan rented a video copy of it for me.

Just before the cameo scene in Around The World In Eighty Days that Frank Sinatra appears as a piano player in a Barbary Coast saloon, I saw my mother in the crowd scene. She was wearing an ankle length brown skirt with a matching suit jacket. She turned her face towards the camera and smiled briefly.

In the late spring of 1956, just before getting out of school for the summer vacation, I had arrived home in the Long Beach house and my mother was gone. She arrived a short time later, and later than she must have intended to do, because she was barely recognizable. It was obvious that she had been profession-ally made up and her hair was styled other than she usually wore it too. Her face was beaming I recalled when I greeted her as she quickly bounded upstairs to change her clothes. When I remarked about her appearance and asked her where she had been, she got around my question saying she had been talking to my father regarding the purchase of our house. That alone hadn't made sense to me because we'd been living there for some time and it was the second time she had used "father" instead of "Mr. Lyma," who at that time I believed was my biologi-cal father. Now, thanks to Dan Kubota's efforts on my part I now I knew she had said it right. She had met with Frank Sinatra. So mother had not ended forever her contact with Frank Sinatra, and since there was nothing listed in the movie credits giving the name Dorothy Lyma, or Hunter, as she was then; this also fin-ished the proof that Alora and Dorothy were the same person. It had been a mys-terious yet pleasant moment for me that day back in 1956 seeing her beaming when she came home ... the only time I can remember being privy to seeing her that happy.

Checkers and Pepper seemed to enjoy the snow as much as I was on our white Christmas on Skywater that ended the year, but in Northern California, it was to be the last holiday season for my mother who passed away from a stroke in January 16, 2002. She was 87.

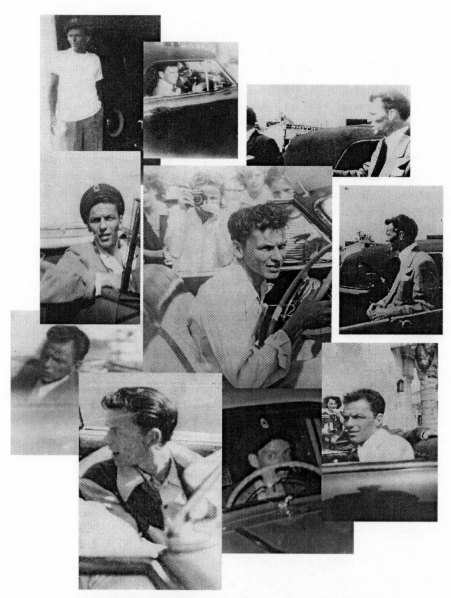

FS in his cars in the early 1940's—courtesy of his fans.

My half-brother, Eric, phoned me from Sacramento saying I wasn't to let Cousin Bob or the other relatives know he had called me. He was afraid of getting in trouble with them if they knew he had contact with me—something they didn't do. I had become the enemy of my mother in their eyes, thanks to her contin-ued efforts to put her cat back in the bag regarding the secret. I suspected my cousin Bob knew I was Frank Sinatra's daughter, but maybe he didn't and the family didn't know the truth either. I was being treated as if they believed I was my mother's crazed child who had been upsetting her in her old age. None of them had a listed phone number and I had not been given an address or phone for reaching my mother after she moved up there among them. I hadn't been told she had a stroke even before the one that had killed her. They intended not to even let me know when she passed away. Unimaginable!

My new friend, Dad's fan, Morgan Heard was gracious enough to list my mother's passing on the internet under her starlet name, Alora Gooding. I felt she had earned the right to be noted and it was placed among information about the movie, Around The World In Eighty Days—the only time I saw her happy after 1947; and I knew at least she could have become one of America's most talented actresses … after all, she had played at least one role so well that she had pulled the wool over my eyes and everyone else's for over a half-century.

My mother had wished to be cremated. Before that happened I wanted to be able to get some of her hair for DNA testing because one the attorneys who had turned me down had advised I would need a sampling. Apparently now this has changed, but then the labs could only test siblings for paternity in common by ruling out at least one of the mothers. With my hopes that Nancy, Frank Jr. or Tina would agree to the DNA testing one day, I phoned the funeral home.

I was told I had to get permission from my Cousin Bob who was left in con-trol of my mother's body. He was less than understanding and I didn't get that lock of her hair—nor was I invited to join the family in saying goodbye to her. Because my mother had always controlled the correspondence that passed her news and mine, all these many years past, I didn't have a current address for any of them to send memorial cards to. But what I would have had to say to the fam-ily, they already had in possession from a poem-song I had written when a tiny cousin once died. The lyric spoke to, "a new budded wild rose that blossomed down stream …" Choose a happy life next time, Mom.

April, 2002

My friend Morgan saw that photos of my dad were being offered on a Web site on the Internet. I got a contact phone number and called to inquire if there might be one of Alora Gooding in this guy's possession as well. Also I was looking for pictures of my Dad in his car, hoping to find one that matched the car in my mother's snapshots from the Garden of Allah. He sent a bunch of them with Dad very young, in Hollywood, driving various convertibles. Young Bobby Soxers had originally taken these candid shots when he was spotted by them. The reader can view them at the end of this chapter. Unfortunately, there were none that matched the car I was looking for, and none of Alora Gooding.

Morgan bought tickets for Frank Jr's show in Las Vegas, "Sinatra Sings Sinatra." He had one for me and I could ride out there with him and a friend of his for the performance scheduled during May. I owned absolutely nothing dressy to wear to an evening Sinatra performance. I agreed to go, I didn't want to miss what Morgan described to be as being my brother singing tributes to my father, doing the songs and the staging just the way Frank Sinatra had done it … because when he'd done it I had missed it every time.

There was a used clothing store in Sedona and I gathered up clothes I rarely wore anymore from my closet and sold them for enough money to buy a silk jersey long black skirt with a matching top and half of the price of a pair of dressy black shoes to go with them. Morgan's mother, Joan, went shopping with me. She gave me money for the balance I needed to buy the shoes but diverted me from the cocktail pumps I was looking at to another pair.

"These will be fine with your outfit and you can wear them when you go to court."

"I'm not planning to go to court." I protested, still torn over what I should do.

"We'll see," she retorted with a knowing look.

CHAPTER TWENTY

A dolphin knew best ...

*T*hirty minutes outside Las Vegas Highway 40 crosses over Hoover Dam. There are three huge angels that stand in memorial of men, two of them a father and son, who lost their lives while working to construct the great heights of concrete that intercede upon the river's flow. This was the second time I saw it. Harry Misfeldt had taken my mother and I on a trip here when I was four or five years old. Now, on May 14, 2002, the fourth anniversary of our father's passing, I was listening to my half-brother I never knew I had back then being interviewed on a local radio station to promote the performance of "Sinatra Sings Sinatra" at the MGM Grand.

"You should call Frank Jr. at the hotel when he get in," Morgan announced to me a little time later when the high-rise hotels with their exaggerated Disney like themes came into view. "This might be a chance for the two of you to meet each other," he added.

"Okay," I heard myself answer already caught up in a mind sweep about entering the city that had credited Frank Sinatra for building the foundation it flourished upon, the place my dad had sung in over and over since the early 1950's. In time for my late arrival there, the Sands had long since been imploded and the voices of Frank, Dean, Sammy, Peter and Joey, The famed Rat Pack, were merely an old echo I strained to listen to on the high desert wind whining through the cracked open car window. We pulled into a cheap rate motel on the Strip. Once settled into my room, I dialed the MGM Grand, gave my name and asked to be connected to Frank Jr.

I got his answering machine in his room and left the message that I was here to attend his concert and that I hoped we could have a cup of coffee together. The phone in my motel room rang less than two minutes later. Here is what I remember from our conversation, which he began, without first bothering to introduce himself on the other end of the line.

"You're not a member of this family!" he asserted, apparently in response to my having stated my Sinatra name when I'd asked to be connected to him. I sighed and took a big breath.

"Oh yes I am," I retorted quickly. "Maybe not socially, but I am in blood a member of this family." My effort earned a short grunt before he attempted to confound my defense.

"Why did you come all this way? What is it you want?"

"My mother steered me far away from anything about Frank Sinatra while I was growing up. Now here you are, my half-brother, doing a special tribute to show what it was like when Dad gave one of his concerts. What you're doing is so special to me I wouldn't miss it for the world."

He softened a little.

"Have you any further proof since we last talked?" he asked me.

"Yes, I finally have been able to put it all together."

"As I remember, your mother was reluctant ...," he began and I interrupted.

"She has confirmed everything, including that she kept me a secret from Dad as well."

"So you really had no knowledge about this before? Nothing was said to you when you were growing up?" he asked, and I knew he was exploring a legal aspect regarding the potency of a claim as the pretermitted heir—reminding me no matter how much or how little each of us may feel about this chance to get to know one another, that big elephant in the room we couldn't help seeing was there with us.

"No—Frank, no. I already told you when we talked before that I learned who I was at age 53. I'm a singer and songwriter as you know—don't you think I would have shown up for his guidance at age seventeen when I got my first guitar?" I implored, hoping he would finally see this was the truth.

"Okay, Okay," he responded somewhat irritated. I wanted him to know how much I cared about our Dad and the efforts I'd made so far to catch up.

"I've spent the time since that learning as much as I can about our father—the man he was, not just the icon. I traveled to the Sinatra Conference on Long Island and even spent three days in Hoboken learning about him. Can't you imagine how it feels to have missed everything about him all my life? I'm now writing a book about this journey."

"I had no idea this has been so epochal," he stated and then continued in a skeptical tone, "So what's the purpose of your book? Do you expect to become famous or something?"

"If being a pubic figure will serve a good purpose," I defended back sensing for some reason he felt my book was a threat. "I want my story to inspire changes to the way young people are being educated … "I began, but he cut me off.

"Are you an educator?"

"No, but my story illuminates the oppression of natural talents and abilities. I would like to see what could be done differently to draw out what is in a child—allow that to be the basis of growth." My words got lost in a sudden knee jerk response from Frank I had no notion was coming.

"I don't think I want to have coffee with you after listening to you," he said coldly.

"That's up to you. I only wanted to give you a head's up that I would be at your concert, in case you or someone with you spotted me. I was just trying to be gracious. I'm not here to get anything from you. I won't be there tonight, on this special date of Dad's passing. I'll be in the audience tomorrow night."

He didn't say anything or attempt to get off the phone, so I continued talking with him.

"By the way, I read Tina's book and I agree with everything she had to say in it."

"You do?"

"All the while Arthur Crowley, acting on Barbara's behalf, had kept telling me that Dad was too ill, I felt there were also times when he might have been up and around, well enough sometimes so we could have met each other. Tina said in her book there were times when she saw him more like himself when he wasn't being kept sedated. It reminded me when I read that of how helpless I felt in not being able to intervene on his behalf then—and, for a time I was made to think if I was just patient I would be allowed to go out there … I can't believe they let him die before we could meet each other." I finished that in tears, adding, "What's the matter with them? How could they do that?"

"You wouldn't believe what they are up to now," he said disgusted I presumed with the in-fighting over the estate.

Morgan knocked on my door and came in saying he and his friend were ready to go to dinner and they were waiting for me. I was still crying and struggling to talk on the phone as he sat down realizing whom I was talking with. Frank Jr. was saying something about ten or eleven tomorrow morning, but I was too emotional to listen, missing most of it. I heard him say he had to go to dinner and realized he was about to hang up.

"You are coming into you own now, Frank," I perked up enough to say, wanting to convey sisterly support for him. "You are in my heart."

I was up and dressed in a nice pants outfit by mid-morning, on time to go and see the dolphins in a huge pool where people could actually visit with them. The door was open to air out a cigarette I had just put out, so my room number was faced to the inside, not visible to the driver of the dark green Lexus sedan who had slowed to a crawl in front of it, face searching the number back and forth on my neighboring doors. It didn't register who that was until after I rushed out, only a fraction aware of what I was suddenly doing, and hollered: "Are you lost?," in a voice that alarmed even me.

I saw the look of horror on his face just briefly as he backed his car out of the area, made a fast u-turn and sped away. His face began to register in my mind. I had left my motel and room number along with my phone number on his answering machine before he called me.

"Oh my God!," I cringed, "I have just chased my brother off."

I immediately looked toward heaven to locate and blame who I guessed was the source of that inexplicable behavior on my part.

"What's going on Dad?!!

Frank Sinatra Junior sang Sinatra that night and he did it beautifully. Our seats were numbered for way in the back of the auditorium and Morgan's friend found an usher and I made an unexpected stroll between the front row and the stage to arrive at my new seat—passing by Frank Jr. who looked down and gave me an amused smile.

After the concert ended I went to dinner with Morgan and his friend and that had taken about an hour. We were outside the MGM Grand waiting for the car to be brought up when Frank Jr. walked up toward the valet booth to retrieve his car. I felt so sad and so stupid when I saw he spotted me there and made a quick exit, handing off the ticket to identify his car to one of his companions. Changed from the elegant tuxedo and patent leather shoes he wore for his concert, I noted somewhat surprised, the Indian moccasins he was wearing dressed now in jeans and a sweatshirt—he could have been me in my usual garbs at home.

Another experience occurred in Vegas to top off the one that I had with the "walk-in," as the Native Americans call it when a spirit takes over a person's body—the only explanation I had thus far for having been propelled through my motel room doorway, scaring off my brother. It happened at the edge of the dolphin pool.

I was a spectator along with other people watching the charming tricks a male dolphin was doing at the bidding of the animal trainer at the side of the pool. I was sitting on my legs to be down closer to the water level. Suddenly this dolphin spun behind his trainer over to me. She was signaling to him to get him back under her control but he ignored her and began a whole speech into my face as he lifted himself half way out of the water at the pool's edge. It was as if he was on a mission because it was obvious, though I couldn't understand anything specific, that I had just received a stern talking to from him … I felt it was something like, "wake up girl …"

During the long drive back to Sedona I thought about both bizarre happenings. My brain clicked in and I got it. If Frank Jr. and I had met for that coffee talk, it was highly possible that I would have fallen into my old habit of trying to please instead of speaking up for my right to have the DNA testing done, for example. I had to admit to myself that wanting to feel I belonged was a fantasy that would have gotten in the way of my moving forward with my identity. There's a hidden word inside of the word "please" it's "asleep." My father and a dolphin knew best.

The news after getting back from Las Vegas was that the ranch had sold. The owner had asked the buyers if they would like me to stay on and continue as the caretaker. They had their own people moving in. I had thirty days to locate a place for the horses and I to live without any income.

The owner, Ron, who understood my financial vulnerability was kind enough to loan me four months worth of rent to help me make the transition. But my real stress was from having to leave Skywater, the little rock house and the eagles. Harley was buried there. Missy Starr was buried there. How could I leave this place, my old home for centuries, and the new dreams I had for it—how could I ever live through this?

All the other tenants had moved out, and the new owners weren't due in for another week, leaving me to enjoy the whole ranch by myself—a special time to say goodbye to every tree, every rock. Down at the creek a Blue Herron flew down and landed on top of a large flat boulder in the water. His long skinny legs seemed so incongruous for standing up on, but he did it just the same.

On my walk back up to the house I passed the old sycamore tree that housed a nest of little falcon size Black Hawks. I called up to them to say I'd miss them. A little one, a youngster probably just now flying circled around my head two or three times and gave a melodic whistle … He was the new life that had been born last spring on Skywater. I was going through a kind of death. The only way to find my re-birth was to stand up for myself. Since the family had proven they were not coming forward to do the right thing; it was my job to stand up and call my spirit back and do it myself. The only place that could happen where I could win my identity legally, was where I did not want to go—into the court in Los Angeles. I went into my study once in the house and began a search on the phone again for an attorney to represent me in regards to my dad's estate.

One among the three who once again turned me down followed up with a letter saying I needed to file my claim at once because of a time faulting in the statutes. I phoned the court in Los Angeles and asked for the clerk in the Probate Department. I wanted her to send me whatever form there was so I could fill it out myself. She told me there was no such form—that the attorneys made up their own following specific guidelines of protocol—she was not allowed to advise me on how I should construct my claim.

"You really need an attorney to help you with this, she said and I thanked her and said just to myself: "No shit".

The last load in my car was ready to take over to a guest-house I rented where there was at least a nice pasture for the horses. It was twilight and the circle of sky over the ranch had a soft lavender blue hue. A young mule deer doe was standing on the road, visible in the headlights of the 'Z," as I pulled out of the driveway. I stopped and she trotted a few steps only and then she stopped and looked back at me.

"I'll be back," I called to her. In what life I wondered.

In my post office box in September, two items were waiting for me. The first was a large thick letter size envelope that dutifully contained the "Fourth and Final Account and Report of Co-Executors; Petition For Statutory and Extraordinary Compensation to Co-Executors and Attorneys, for Authority to Retain and Reserve and for Final Distribution the attorneys at Loeb and Loeb who represented my dad's estate had sent me to give me notice that probate was closing in the coming month of October, 2002.

It had taken four years to probate Dad's estate. During that time the family had settled their differences with a tolling order to pacify the dispute over Sinatra recordings' royalties going to the kids and those going to Barbara; that took a year. The second year was spent mainly gathering up and categorizing all of Dad's furniture, paintings—his stuff from his homes—and the sorting of community property vs. what goes with the kids trusts etc. A beer company was sold as well that involved income for the trusts that mainly went to the kids. The third year was a battle over his grand piano that sat in the living room in the Beverly Hills house that remained in possession with all its possessions with Barbara Sinatra. That should have been a no-brainer—a phone call to Frank Jr. the day after Dad died to let him know it was coming over to him—the son who composed music, arranged orchestration for Frank Sinatra and also himself … Who else could make use of the piano? This past year there had been an inquiry Barbara had raised over some of the monies Dad had given to unlicensed charities in the past, clarifying what Frank Jr. had been referring to. It was thrown out of court.

It wasn't my place to judge what had gone on between all of them during these years—especially because the outsider is just that—outside of the complete facts. But clearly they had all made the team of attorneys much wealthier, with the exception of Harvey Silbert, whom I had learned was a wealthy man himself and well known as a philanthropist. In the paperwork I saw that Harvey, an old and dear friend of my dad's, had refused any payment for his services as a Co-Executor.

The only item left unresolved in Dad's probate was me.

The other item in my P.O. Box was a small package sent to me from my brother, Eric up in Sacramento. It contained my baby shoes that had been my first pair and that my mother had bronzed in tribute of the first few steps I took on my walk in life. I couldn't miss the astuteness of the timing of their arrival.

In the morning my phone rang. It was Bob, the man who had once owned Pepper. You may remember Pepper came to live with us to be the new companion for my horse Checkers—saving his life after Missy Starr died. A little note had been included along with her medical vet records when she'd arrived. She had once belonged to Bob's wife who had passed away from Cancer. The horse had been a long companion of his wife's, and Pepper was elderly when the woman died. Her wishes had been that her horse, believing care would not become available for her at her high end years, be put to sleep. Bob could not bring himself to do that and Pepper had been donated to an equestrian facility where horses were used with handicapped kids. She was too high spirited for that kind of quiet, standing still work and needed a more suitable home. The facility gave her to me and asked a simple request that I contact Bob to let him know of her new fate, to give him peace of mind about his having gone against his late wife's wishes. Over these past two years I did stay in touch with Bob and we became pals. He perked up each time I had a funny cheery story to share with him about how Checkers and Pepper were getting along together. In return he often cheered me on knowing what I was struggling through. On this morning during our conversation I told him about getting the closing papers for the probate out in Los Angeles and even though I had just tried again to find an attorney to help me, so many had turned me down it seemed useless to hope one would now so late in the game.

Pal Bob didn't agree.

"You must go to that hearing with or without an attorney, Julie," he urged. "You will regret it for the rest of your life if you don't go in there and stand up for your rights, regardless of the outcome—whether you get your DNA from the court or not. This is for you to do for yourself, and if you'll agree to it, I will pay your plane fare and hotel so you can go."

The first attorney agreed to "have a look." I sent out all the facts I knew from my mother along with photos of my self and my son to show our likeness to Frank Sinatra, copies of the probate filings he asked for and additionally new information that related to scientific evidence I found by reading Tina's book, "My Father's Daughter," by Tina Sinatra with Jeff Coplon.

Dad had once needed blood for an operation and had called on Tina to donate it, hinting at a rare blood type, like my own. But more specifically, she mentioned another operation he had in 1969 to relieved the unnatural tightness of the skin on his hands which made even gripping a microphone painful. It had been caused by his having Dupuytren's Contracture—a rare condition I also have, and why both of us grew very small fingernails.

A few days later Paul Livadary called me back.

"I wanted to phone you myself, Julie, to tell you that unfortunately, I will be unable to take your case. It isn't because I don't believe you are who you say you are. Personally, I am convinced you are Frank Sinatra's daughter, but the final accounting closing out his estate is now just a little over two weeks away. There isn't enough time to do the work that would be involved, and you are un-able as you said to pay my fee. I'm sending back to you all the photos and documents. I'm sorry, and I wish you luck."

"I appreciate the time you've spent and I understand your position, Paul, but I really need this help."

"If you are determined to see this through, then there is something you can do yourself. You can write a letter to the court. It's a way to let the judge know that you are a pretermitted heir and that no attorney would help you with your case."

"I didn't know this existed. No other lawyer mentioned it to me."

"You just address your letter with a cover sheet like the ones that come to you from the estate attorneys when you have been given notice of hearings. Write the letter to the judge himself and include what you have been told from your mother about being Frank Sinatra's daughter. This is your last chance to get this resolved, including your DNA proof. Ask the judge to order the testing on his own motion from your other siblings. Address it all to the court. Oh—and be sure to attach a photo of yourself with the letter."

"Thank you. I will do that."

"Everyone deserves their day in court," Paul added, "So send your letter now.

Then on the hearing date for the final accounting on September 30th—show up."

CHAPTER TWENTY-ONE

"Somewhere under a sky on fire alone on a burning sea, A sailor searches for his dreams unyielding in his need ..."

—Julie Sinatra

September 29, 2002

L anding through an unusually clear blue sky into LAX in Los Angeles was an easy metaphor for my flight that had lifted out of Phoenix—out of the ashes—into a leap of faith. I had made reservations for the shuttle to take me from the airport to my hotel downtown so the driver already had my name.

"Any relation?" he asked as he checked me off his list to board the bus.

"Same dad—different mom," I answered with the simplification I traditionally used for this kind of inquiry.

"You look like Frank with those blue eyes," he grinned.

I fed his response into my self-confidence, needing this little boost. At nine AM the next morning I would be crossing over the threshold at the doorway of the Probate Division of the Superior Court of the State of California for the County of Los Angeles with mostly just my self-evidence to present my case with. If the outcome became successful this would mean I would be able to enter my culture under my true identity.

Before going to bed I ran a careful inspection of my apparel I would wear to court. The shoes Morgan's mother, Joan, had said I would need one day for this, got an extra buffing; my black flannel skirt was examined for any trace of lint. My briefcase was organized in such a way that I could pull out any documentation instantly that I might get asked to present in front of the judge. The next thing I needed to do was spend some quiet time centering myself.

My mind was racing through my fears ... would the judge throw me out without having my DNA proof on me? Would I be belittled in that public arena—considered to have brought a frivolous case into his courtroom as Carol Lynn had said she didn't want to risk a few years ago? Ed Shirak's words on my last morning

215

in Hoboken floated into my head: "You have his heart," he'd told me. Heart in Hoboken language represents having courage. I decided I needed a warrior's shield to go into court with.

I tore off a piece of note paper from a pad by the phone in my room and began thinking about how I wanted to present myself. I made a list of names of colors and wrote out beside them what they symbolized ... Red for heart—Blue for truth—Yellow for intelligent thinking—Grey for remaining neutral and listening—and Green with White in a checkerboard to keep the subject of money on a high ethic. I put the little paper shield in my purse to carry with me the next day.

September 30, 2002 ...

The wake-up call for 6 AM I'd requested came after only three hours of sleep. My brain had been busy all night long broadcasting every point of fact and circumstance I must have believed I would blank out on or something of that horror. But while I showered and dressed a calmed poise came over me, and just the thought that in an hour or so I would be inside that courtroom seemed to feed the energy I needed into my body. After downing the two cups of coffee, all the little pot held, I gave myself another scrutiny for a new lint bandit or loose strand of my long hair I had tied back that may have landed on my blazer. Finding no trace of lipstick on my front teeth in the mirror in the hotel elevator, I picked up a brisk pace through the lobby doors and maintained it for my two-block walk to the courthouse. I stopped just long enough to gaze and take in the meaning of the statue of Justice holding the balanced scales in her hands before going up the broad concrete steps. "Truth in its final stage is considered self-evident." ... I had to trust that my truth would earn that justice.

Once inside I didn't know where to go. A policeman there in the entrance area motioned me to a window where a clerk advised I needed Department 11. She said it would be marked in the hallway and I would see the Probate Division sign. I went in and sat down.

The Honorable Thomas W. Stoever—Judge, was not yet at his bench. I noticed several people, mostly men I assumed were attorneys were going over one by one to the court clerk's desk. One sitting behind me got up I noticed and I turned and asked him what everybody was getting over there. He said the cases were called by number and not by name. I asked him to please get me the number that would be called for the Sinatra case.

I realized I had no idea what was going to take place in a hearing. To calm that unknown building imagined fear scenarios in my head, I reviewed what I had included with my letter to the judge he already had. I cheered myself up a little by remembering I had included a copy of Arthur Crowley's letter that had stated that Frank Sinatra had never heard of me. His stonewalling would serve now as further evidence toward my claim as the intestate child. Along with that document I had included a lab copy report of my rare blood type, and a copy of my court decreed legal name of Sinatra, photographs of my dad and of me and of my son to show our likeness, a straightforward clear and simple statement that my mother had confirmed Frank Sinatra was my biological father and how it was that this had been kept from me and from him for over a half-century. I also included quoting Frank Jr.'s statement that "nothing I sent out there was ever put in front of him(Frank Sinatra), and a quote from Crowley who stated, "the shock of you could give him(Frank Sinatra) a heart attack," and one more from Harvey Silbert, Co-Executor, who stated to me that my father had never mentioned me while he was preparing the first will. In my briefcase I had a copy of every letter that had gone back and forth between the attorneys representing the other Sinatras, myself, and my original attorney, Carol Lynn who was no longer on board. I concluded mentally that there was nothing to be afraid of.

"Number 127—Sinatra," the clerk called out and I stood up from my seat and moved into the aisle.

The judge spoke first.

"We're here to close this up unless there are any objections," he stated looking right at me.

"Your Honor, I am Julie Sinatra. I am here to object to the final accounting because it does not include my fair share because I am an heir," I managed, praying my feet would not go out from under me—grabbing that image of the Blue Herron standing solidly on his flimsy legs by the creek back on Skywater.

The judge gave what seemed a slightly amused smile and motioned me to come forward to a table just below the bench. I already had my briefcase in my hand. I went up and stood behind a microphone at the left side of the table.

"I sent a letter to the court a couple of weeks ago, Your Honor."

"I have not read your letter because it represents an ex-parte in this matter," he stated pleasantly, firmly, and my heart got caught in my teeth when my chest caved in. He must have seen what I supposed was a look of horror on my face, because he quickly added, "But I am aware of it. Ms. Sinatra, you will have to file a formal objection with this court, and once you have done that, I will be able to read the letter—okay?"

In a flash of movement from their seats, two attorneys leaped up to the table. One stepped up to the microphone on the right side of the table. The one coming up on my left bumped me with his shoulder knocking me out of his way as he took over the microphone I'd been using. This left me behind the middle of the table where there was no microphone.

For an instant I thought maybe I was supposed to leave and go sit down, but that idea was quickly cut off when I suddenly felt someone place their hands my shoulders, as if to steady me. I took a quick glance behind me, but no one was there. The gentle pressure on my shoulders would remain throughout the balance of the hearing. The two lawyers then both introduced themselves to the court. My bully on my left spoke first.

"Good morning, Your Honor. Jeffrey M. Loeb, of Loeb & Loeb, same spelling(he spelled it) appearing on behalf of Petitioners, Harvey Silbert and Eliot Weisman, Co-Executors of the Will."

Next Barbara's lawyer:

"Good morning, Your Honor, I'm Alan Watenmaker (he spelled his name) of the law firm of Hoffman, Sabban & Watenmaker, appearing on behalf of Barbara Sinatra, Beneficiary."

The Judge just gave them each a nod of acknowledgment and turned his attention back on to me as the clerk asked me to give my name and spell it. Then His Honor spoke to me.

"When will you be filing objections? You've written a letter than does not qualify as formal objections."

"Okay," I answered, not knowing how to proceed.

"I will give you time to file formal objections, if you choose to do that," he said and gave me a smile. The full bearing of his offer and the miracle it implied for me didn't register at that moment, that he had just offered to halt probate on my behalf. I did sense that he had taken me under his wing and I asked him for help.

"Yes, all right. Can you direct me?"

"All right," he said continuing with, "You will be filing with the court Formal Objections. You must pay a filing fee, a hearing fee, and have the matter set for the date that I am about to give you."

I sensed each of the attorneys at the table with me ready to jump out of their skins. The judge was making it clear that he did not consider me at all "frivolous."

"Is that what I should write down? Is that the name of what I will be doing?" I asked next, ready to add to his other instructions I had written on a legal pad from my briefcase. But before the judge could respond, Jeffrey Loeb spoke up.

"Your Honor, can I be heard briefly?"

"Sure," the judge answered him now grinning.

"Historically, this matter—Probate began in 1998 following Mr. Sinatra's death. At that time, Ms. Sinatra filed a request for special notice. We knew her then by her name of Ms. Speelman, which was the name she provided on the

Request for Special Notice. We corresponded with her shortly there after in 1998 asking her to provide us the basis upon which she thought she was interested in the estate. We did not hear from her at all. Over the course of the past four years, I've heard from two different attorneys in Los Angeles County asking me for facts relating to the estate because they have been approached by her for the purpose of representation. We never heard anything further from her."

The Judge then turned to look at me for my response.

"As I explained in my letter, Your Honor, no attorney will help me with this case. I did receive a letter from a Mr. Andrew Garb of Loeb & Loeb that Mr. Loeb is referring to, and I have a copy of my letter I sent back to him at that time with me," I stated and pulled it from where I knew it was in my briefcase and held it up for the judge to see it in my hand. The judge smiled and turned his eyes back to Jeffrey Loeb who had begun speaking again.

"Your Honor, I don't understand why she filed her special notice under the name of Speelman and is here today using the name Julie Sinatra?"

"I went to court over a year ago, Your Honor, the name Speelman was my x-husband's name, and I had my name changed to reflect my true maiden name," I said with my copy of it half-way out in sight.

"All right," the Judge nodded at me and his eyes twinkled with delight—I guessed must be from the entertaining performance going on in front of him. I was smiling by this time too.

Jeffrey Loeb spoke up with another try to dislocate me from favor. He told the Judge about the time I had phoned Loeb & Loeb and asked them to go ahead and send me the form to withdraw my special notice. They did so at once as you can imagine they would jump at that. But when the form arrived my common sense kicked in and overcame the emotional frustration I had been feeling when I wanted to give up—that took place somewhere between number ten and number 15 attorney who had turned down my case … looking at the form I realized I could not sign it and threw it away. The judge was now looking back at me again, waiting for me to give some explanation of this, but I just kept silent. It didn't seem appropriate to bring my emotional drama into court. Loeb jumped back in.

"To delay the closing of the Probate at this point in time, Your Honor, particularly in view of the fact that the Will itself provides a basis to deny Ms. Speelman(I looked down my glasses at him and he corrected)Uh, Ms. Sinatra any relief, it defines children as being the three named Sinatra children and further defines children as only those born in wedlock. Those born out of wedlock are not children. So even if you were to somehow view this as an opportunity to rule on the pleadings, if you deemed her letter to be objections, she doesn't fall within the scope of the Will and it's far too late for her to revoke the Probate," he concluded and I was proud of myself for not acting upon the sudden urge I felt to clock him when I'd heard him refer to me as an, "unchild."

The Judge was frowning down on the lawyer and I thought maybe he too didn't care much for his callus disregard for me either. That clause about the child out of wedlock I had already learned some time ago appears in wills as a tradition the attorneys automatically write into them, not necessarily from a specific request the deceased has indicated wanting. It was in my mother's Will and Testament also … it doesn't carry much legal weight.

The response from the bench was simply: "We'll see." At that point Jeffrey Loeb kicked in again.

"She's received Special Notice for these past four years, Your Honor, she's been served all the papers. We've had three interim accountings and she's never once appeared in this court."

"Are you willing to submit the matter on the basis of your documents in the file and this lady's letter to the court?" the Judge asked him.

"I haven't seen the letter Your Honor," Loeb said back.

"I haven't either," the Judge retorted.

"Is that a 'No' or just exactly what is that?" the Judge inquired.

"Until I see the letter it's a 'No' Your Honor."

"Good decision," the Judge commented back.

"On behalf of Mrs. Sinatra we would also object," Mr. Watenmaker spoke up.

"Okay," the judge acknowledged him.

"May I speak Your Honor?" I interjected, and the judge told me to go ahead. "When I wrote the letter back to Mr. Andrew Garb of Loeb & Loeb when they wanted to know what my interest in the estate was … I did state back then that I was Frank Sinatra's daughter and that was my interest."

"All right," the judge responded and began giving me instructions again.

"Julie Sinatra will file Formal Objections in this matter not later than October 18th," he then looked directly at me and added: "That gives you three weeks."

Jeffrey Loeb wanted to get paid even if Probate, I realized myself, just at that instant, was not going to close on this hearing as had been scheduled. He asked the Judge for "interim relief."

"I'm not finished yet," the Judge said cutting Loeb off, and continuing, "The hearing on the account and objections, if any, will be heard on November 21st," he announced and then turned to me once more saying, "Now Julie Sinatra, understand this: If you have not filed your Formal Objections and paid the fees and had them set for hearing on November 21st, they will be deemed denied."

"Yes, Your Honor," I said gratefully.

The Judge had said the date wrong and Mr. Watenmaker corrected him to the filing deadline originally set which was October 18th. The judge then clarified the dates and repeated that it was the hearing date set for November 21st—the filings by October 18th, and I wrote it all down.

Jeffrey Loeb spoke next to be sure my objections to the court would be provided to all the parties by me by October 18th also. The Judge instructed me to send copies of what I filed to all the attorneys and parties that had been listed on having special notice throughout the Probate. Jeffrey Loeb had more to say.

"One of our Co-Executors is incapacitated and may not survive until the hearing date, Your Honor, we'd asked in our supplement for the relief that the remaining Co-Executor, Eliot Weisman, be authorized to conclude the administration of this estate alone," he told the Judge, and I realized that Harvey Silbert was dying.

"I'm sorry to hear that, he was an old friend of my Dad's," I turned and said to Loeb.

Mr. Watenmaker spoke up that Mrs. Sinatra would not object to Eliot carrying on alone, and the judge turned to look at me next. I realized I had to say I didn't object to this either … so I said that. Watenmaker had more to address the court with.

"My understanding that Ms. Sinatra's objections will go to the issue of her entitlement to the estate as a beneficiary and do not relate to the specific items that will remain JTD's for purposes of this hearing," he said to the Judge who then looked at me and grinned out:

"I have no idea. She is entitled to object to anything she chooses to object to," he finished his statement with a smile at me.

I gathered that Watenmaker was trying to say his client would not be affected by what he expected I would file which I guessed he thought would only affect the other siblings … In another word, this attorney also had wanted to have a basis to get paid today which the response from the Judge had just denied. He was putting the pressure on them where I was concerned. Their stonewalling days were over.

After a brief exchange to discover whether or not Robert Finkelstein was listed as one who would need special notice of my filing; it was determined he represented the other kids. I already knew he was on that list, and planned to include him. "See you all back here on November 21," the Honorable Thomas W. Stover announced that this hearing was over.

With that, the two attorneys sped back on their heels and exited the courtroom as if they were on jet skates. After thanking His Honor, I turned around to leave.

Suddenly in my mind's eye that bronzed golden horse was galloping toward me, alive from the garden in front of my dad's house in Palm Springs. I leaped upon its back and rode him down the center aisle and across that mystical threshold ... And somewhere between the courthouse steps and my hotel, I looked back over my shoulder in time to see the victim of my childhood as she disappeared.

CHAPTER TWENTY-TWO

2nd Hearing ...

Not over were the challenges I still faced ahead of me. When I returned home to Sedona on October 2nd, the answering machine on my phone was blinking. It was a message from a gal who handled permissions for the publishing business. She got signed-off okays to use photographs in books taken by independent photographers and the like. I had talked with her once to learn about this and she had shared that she was in fact doing that for a book Barbara Sinatra was writing. She had expressed being very sympathetic towards Barbara versus the other Sinatra children. That conversation took place well over a year ago. What was she doing on my phone now asking me to let her know if I had ever gotten an attorney to take my case??? I didn't call her back. Her timing to casually see how I was doing was highly suspect. That night, my dad came into a dream.

He was in his late 50's I could tell from photographs of him I'd seen him at different ages in. Also he had Barbara on his arm. He seemed very concerned as he began speaking to me. She was looking off somewhere else, seemed just there passively documenting a time period of his life because she looked just as I had seen her in pictures when they first got married and lived at his home in the desert.

He was saying as he began walking through his house and pointed to an item of his: "Use this for your DNA to prove to others what we both know is true." Then he disappeared and the dream was over.

Did the dream and the phone message mean I was supposed to do some under the table deal with Barbara to get my DNA? And how would that play out? Without the court ordering the DNA and monitoring it ... How could I trust that something screwy wouldn't occur? Once again, without an attorney, I didn't know how to proceed. It was enough for right now that my dad was behind me in all this.

I decided to try again to see if Paul Livadary might feel differently about taking my case if he knew the judge had halted the probate for me.

"Good for you!" Paul said when I shared what happened in court. I asked him point blank to re-consider my case. He turned me down.

I told him I had only a sketchy idea along with a few directions from the judge about how to fill out my Formal Objections. Paul gave me a list of what I should include such as asking for blood tests and DNA from the surviving siblings and to include a copy of my letter I had written to the court with all of its exhibits I'd attached to it. He said I would find all the right language to use in presenting my objections by looking at the notices from the filings that Loeb & Loeb had sent me during these years.

"Now, I've just spent twenty minutes on the phone with you, Julie, for free. You'll be fine. That's all the time I can give you. Good luck," he said and we hung up.

So I was still on my own. I about went crazy trying to figure out what part of the Formal Objections I was "praying for" and what part went into the subject area of the form before the prayer was supposed to begin. Additionally, just handling the creation of the form itself was a nightmare. It took me at least three or four tries, hours of effort, until I had the first page lined up in my computer to print out the same format used that the ones from Loeb & Loeb did. What I wouldn't have given for a good old IBM Executive typewriter. I also remembered from once having worked as a legal secretary that the title for me representing myself is called, "pro per" which went up in the top left hand corner of my document along with my address, etc. Within a few days more I had it all completed, and ready to make copies to send to all the parties I needed to according to the judge's instructions to me. A special reward awaited. Tony Bennett was giving a concert in Sedona that coming weekend and his son, Danny Bennett had arranged for me to have front row tickets and a back stage pass to meet his father in person ... my dad's favorite singer and the man who had directed me to the truth about who he was.

"You're beautiful," he said approaching to meet me back stage after the manager of the venue had just alerted him that a daughter of Frank Sinatra was standing there hoping to meet him.

I became tongue tied. I was overwhelmed because Tony seemed like the closest I had come to being with my dad. We shared a hug and I told him I could feel my dad was there with us. He graciously offered and we had our picture taken together. I wanted to tell him how I had just stood up for my own justice and triumphed, knowing he would be someone who appreciated that. But I didn't want to put my dad's old friend in an awkward position because these legalities were still on going. So, when he said how nice it was to have met me, exploring my face probably for more information, I just said back in regards to meeting him:

"It was my honor and privilege." Then after I got home I realized, like an idiot I had forgotten to tell him how great he sang.

Tony Bennett and Julie Sinatra
Backstage at Tony Bennett's Concert Sedona, Arizona, October 5, 2002

Pal Bob had already told me that if I had to go back to California for court again, he would foot the bill once more. I knew what a lucky girl I was to have this support because without it I had no way to show up again as legally required to do at the November hearing. My Formal Objections were both filed and paid for more than a week before the October 18th deadline. Additionally the copies all went out to the parties I was required to give special notice to, including Finkelstein who represented the other kids—all well ahead of the deadline.

It felt great and I was inspired to give a concert myself. And, there was another reason I felt compelled to go out and sing ... I wanted to act on being who I am.

The venue was smaller than where Tony Bennett sang, of course. I chose one that held around 200 seats. Musicians in town joined me to rehearse my original music and the Creative Life Center, where we would perform had assured me with the publicity they had planned I would make enough monies to pay for the hall and the musicians. That's exactly to the penny what I did make. But I was rewarded by a fan and his wife in the audience who had been skeptical about who I was claiming I was, but decided to attend to see for themselves. Within a short time after the concert where everybody got paid but me, they approached me to do a cover story about me in the magazine they published in Sedona.

I wanted to be able to get my hair cut before they came to shoot the photographs, but I didn't have any money for it. I got a call out of the blue from the owner of a beauty salon where I had gone before. Her father was coming in to visit from Miami. He was a big fan and also had known Frank Sinatra and he was hoping to meet me ... not only did it result in my getting a free haircut, I also learned something about my dad that would topple a myth that followed him for years and years. Dad's hand in all this seemed obvious.

Gerald (Gerry) A. Grande began by telling me he and his now deceased wife had been fans of my dad's for sixty years.

"We were bobby-soxers back then—In the audience at the Paramount where your father first began," he shared cheerfully adding, "My wife used to say Sinatra could put his shoes under her bed anytime," he laughed.

"I missed it all," I told him. It was my mother's secret. I learn a lot about him when I meet people like yourself."

"I used to be the MC at Our Lady Queen of Peace church in Brooklyn," he went on, "Frank Sinatra and Vic Dimone would come in to sing at our fundraising shows for the poor. Frank did this for many years from the late 30's into the early 40's," he told me, and then he got very serious and leaned forward in his chair to talk more intimately with me.

"Frank was accused all his life about being connected to people who later on became known as the Mafia," he said, shaking his head to indicate 'No'. True, he knew the Freshetti brothers, you've probably heard about that?"

"Yes I have. They, along with a guy named, Moretti had approached him to go down to Havana, Cuba for Luciano's summit," I said and waited for him to continue.

"I knew the Freshettis. We all did growing up then in the neighborhoods. These guys were around and sometimes stood up for the little guy, like they did for your father when he was growing up in Hoboken. A kind of unspoken loyalty existed, was expected, when you became a recipient of help from guys like the Freshettis. You're Frank's kid, I can see that. I know he would want you to know that it's true he knew these guys, but I can tell you straight—Your father never crossed over that line to become one of them."

Mid-November, 2002 ...

A day or so added to the week before the scheduled court hearing for November 21, Paul Livadary phoned me. I had not expected to have contact with him again.

"Your case has been nagging at me, Julie," he began. I know you will soon if not already have something from the opposing attorneys that is called, "Points and Authorities." It will be over your head to file a necessary brief to answer it. Additionally, I recently talked with an entertainment attorney here in town whom suggested that there may be monies in Frank Sinatra's publishing companies that are not part of the trusts out there. If you are willing, I would be willing to begin to represent you and write the briefs and appear in court on your behalf for one-third of anything you inherit plus my expenses.

"What are points and authorities?" I asked him.

"They are taken from old previous cases that show rulings that have set precedents regarding, in your circumstance, the treatments for the pretermitted heir. You will be defeated at the hearing without this."

"Remember when you shared that you were once a young attorney just out of law school and volunteering for the Boys & Girls Club in Los Angeles ... you said you wrote my father a letter asking him for a donation and you got his personal check back within 24 hours for the amount of $25,000.00.?"

"Yes. I do remember telling you about that. Frank Sinatra would want you to have what you deserve from his estate. The publishing monies that might be available would likely amount to a great deal."

"I think you're on my phone now because my dad picked you for me ... You're it kid!"

He laughed.

"Would those funds be separate from the other kid's inheritance?

"From what I remember, there wasn't anything scheduled in his will about the publishing," Paul said, but then I remembered I had read something in regards to this.

"I believe I read that my dad gave his publishing away years ago to his manager, Hank Sanicola, when they parted ways with one another."

"That can all be looked into but if you want me to come on board we will have to get moving in getting a contract signed between us and you will have to file a form with the court right away telling the court you are no longer a pro-per and have attorney representing your case."

"Okay, Paul, this is another miracle for me but I wish you'd been on board when I had to go it alone out there in September."

"Think of it as a tactic," he chuckled, "The judge did get on your side ..."

"A tactic?!" I kidded back, but I hoped that Judge Stoever wouldn't take it that way when I suddenly showed up as the underdog who now had a tough reputated litigator with her.

The next day I got a call for the paralegal in Loeb & Loeb's office. She dropped her snippy tone she'd used to inform me they were sending out "Points & Authorities" to me, when I told her to forward them to my attorney instead. Boy that felt good!

Paul, along with Bill, another attorney he brought in, stayed up until 3 AM in the morning finishing the arguments to answer the opposing lawyers within time to file them in a brief. I recognized that he, like me, had interpreted the US Supreme Court's "Mary Queen of Scotts" law the same way … and Paul found a brilliant link to swallow the gap in the California probate statutes that attempt to get around the law of the land. He saw a way to combine family law statutes with the probate statutes for California—linking me into a natural position to be considered for ordering the DNA testing under "Special Circumstances," a clause in the probate statues as an exception to the rule that a judge is not allowed to order it. Additionally, Paul attached a copy of my birth certificate that I had been unhappy about not being able to get changed from Lyma as father, to Sinatra, as father on it … but now it was going to serve me as is to add proof that Frank Sinatra and I had never had a clue about my true paternity. The brief and all the required paperwork got in before the bell rang.

November 21, 2002 …

Walking into this hearing I felt some apprehension, I guessed maybe because I had given up my control of what would be said in my behalf. At the same time I understood that this would be very different than that 'day in court' everybody deserves I'd already had, and having an attorney was paramount now. But it was only moments later after our case was called that the judge spotted me and he gave me a miffed look. I wondered if this was because he really had expected me not to be able to continue and hold back the closing of probate—he was there to see it got closed; or, maybe, I hoped not, he believed I had pulled that tactic Paul commented on, which I was innocent of. Another few minutes I would know.

Jeffrey Loeb argued that I had not specifically listed characterization of assets when I filed my objections. Paul reminded the judge that I had been pro per …

"So?," His Honor challenged him, and Paul continued.

"A pro per who has put their best foot forward and now they have counsel who is able to argue that and out of efficiency for this court's time, as you just stated, if the court decides that she can't have DNA testing, for all intents and purposes, she can't pursue her claim further because she can't rise to the standard of clear and convincing evidence, probably. Under those circumstances, then all the rest of it is moot," he said and went on to argue, "The business about asset characterization is only a part of the accounting possible issues, if indeed she were an heir. Loeb & Loeb had only provided accounting for the assets in their inventory they filed, and in regards to the fact that debts and taxes were prepaid out of community property, no adjudication had been done," he concluded.

"Well there was never really a reason to adjudicate up until your client made this claim," Judge Stoever retorted.

"Exactly, I'm not faulting their accounting. If there isn't an intestacy involved, then they've done everything fine. But statute 11700 allows this petition to have been brought at anytime prior to final distribution. That she has done. She is not a "late-comer" as Mr. Watenmaker (for Barbara Sinatra) has argued. She warned Loeb & Loeb in writing that she considered herself to be a child. They knew. They could have brought a petition under 11700 years ago, if they chose to, to clear the deck. They knew this was a possible problem," Paul defended and here it came …

"Counsel, just to clear the decks on your comment about your client being a pro per, indeed she was a pro per and a very experienced one at that. She's had a lot of time in the courts. She's quite good at it what she does," His Honor said back, alluding to his belief that indeed some tactic had been in mind when I appeared at the previous hearing alone. My heart sank.

"Your Honor …," I began in an attempt to re-align the truth … and he swiftly cut me off.

"No!" he shouted down at me. "You have an attorney now!"

Paul spoke up quietly addressing the judge saying, "I'm unaware of what you're referring to, Your Honor," but the judge waved him off with his hand.

"Well—go back in the file. You'll see she's been in this a long time," the judge defended back.

"She's had special notice, Your Honor, They've been stonewalling her." Paul answered.

"Okay. Are the parties at this point in a position to submit the matter of DNA testing?" His Honor asked looking out into the courtroom. My heart was back in my teeth waiting for the next second to occur.

"I am, yes, Your Honor," Paul stated. Then Jeffrey Loeb spoke.

"Your Honor, I think, in fairness, Mr. Finkelstein, who represents the three natural children, who is present in court, should be asked that question as well."

"All right. He's welcome to come up," the judge smiled his permission.

In the meantime, Barbara's attorney spoke up saying what amounted to that his client should not have to wait for her share of the estate while testing issues could drag on. Paul responded to this as the legal garcon battered back and forth.

"I think that to approve undercuts the share or effects, let's just say, the possible share of her(meaning me) intestate share, if indeed she establishes her heir ship, and for that reason we have a process here."

"Okay," Judge Stoever acknowledged as I saw Paul apparently won that point. No one was getting paid yet. "Now let's get back to the original question—Will all counsel submit the issue of DNA testing to the court today?"

Robert Finkelstein spoke next.

"Your Honor, I have acted as a transactional attorney for the Sinatra children and they have not been noticed in this proceeding and I would not be willing on their behalf to submit to anything today."

I shot a look to Bob Finkelstein—I could not believe he would actually lie in court. Paul quickly spoke up, turning to Finkelstein.

"You've been noticed all the way through this." Then Paul turned to the judge and added, "Your Honor, Mr. Finkelstein has been noticed."

"All right. All matters are ordered to mediation," His Honor responded, ending further discussion about the DNA that I knew now was not to be ordered from the bench. The opposing attorneys reaction to this is where I got the clue that this hearing was coming to an end.

Both Loeb and Watenmaker argued that there was over $2,800,000.00 in community property, meaning that part of the total monies coming to Barbara Sinatra. They said that even if my claim was to become successful, they should still get paid their fees for handling the community property because I would likely not become entitled to any of it anyway.

"Maybe," His Honor warned them—keeping the pressure on—giving the underdog some deserved power.

The judge ordered and set a date for the next hearing on December 19th and advised the attorneys that the arbitration needed to be binding so this could all, "be wrapped up," as he put it, and when he said that he looked right at me. He also told us he would set a trial date at that hearing if the arbitration failed to produce an agreement. I couldn't help feeling a little cheated when he opted out on ordering the DNA for me ... Paul had made the point with the judge also that I needed it to go *into* the arbitration with. But at least I had arrived through these procedures to a point where I had a chance to get that resolved through this next legal process. I chose to remain positive.

Outside in the hallway the opposing attorneys approached Paul to offer some crummy deal that did not include my DNA. Paul turned it down and we sat to discuss things over a cup of coffee at Starbucks in the patio area beside the courthouse. He was upset that Robert Finkelstein had lied in court, explaining that what Bob had used was a tactic that obligated the judge to vacate the avenue he was proceeding along towards ordering my DNA.

"It makes it very difficult if they are willing to lie in court," he said, shaking his head.

"You're not going to like what I have to say, Paul," I began. "I want you to write an offer to the family—the kids I mean, and tell them I will exchange my DNA testing with them for receiving no inheritance."

He was taken aback, but regained his composure, and I continued. "I've written a manuscript that I will have to add the court experiences to, but when it's finished and published I will pay you a percentage to cover the work you have done for me here."

He agreed, and within a couple of days he sent out a confidential agreement expressing my wishes to the home addresses I gave him for Nancy, Frank Jr. and Tina—and also a copy over to Robert Finkelstein.

There was no response as Paul had told me he had expected there would not be. But I was hard pressed to come to any understanding of their behavior. Ahead of me was now the court ordered arbitration. It would be overseen by a different judge all attorneys agreed could be trusted to be impartial. It began in early December, 2002 around the time my psychotic landlord was threatening to kick me out because he didn't want horses there anymore. The rent was due I wasn't sure I would come up with in time and I knew that holding out with my high ideals could prove to be life threatening. Still I wanted a way to maintain my integrity in the upcoming litigation.

Clued in from reading my copy of the last filing for accounting I'd received before I went to court the first time, I knew there were residual monies in Dad's estate left over after taxes had been paid that would not subtract anything from a family member's inheritance. I asked Paul to once again stress their agreeing to do the DNA testing.

Paul phoned me in the evening after spending five hours or more in the arbitration. No agreement had yet been reached and they were flatly refusing to do the DNA testing. He said that because of the course of things that the arbitrating judge had a message for me. She felt we had won the briefs(legal arguments each side filed with the court)by providing clear and convincing evidence to back up my claim and would therefore win the trial and the appeal, but fail to succeed in having my DNA testing ordered for me at the Appellate Court—they would do it more likely for an infant or baby child who would be growing up without a father who had passed away before knowing about the paternity ... I would be viewed as having lived all my life thus far just fine without a father's help in their eyes.

"It would take at least up to two years," Paul finished, and I could hear the reluctance in his voice. "They have made an offer that at least exceeds what you would likely receive as the outcome from the Appellate Court," his voice was trailing off somewhat. "It's not what I hoped for you," he added, wearily.

"Wouldn't there be a chance the trial judge could order the DNA?" I interjected.

"Julie, I am your attorney on contract with you and therefore obligated to proceed on your behalf if you decide we should go to trial. They have already demonstrated their willingness to lie in court and you have already won legal recognition as Frank's daughter from the judge in the past two hearings, so you have that. After much time and money spent you could come out of it where you are right now."

I resented his sales pitch to give up, but I also knew that if I continued to go on I would have to come out of it with a huge money win to cover the costs. The tax residual monies would not begin to do that and that meant I would be forced down an avenue to demand money from the trusts my dad had set up years ago for each of the children he knew he had. I hadn't made this journey to do that. I knew my Dad would have included me if he'd known of me, and that was enough. I was disappointed that the family's offer would not cushion more than a year of finances, as my mind quickly traced through costs of moving, fixing or having to replace my car, paying back personal loans from friends—all the stuff I would have to cover until I could land a publishing deal for my book and see myself more secure in the future. Like a good salesman, Paul was silent, leaving the ball squarely in my court. I couldn't blame him. He would have to be out on the limb knowing the possibility that he might end up out of pocket. I knew what I had to do.

"Make the deal, Paul, but go back to them adding your contingency fee to the sum if you can. Tell them I won't sign anything that negates my being Frank Sinatra's daughter."

He phoned the following day saying he had been able to win the wording that would allow me to use my name and do anything with it, i.e., publish my book, my music, anything in my life as Frank Sinatra's daughter without interference along with the settlement amount which did not include his fees. I would not be allowed to publish the Confidential Contract, as it was called and would be allowed in referring to it to say only that we came to an agreement "in consideration to the benefit of our mutual undertakings." All parties signed it on December 18, 2002.

The proof that I had been legally recognized by the Court in my true identity is there on public record and in the pudding when the attorneys for my dad's estate filed the Second Supplement To The Fourth and Final Account and Report which includes me in receipt of an amount in the six figures among the final disbursements of inheritance that the judge approved. I had won the right to enter my culture under my true identity.

"It's over," I thought to myself as I drove back from Sedona with a copy of it retrieved from my post office box. But as I passed the forest road that winds its way down to "Skywater," a lump came into my throat and all those merciless what-ifs surfaced to cast doubt on the decisions I had made all along the way.

"Oh, Dad," I sighed to him mentally. "Will I ever truly find my place in this world?"

He spoke up quickly and put me at ease.

"It's the start."

EPILOGUE

Dear Readers: Some afterwords.

A cover story was done about me this past summer (2006) published by the Daily Telegraph in London, a conservative and prestigious newspaper widely read around the world. I got an e-mail from a person who read it on the internet who commented that denying someone their identity is the same as killing them. Well you've just finished a book about this someone who refused to stay murdered. It's my hope that I've rocked your boat a little with this story that is not mine alone, but yours too. I sailed my boat across the seas of my dad's life to find what I was missing—when I found him, I found me. And my life at least has me in it now. That's not to say it's easy. Sometimes I still feel like, how did my dad put it? "It's all Mondays …" There are always those who seek to oppress us, but I no longer allow that to cause me to drift from my heart. It's my deepest wish that you will, if you are not already doing it, reconnect to your own personal truths. Trust your heart voice and create your life based on who you are. There's a line from one of my songs: "They are true sailors who sail to freedom."

It seems my journey to my father is still ongoing and marked by little destinations. Recently I dined with my friend, Masako, at Vince's Little Star, a local family owned Italian restaurant I had passed by many times en route to get feed for the horses. I cook Italian food often at home and I like to try other menus when I go out, but my friend had insisted we eat there and had said she had a surprise for me. We sat at a booth where I quickly spotted a poster picture of Frank Sinatra hanging on the wall. My friend knew the owner, Vince Scaturmo. He came out of the back where he'd been cooking and she introduced me as Frank's daughter. He grinned and told me he had a story about my father as he picked up the placemat in front of me. It had a map of Italy and Sicily drawn on it. His eyes were shining as he turned it over and wrote the names of the villages in Sicily and inked in a dot at their map related locations.

Vince pointed to a village called Sclafani, four dots down from Palermo at the top, and three dots south of Carleone famous for the godfather and origin of the mafia. He explained that his grandparents had come from Sclafani and that they knew my grandfather Marty Sinatra's parents who had been born and raised there also, that is until the Sinatras moved to Catania (a couple of dots over on the coast). He said the people still spoke Italian in their old village dialects when they came to America, and that was the Italian his father, also named Vincent, spoke when he went to Hollywood and worked as a dishwasher at the Casa D'Amore restaurant owned by the Salvatore and Pasqualle brothers in the summer of 1948.

The father, Vincent Scaturmo, Sr., had told his son that Frank Sinatra came in often to eat at Casa D'Amore and how he met Sinatra there. Vincent Sr. was a new employee when his boss, Pasqualle called him out from the back to meet someone (Sinatra). Pasqualle had already told Frank Sinatra that the man was from Sclafani. As the story went, my dad began speaking in perfect Sclafani dialect to Vince's father, using it as old friends would, instead of formal Italian considered proper for first meeting someone. Vince said his dad was thrilled to speak with someone from home, and he told me that Frank Sinatra asked his father: "Do you know who I am, Vincent?" His father answered: "No but you look familiar."

Each village a different language depicting a unique culture—and Sclafani many miles away from Corleone where another myth persists the Sinatras had lived and courted the Cosa Nostra, implying a heritage connection with Frank Sinatra ... But my dad didn't speak Corleone dialect. He spoke Sclafani.

Vincent Scaturmo became a chef and the son prepares his father's delicious food at the "Little Star" in Cornville, Arizona.

Additionally, speaking of Italian food, my dad's trusted and loved barber of many years, Eddie Carroll (now my good pallie too), told me on one of his visits out to the desert Sinatra abode how Dad spent hours upon hours in the kitchen cooking up my grandmother's recipe for spaghetti sauce. He touched me deeply when he also told me after reading the Sedona Monthly cover story about me: "Your father would have loved you, Honey." Eddie's promised to send me the recipe.

I sailed into another little harbor when a letter addressed to me came to the old post office box I had in Cave Creek years ago that a friend of mine now rented. She phoned and the letter turned out to be from Tom Lyma's daughter. I didn't recognize her last name of Malvino that was on the envelope, but when my friend at my request read the letter to me I was astounded. Joan Lyma Malvino had spent the past 12 years trying to locate me in her belief that I was her long lost half sister. When we were finally re-united over the phone I told her the news and she agreed to do DNA testing immediately with me. The lab results showed she and I had no blood relationship between us. Although we are not sisters ... we have become good friends.

Joan Lyma Malvino

A photo finally documenting my mother, Dorothy Lyma as the starlet, Alora Gooding finally surfaced on the internet just in time to include in this book.

A lucky find! Mom captioned as Alora Gooding by unknown photographer at Mickey Rooney's swim party for the cast. Alora was a stand-in for June Presser.

My son, Dan sent me a very special gift last Christmas. It was a recently published book about my dad entitled, "The Sinatra Treasures," by Charles Pignone. It is filled with personal mementos of Frank Sinatra. More than that the gifted book was Dan's way of showing me he was finally on board.

"Tally My Chex (Checkers)," my beloved companion for over 30 years passed away in the spring of 2004. I buried him on Good Friday with a sprig bouquet of yellow roses that seemed to defy gravity as I tossed it into his grave. It floated gently down to lay along his mane as if it had been carried and placed there by an angel. He shared his power with me until I came into my own.

People I meet for the first time often ask me if I had a relationship with my Dad. "Not the way you think," I tell them, but we do have one and our relationship is still strong. He finds a way he knows I can recognize and shows up just when I need him the most … Love doesn't die. His energy is still around … can't you hear him saying: "Let's start the action now."

With heart,

Julie Sinatra

SINATRA AT THE CENTER

JULIE SINATRA IN CONCERT

SEDONA CREATIVE LIFE CENTER
SATURDAY NIGHT DEC. 7 at 7:30 PM
Pre-sale Tickets $15 or $18 At The Door
333 Schnebly Hill Rd. in Sedona, AZ
info: (928) 282-9300

Julie Sinatra

Daughter of" Ole Blue Eyes "Performs Her Songs
Mixing It ALL UP For A Special Evening
Of FOlky BlueSY "Desert Prairie Jazz"
and some familiar SINATRA stuff too!

JULIE SINATRA And Her Band
FEATURING BOBBY COTTONWOOD, Vocalist / Drummer,
RAMONE DANA, Jazz Pianist and MIKE REED, Sax 'n Flute

Grandmother, Dolly Sinatra—1923, playing her guitar
(where Dad and I got our music ability)
Dad is sitting in front of her at summer vacation camp

Dad chose, *"The Best is Yet to Come"* for his last song in his last public appearance singing, departing from his traditional concert finale, "Put Your Dreams Away."

Visiting Dolly and Marty

"The Best is Yet to Come"

MADE ME STRONG

lyric & music by Julie Sinatra

I know it's late but could I sit with you awhile
I've thought a lot on what I'd say
The time has passed for getting to the heart of things
We won't get lost in the remembering

Chorus:
Everybody says I've got your famous eyes
Blue as the sky
And from your best I want to thank you for my song
And the rest you gave me Dad made me strong

Seems you and I have turned a whole world upside down
It's easy now to see the clowns
Then you should know life is perfect to the day
When souls in heaven planned it that way

(chorus)
Bridge: Some people turn away their peace in mind
Some who seek it walk through fire
Sad I couldn't swim with ducks or swans
Then I saw an eagle who flew higher

verse 3:
Well yes it's late the rest is better left I guess
Where angels know you want to be
All said and done as the truth rides in the dawn
The best is yet to come on this road I'm on

(chorus)
© 1997

"It isn't until you come to a spiritual understanding
of who you are—
not necessarily a religious feeling but deep down the spirit within—that
you begin to take control."—Oprah Winfrey

APPRECIATION

A Special Thanks To: Dan Brown, Eric Hunter, Joanna Sullivan, Cathy Huffman, Deb Ball, Susan Lanci, Heather Dionne, Elaine Gragg, Jon Iger, John & JoAnn Braheny, Dan Howell, Jon Yingst, R.J. Bowden, Toni Irving, Jerry & Kurt Florman, Bernard Perry, Samuel Pielet, Doris Grayson, Charles Realmonte Esq., Gavan Weiser, Sam Brown, Jim Moorhouse, Steve Parrish & Mom, Janice's bargain vegetables, Darrell Peterson for her intuitive questions, Terry Rudd, Ron Peterson, Sondra Peterson, Rod & Carol Lynn DeSzendeffy, Paul Livadary, Joan Manning, Morgan Heard, Eddie Carroll, and Evan Imber-Black, Ed Shirak Jr., Mario Lepore, Diane and Carla Faggio, Bernice Perry, Dan Kubota—for his archival research, Hal Blaine, Doug Haywood, Gerry Grande, Don Crutchfield, Frank Sinatra Jr., Tony Bennett, Dan Bennett, Ellen Geiger, George Schlatter, Rick Apt, "Gordo" Lightfoot, Courtney Pledger, Skip Thomas, Ellen Davis, Phil Moyer, Joan Malvino, Rick Rauch—excellent farrier and shaman, Masako Shirai who is wisdom joy, Beth Stevens for timely e-mailed encouraging words from Santa Fe, Dary Matera for locating the long hoped for photo of my mother captioned as Alora Gooding/1940's, Roseanne Welch for her astute editing, Thanks Jeff Cook for your technical help! And Debby Weinkauff & Joe McNeil for the impeccable cover story about me, and Debby's honest photographs in their Sedona Monthly Magazine plus all Joe's good advice … and a deep appreciation goes out to Stefan Bickel and for my great pal Bob Schmidt, and Dad's fans who embraced me with Sinatra stories. No one makes it here alone … Thanks Dad!

RESOURCES

"Sinatra," the mini-series for TV, produced by Tina Sinatra/Warner Brothers TV

"Frank Sinatra an American Legend"—book by Nancy Sinatra, copyright 1995–1998, General Publishing Group, Inc.

"My Father's Daughter"—book by Tina Sinatra with Jeff Coplan copyright 2000, Simon and Schuster publisher.

"Sinatra, Remembering—A Life In Pictures" by Robert Sullivan and the editors of Life, and the Farewell message words and drawings by Tony Bennett therein, copyright 1998.

"The Way You Wear Your Hat—Frank Sinatra and the Lost Art of Livin'," book by Bill Zehme, copyright 1997, published by Harper Collins.

"Why Sinatra Matters"—book by Pete Hamill, copyright 1998, Little Brown and Co. Pub.

"Our Way"—book by Ed Shirak, Jr., copyright 1995, Lepore's Publishing.

"His Way"—book by Kitty Kelley, copyright 1986, Bantam Books publisher.

"Frank Sinatra"—book by Jessica Hodge, copyright 1994, Brompton Books Corporation.

"Sinatra—Ol' Blue Eyes Remembered"—book by David Hanna, copyright 1990–1998, Bell publisher.

"One For The Road—an open letter to Frank"—article by Shirley MacLaine, published in Newsweek Magazine, copyright 1998.

The Motion Picture Academy of Arts and Sciences in Los Angeles

978-0-595-68589-9
0-595-68589-7

Printed in the United States
86982LV00008B/34/A